GREAT CHIEFS

CHIEFS

VOLUME II

BY TONY HOLLIHAN

FOLK
LORE
PUBLISHING

© 2002 by Folklore Publishing
First printed in 2002 10 9 8 7 6 5 4 3 2 1
Printed in Canada

The Publisher: Folklore Publishing

Distributed by Lone Pine Publishing
10145–81 Ave.
Edmonton, AB T6E 1W9
Canada
Toll Free: 800-661-9017

Website: www.folklorepublishing.com

National Library of Canada Cataloguing in Publication Data
Hollihan, K. Tony (Kelvin Tony), 1964–
Great chiefs / K. Tony Hollihan.

(Legends series)
  Includes bibliographical references.
  ISBN 1-894864-03-4 (v. 1).—ISBN 1-894864-07-7 (v. 2)

  Indians of North America—Kings and rulers—Biography. I. Title.
II. Series: Legends series (Edmonton, Alta.)
E89.H64 2002   970'.00497'00922   C2002-911043-2

Editorial Director: Faye Boer
Cover Image: Rides to the Ghost Dance; artwork by Dale Auger, with thanks to Duval House Publishing
Photography credits: Every effort has been made to accurately credit the sources of photographs. Any errors or omissions should be directed to the publisher for changes in future editions. *Photographs courtesy of* Arizona Historical Society (p.154, 4689); Denver Public Library, Western History Dept. (p.103, X-33351); Glenbow Archives, Calgary, Canada (p.178, NA-1494-2: p.196, NA-1654-1; p.204, NA-1315-18; p.218, NA-40-1); Indiana Historical Society (p.41, C2253); Library of Congress (p.64, USZ62-10173; p.84, USZ62-131515; p.172, USZ62-124430; p.269, USZ62-103622); National Anthropological Archives, Smithsonian Institution (title page & p.235, NAA-3404-A; p. 317, NAA-560,782); National Archives of Canada (p.13, C-016744; p.56, C-36181); National Archives, Still Pictures Branch, College Park, MD (p.129, NWDNS-111-SC-83726; p.169, NWDNS-106-BAE-251-7A, p.252, 533060); National Museum of the American Indian, Smithsonian Institution (p.71, 16/1351); Nevada Historical Society (p.274, p.281, p.313); A Pictographic History of the Oglala Sioux, by Amos Bad Heart Bull, text by Helen H. Blish reproduced with permission from the University of Nebraska Press, © renewed 1995 (p.115; p.123).

PC: 6

Contents

For Mom & Dad
—Thanks—

INTRODUCTION

As WHITE SETTLERS SURGED RELENTLESSLY westward across the
North American continent in the 19th century, they
encountered the Native tribes that had occupied the land
for centuries. The traditional Native way of life became
impossible to maintain in the face of changes that were
dramatic, rapid and unlike any the Native people had ever
experienced. The Great Spirit saw the people's struggle and
provided them with a handful of leaders with wisdom,
bravery and strength. These leaders were relied upon to
negotiate treaties, and when those failed, to help them
withstand the inevitable armed forces that were sent to
eliminate them or relocate them to distant reservations.

As I understand it, Native leaders have special powers—
beyond wisdom and bravery—usually associated with
a spirit helper that gave assistance, often through visions.
But having spirit helpers and visions were not enough for
a man to become a leader. Individuals had to travel paths
worthy of respect. The choices he made, especially as those
choices conformed to band values, demonstrated leadership
potential. Power and behavior made a chief, who then
shouldered great responsibility because his only concern

was the welfare of his people. Volume II of *Great Chiefs* explores the lives of six such men.

Tecumseh, a Shawnee, created one of the greatest Native confederacies in the early 19th century. Founded on the philosophy of "a dish with one spoon," Tecumseh tirelessly organized Native tribes in an effort to stop American expansion into traditional Native lands. While he was an orator who mesmerized Native and white men alike, Tecumseh was also a respected warrior who backed up his words by leading his people in battle.

Geronimo, a Chiricahua Apache, was feared both in the southwestern United States and in northern Mexico as one of the most terrifying warriors of the second half of the 19th century. Fire burned in his belly because Mexican soldiers killed his family and American officials betrayed his people. Geronimo was captured several times, but it wasn't until the government relocated him to distant Fort Marion, Florida, that he was finally removed as a military threat.

Crazy Horse, an Oglala Sioux, was a warrior without equal on the mid-western plains. Dedicated to fighting the white men who invaded traditional Sioux lands in increasing numbers, the uncompromising Crazy Horse owned only a horse and his war equipment. He fought General Crook at the Battle of the Rosebud and General Custer at the Battle of the Little Bighorn and was the strategist behind many Native offensives.

Crowfoot, a Siksika Blackfoot, was a leading chief of his people by the early 1870s. He measured men by what they could do for his people rather than by their skin color. When the North-West Mounted Police stopped the illegal liquor trade that was decimating prairie Natives, Crowfoot declared that they were his friends. He buried his war club and made treaty with the Canadian government because he believed peace was in the best interests of his people.

Despite vigorous calls from Native leaders to fight the white man, he remained true to his word.

Plenty Coups, a Mountain Crow, was recognized as a leading warrior and a chief by his mid-20s. A vision in his youth had revealed to him that the white man would inevitably blanket the West as the buffalo had once done. Believing that the Crow would be best served by a friendship with the newcomers, he chose to ally with the Americans rather than go to war against them. As an army scout he fought against the Sioux and Cheyenne in the 1870s. Later, he worked tirelessly to further the interests of his people, and in 1904, the Mountain Crow selected him as their principal chief.

Wovoka, a Northern Paiute, was a dreamer whose visions affected Natives across the continent. There was little remarkable about young Wovoka, who worked as a laborer for white ranchers throughout his mid-20s. But in the late 1880s, he had a vision that planted the seeds for what would flourish in many Native communities as the Ghost Dance. The ceremony was one that preached peace and promised renewal, but in some quarters the Ghost Dance took on warlike characteristics. Wovoka disavowed such practices and continued to serve his people as a visionary, a healer and a voice of wisdom.

Finally, some notes of explanation. Native tribes called white people, including government officials and the British monarchy, by different names so terms will vary from chapter to chapter. Usually, a Native's name changed over his lifetime, so the same individual may have different names. Often, when a young Native performed some notable feat, he was given his father's name whereupon his father took another name.

CHAPTER ONE

Tecumseh

~~

Kispoko Shawnee, 1768–1813

WHERE THE TIPPECANOE RIVER BRANCHES off from the Wabash River (in present-day west-central Indiana) rose the village of Prophetstown, a Shawnee village led by Tecumseh. With its great council house, medicine lodge and rows of *wigewas* (lodges), the village looked like any Native community in the northeastern woodlands. A careful observer, however, might notice the House of the Stranger, a substantial lodge built for visitors. Most of the countless visitors flocked to see and hear Tenskwatawa, the Prophet, who had experienced a vision from *Waashaa Monetoo* (the Great Spirit). People came expecting to hear him preach of the value of a traditional Native lifestyle, free from the corrosive influence of the Big Knives (white men). Not so many years ago they would have heard just such words. In 1809, however, visitors listened to Tenskwatawa speak of the value of a Native confederacy, a political and military union that might stand against the Big Knives. It was a message that went far beyond

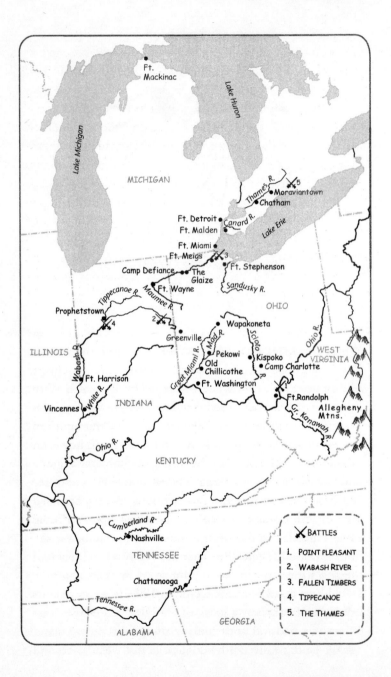

his previous calls to avoid liquor and white trade goods and to seek isolation from the growing white settlements. Tenskwatawa's new message was that of his brother, Tecumseh.

Prophetstown was only a year old in 1809. Building it had consumed the time and energy of the community, and adequate preparations had not been made for winter. Despite Tenskwatawa's successful efforts to secure supplies from William Henry Harrison, the governor of Indiana Territory, there was not enough food. Hunger soon became the least of the community's problems when a cholera epidemic struck. The sick and dying appealed to Tenskwatawa, a healer with special abilities. Could the Prophet not help? He was powerless against this new disease, and doubtful Natives began to slip away from Prophetstown.

Harrison, wary of the increasingly political nature of the Prophet's message, welcomed the dissension in Prophetstown and tried to turn it to his country's political advantage. He knew of Tecumseh's efforts to forge a Native alliance, but he was uncertain about its purpose. While the Shawnee chief was interested in a united Native front in the matter of land negotiations, Harrison suspected that armed resistance hid in the shadows. But the problems at Prophetstown suggested that Tecumseh's alliance was not as solid as the chief supposed. Harrison moved quickly, and in September 1809, he made the Treaty of Fort Wayne with the Delaware, Miami and Potawatomi. Those tribes ceded three million acres in Indiana and Illinois for increased annuities and $5000 in trade goods.

Tecumseh was incensed. The Fort Wayne Treaty struck at the heart of his objective as effectively as a stout ash arrow. For some years he had traveled throughout the Northwest, as the lands to the south and west of the Great Lakes were then called, and met with tribes to promote the concept of a dish with one spoon.

"The land belongs to all Natives," thundered Tecumseh, "and none of it should be ceded by one tribe without the consent of all."

It was not an original idea. Other Native leaders throughout the 18th century had promoted it. But with Tecumseh, the idea found a voice whose ability matched its grand scope. The Shawnee chief issued a declaration. He would kill the treaty chiefs who selfishly gave up the land that belonged to all Natives, just as he would kill any white settlers who tried to occupy it.

Tecumseh took his message west to the Osage, Sacs, Santee Sioux and other tribes that had seen the erosion of Native territory in the East but had not yet been forced to cede any of their own. At Prophetstown, Tenskwatawa's words were sharper, more closely reflecting Tecumseh's position. Tenskwatawa argued that it was time for the Natives to reclaim what was theirs, by force if necessary. The brothers' message struck a responsive chord with other Natives.

Perhaps it was time to resist, they thought.

White settlers also heard the message, and it caused their blood to run cold. Governor Harrison's own spies confirmed the rumors. Tecumseh could raise 10,000 warriors in a week and another 10,000 in a month. The United States could not afford to fight such a war, especially since it was on the brink of war with Britain. Harrison sent word to Prophetstown, to Tecumseh, whom he had finally come to sense was the greater threat of the two brothers. Anxious to determine Tecumseh's intent regarding the cession of lands, Harrison proposed a meeting. Tecumseh agreed, and he arrived at the governor's residence at Vincennes, Indiana Territory, with some 300 warriors in

July 1811. Eight hundred militia greeted the warriors. The
meeting began with little ceremony before Harrison
opened the discussion.

"Last year you declared that the Treaty of Fort Wayne,
fairly negotiated with the representative tribes, was some-
how underhanded and deceitful. You declared as much on
behalf of all tribes of the continent," he noted. "The matter
has been taken to the President. Until he responds, I can
say nothing more about it. I can offer you safe-keeping
should you and your brother wish to travel to Washington
to address the matter directly with the President."

"I have meetings of mine own to attend to and cannot
meet with the Great Father. After much trouble and difficulty, I have united the northern tribes," replied Tecumseh.
"When this council is concluded, I go south to unite those
tribes. Do not be alarmed," he added hastily. "I look to your
own country as an example of uniting all the fires that
compose your confederacy. We did not complain of yours,
and my white brothers should not complain of me doing
the same thing with regard to the Indian tribes."

"Will you try to stop the settlement of the new purchase?" asked Harrison.

"I hope that no attempts will be made to settle it until
I return in the spring. I expect the Wyandot and the
Iroquois to arrive this fall. They must occupy that tract as
a hunting ground and...they might kill the cattle and
hogs of the white people, which will cause disturbance,"
admitted Tecumseh. "I wish everything to remain in its
present state until I return. I wish no revenge sought for
any injury that had been or should be received by the
white people until my return. I will then go and see
the Great Father and settle everything with him. The
affairs of all the tribes in this quarter are in my hands, and
nothing can be done without me."

"The moon which we behold…will sooner fall to the earth than the President will suffer his people to be murdered with impunity. I will put my warriors in petticoats sooner than I will give up a country that I have fairly acquired from its rightful owners," Harrison replied calmly.

On that sour note, Harrison brought the council to a close. As Tecumseh headed south, Harrison reflected on the Shawnee chief, thoughts he later put to paper.

> *The implicit obedience and respect which the followers of Tecumseh pay to him is really astonishing, and more than any other circumstance bespeaks him one of those uncommon geniuses which spring up occasionally to produce revolutions and overturn the established order of things. If it were not for the vicinity of the United States, he would, perhaps, be the founder of an empire that would rival in glory that of Mexico or Peru. His activity and industry supply the want of letters. For four years he has been in constant motion…and wherever he goes he makes an impression favorable to his purposes.*

Harrison wasted no time in formalizing his plan. He would preempt the Native occupation of the lands ceded by the Fort Wayne Treaty by attacking Prophetstown while Tecumseh was absent, thereby circumventing Tecumseh's influence. It was an effective strategy because Tecumseh did not expect Harrison to attack. Despite his angry words about killing settlers, Tecumseh envisioned a peaceful Native alliance that would reject land sales to the U.S. Therefore, his travels to the southern tribes were imperative. Harrison, however, took Tecumseh's words at face value and expected violence. Tecumseh might not have anticipated Harrison's hurried strike, but he was a thoughtful leader who considered all possibilities. Before traveling to Vincennes, he had

A drawing of Tecumseh by Frederick Brigden. The date of the drawing is unknown, but like all known portraits of Tecumseh, it was rendered after his death. There is no fully authenticated portrait of the Shawnee leader. Brigden's portrait is accurate in many of its details. In his mid-30s, Tecumseh purged his life of the white man's influences after Tenskwatawa experienced a vision advising Natives to reject white ways. Tecumseh dressed in obsolete Native styles and included little of the white man's trappings, except his silver-mounted tomahawk and knife and a musket. Tenskwatawa had declared those appropriate to use if fighting the white men. Tecumseh also gave up alcohol and foreign foods, his rejection of white influences being in line with his own political ideas. He argued that Natives should unite to resist the white man's encroachment on their lands.

instructed Tenskwatawa to avoid fighting. If Harrison's men moved on Prophetstown, the Prophet was to abandon the village.

Tecumseh was not long gone when Harrison took the offensive; he ordered the Natives to leave Prophetstown. Tenskwatawa tried to appease the governor by sending a delegation to Vincennes. They arrived to find a gathering army. Harrison was not mollified by promises that matters would be settled in the spring. By the end of September, more than 1000 soldiers and militia were marching towards Prophetstown. Leaving some men at the hastily constructed Fort Harrison (just east of the Wabash River at present-day Terre Haute), the soldiers were camped a mile northwest of Prophetstown by early November. Tenskwatawa knew of their presence, and as he looked to his own forces, he was not confident. He had perhaps 500 warriors, and few of them had weapons to match those of the enemy.

To buy time, he sent word to Harrison that he would meet the following day. Then he addressed his warriors. Realizing that he was not a military man, the Prophet turned to his strength.

"*Waashaa Monetoo* has spoken to me! Half the Big Knives' warriors are already dead! The rest have lost their minds. Our tomahawks will be enough to kill them. Do not fear bullets. My magic will make them useless. The enemies' powder will be as harmless as sand and their bullets as soft as rain."

Tenskwatawa's dramatic words were effective, and despite Tecumseh's direction, the warriors prepared for battle. Before dawn of the day that Tenskwatawa and Harrison were to meet, the warriors attacked. Harrison had prepared his men for such a move, and sentries roused the camp rendering the ambush a failure. It did not dampen the enthusiasm of the warriors, who charged Harrison's men in rolling waves. But confidence melted when the warriors realized that the Prophet's magic was not working. Bullets caused injury and death. At daybreak, Harrison ordered a counter-attack that forced the Natives into retreat. Rather than pursue them, however, he burned Prophetstown to the ground.

The razing of the Shawnee village was the only success that Harrison enjoyed on this occasion. At the Battle of Tippecanoe he lost more men than the Natives had, and despite his superior forces, he could not justly claim victory. And, while the battle had thoroughly discredited the Prophet, it fueled the flames of hatred in the heart of one who had desired that there be peace on the frontier.

Tecumseh returned shortly after the battle. "I stood on the ashes of my own home, and there I summoned the spirits of the warriors who had fallen. And as I snuffed up the smell of their blood from the ground, I swore once more eternal hatred—the hatred of an avenger!"

〰〰〰

In the late summer of 1774, the Shawnee village of Kispoko Town on the Scioto River (in present-day south-central Ohio) was in an unusual state of commotion. Tecumseh, a young boy of about six, had been aware of the excitement for some days. He had picked up bits and pieces of news although he understood little of it. There had been talk of a red tomahawk delivered to his father, Pukeshinwau, the local chief. Tecumseh had seen the strangers who brought it when they arrived in his village, but he did not see the tomahawk. The council house was well used as the community met to discuss the symbolic weapon.

Tecumseh heard parts of the debate as it spilled out into the village and animated those gathered around the fire pits. Should the Kispoko prepare their warriors for battle? Tecumseh guessed that they would, because he saw that the warriors were preparing themselves. Painted and covered only in breechcloths, they performed dances. They also fasted and sat with the holy men, who asked the spirits to bring strength in the forthcoming struggle. On this day, Tecumseh watched as the warriors finally left the village. His eyes grew wide as he saw the men fall in behind Pukeshinwau. Never had he seen them dressed for battle, painted red and black with feathers attached to scalp locks, the only hair on otherwise shaved heads. They disappeared along the Warrior's Path, their whooping, gunfire and war songs soon lost in the trees.

Tecumseh didn't know it, but the men led by his father were part of the largest force of Native warriors since Pontiac's War in 1763. Shawnee, Iroquois, Wyandot and Delaware warriors rode to protect traditional homelands and their families who lived there. The Natives had endured the loss of land and suffered its accompanying effects for many years, but the problems intensified after 1768, when the Iroquois and the British government signed the Treaty of Fort Stanwix. For £10,000, the Iroquois ceded vast amounts of territory west of the Appalachians. But the Iroquois did not own the territory. Most of the region (notably present-day Kentucky) was the traditional hunting ground of the Shawnee.

Settlers who came to the region after 1768 were indifferent to the finer points of historic title. The tension between the local Natives and the newcomers simmered and finally boiled over in the spring of 1774 when Big Knives killed 13 Native women and children on the Scioto River. Many settlers were quick to condemn the massacre although their concern was not humanitarian. They feared that the Natives would seek revenge, thereby reducing the frontier to a bloody stage of violence. Under pressure, Lord Dunmore, the governor of Virginia (at this time the colony extended just south of Lake Erie and west to the Mississippi River) decided to take action before the Natives could mount an offensive. He organized a militia of 1500 men, divided them into two columns and marched on the Native villages along the Scioto River in what became known as Lord Dunmore's War.

In response, the prominent Shawnee chief Cornstalk had sent the red tomahawk to his brothers. Many Shawnee agreed to join him, as did others who were upset with the Fort Stanwix Treaty. As many as 1000 warriors met Colonel Andrew Lewis's force of 1100 men in a decisive battle at Point Pleasant, at the junction of the Great Kanawah and Ohio rivers on October 10, 1774. It was a hard fought battle that lasted the entire day. The determination of the Native warriors caught the Big Knives by surprise.

One of Lewis's men remembered, "I cannot describe the bravery of the enemy in battle. It exceeded every man's expectations....Their chiefs ran continually along the line of battle exhorting the men to 'lie close' and 'shoot well,' 'fight and be strong. ' "

Their words of encouragement contributed to significant militia losses of 140 men. But it was not enough to win the day. The Natives retreated, leaving 50 of their own on the battlefield. Among the dead was Pukeshinwau. The war chief took a bullet in the chest, probably as he rode along the line of battle inspiring others with his courage. He did not die immediately and was able to gasp his dying wishes to his oldest son, Cheeseekau, who was 13 years old and participating in his first war party.

"You are my first born. To you falls the responsibilities that were mine. Lead forth your younger brother in battle. Preserve unsullied the dignity and honor of our family."

After the battle, Cornstalk led the warriors back to his village of Chillicothe, where he called for a war council. All were aware that Lewis's militia was in pursuit, and scouts brought news that more men were approaching from the Ohio River. No one was confident that they could defend their villages against such numbers. Discouraged, the gathering fell silent.

Finally, Cornstalk slammed his war hatchet into the center post of the lodge and proclaimed, "Since you are not inclined to fight, I will make peace."

Cornstalk traveled to Camp Charlotte to meet with Lord Dunmore. Since no written record of the meeting was kept, their agreement remains uncertain. Dunmore claimed that Cornstalk accepted the Fort Stanwix Treaty, while the Shawnee chief maintained that he had only consented to a truce. The disagreement soon made little difference because settlers decided the matter by renewing their migration into old Shawnee hunting territories.

While Cornstalk and Dunmore were negotiating, Kispoko Town mourned its dead chief. Methoataaske, Tecumseh's mother, faced difficult times. Following the funeral rites, Pukeshinwau's relatives spent 12 days in mourning. They then had a feast and returned to the normal village life. But as the wife of the deceased, Methoataaske was required to mourn for 12 moons. She could not mingle with others, had to wear the same clothing for the entire period and refrain from washing. The demands were challenging, but they were particularly a trial for Methoataaske. She had four sons and a daughter, and she was pregnant. She gave birth to triplets, an unusual occurrence among Natives. One died, and another would grow to become Tenskwatawa, the Shawnee Prophet. Methoataaske never fully recovered from the ordeal, so those most influential in raising Tecumseh were his sister Tecumapease and his brother Cheeseekau.

Tecumseh was born in the spring of 1768 on the Scioto River, likely at Kispoko Town, the village founded by his father. His family had not been long in the region. Pukeshinwau and Methoataaske were born and raised in the south (likely present-day Georgia or Alabama) and moved north only in the late 1750s. The move is not surprising because the Shawnee were a migratory people, comfortable with nomadic ways.

The Shawnee tribal name came from the Algonquian word *chawungai*, meaning "southerners," reflecting the Shawnee's position to the south of other Algonquian tribes. It is probable that the tribe originated near Lake Erie, but early in their history they separated into five divisions—Mekoche, Hathawekela, Chillicothe, Kispoko and Pekowi—each of which traveled easily throughout the territory west of the Appalachian Mountains. For the most part, the divisions were autonomous, although they were linked by custom, language and mythology, which created a shared sense of tribal identity.

Methoataaske was a Pekowi, but since Pukeshinwau was a Kispoko (who also had a white ancestor) that became Tecumseh's division. The Shawnee were also organized along clan lines. Clans were symbolized by animals from which clan members derived special powers. Pukeshinwau belonged to the panther clan, but the name did not refer to a creature of flesh and blood. It was of the skies, a starry being that leaped through the constellations. Tecumseh's name is linked to the sky creature. "Tecumthé," as the Shawnee pronounced it, translated to "I Cross the Way," just as the panther journeyed across the sky. As tradition dictated, an elder from another clan gave him the name about six months after his birth.

Tecumseh was born during a brief sigh of tranquility in an otherwise tumultuous time. During the late 1750s and early 1760s, the French and Indian Wars were waged for control of North America west of British settlement. The Shawnee allied themselves with the French and found themselves on the losing side. All was not lost, however, because the British wanted to maintain the lucrative fur trade that had brought the Shawnee and the French together. The Shawnee did not object because they had already integrated European trade goods into their lives. As with most northeastern tribes, the Shawnee had no desire to give up muskets, knives and kettles, and they willingly began trading with their erstwhile enemies. The British, however, were poor trade partners. Their gift giving paled horribly compared to past French practices. They did not recognize the Natives as equals in trading and tried to cheat them. And, worst of all, they wanted more than the furs that had satisfied the French. They wanted the Natives' homeland.

In reply, the Ottawa chief Pontiac forged an alliance among the tribes west of the Appalachians, and in 1763 he launched an attack on the Great Lake forts. His confederacy enjoyed considerable success. They took eight forts and made it necessary to evacuate a ninth. But Pontiac's weakness was his dependence on the French, who thumbed their nose at his Native alliance. Eventually, British support arrived. Perhaps cunningly, but certainly cruelly, they came bearing blankets infected with smallpox. The Natives took the gifts and died in great numbers. Those who lived were forced to abandon the warpath so that they might hunt to feed their families. A resistance that started with a bang of promise, fizzled. Pontiac made peace in 1764.

The late 1760s were relatively quiet years for the Shawnee along the Scioto River. Settlers were crossing into their traditional territory, but not in great enough numbers to cause undue concern. Everything changed with Lord Dunmore's War in 1774. Matters further deteriorated in

1775 with the outbreak of the American Revolution. Led by Cornstalk, many Shawnee stayed committed to the Camp Charlotte agreement and remained neutral. But as the number of settlers into Kentucky increased—an estimated 10,000 by this time—it became difficult for Cornstalk to control aggressive young warriors.

By 1777, Cornstalk could no longer keep the peace. He felt obligated to inform the Americans of the situation. In October he traveled to Fort Randolph on the Ohio River. Upon hearing Cornstalk's news, the fort's commander had him thrown in jail. Cornstalk wasn't in jail an hour when a mob of Americans overpowered the guards and killed him. With news of the murder, the Shawnee joined the British and went on the warpath. Under these threatening conditions, however, some Shawnee decided to move. Methoataaske took her family and moved northwest to live with relatives at Pekowi on the Mad River (just west of present-day Springfield).

Tecumseh was 11 years old at the time of their relocation. He was a spirited and mischievous child who was often punished by a struggling mother. With three infants and no husband, she found the responsibility of child-rearing challenging even with the assistance of other villagers. Already Tecumseh's older sister, Tecumapease, had begun to shoulder many of her mother's duties. She and Tecumseh grew close, but the relationship was interrupted when Tecumapease married in the early 1780s. While his brother eventually played an important role in Tecumseh's education, during these years, Cheeseekau was busy proving himself as a warrior, and he was away raiding as often as he was in the village. As difficult as the boy was to control, Methoataaske looked with satisfaction upon the development of his skills. He was often the victor in games and competitions, he mastered bow and arrows at a young age, and she took note that he often delivered the small game that he killed to the elders in his village. At an early age, he had learned the lesson of communal responsibility.

Once settled in Pekowi, Methoataaske had additional help raising Tecumseh. Just south of the village was another Shawnee village known as Old Chillicothe, home to the war chief Blackfish. Blackfish may have adopted Tecumseh, but he certainly did serve as a father figure. The relationship was short-lived, however, when in the spring of 1779, Blackfish received a mortal wound defending Old Chillicothe from Kentucky militiamen. Tecumseh witnessed the six-week ordeal of his death. But warfare did not only bring grief to Tecumseh. In 1780, the British captured some 350 prisoners in Kentucky. They were taken back to Pekowi, and while most were released, a 12-year-old boy named Stephen Ruddell remained in the village. He was renamed Sinnamatha and became Tecumseh's inseparable companion.

Tecumseh and his family were driven farther west in August 1780, when 1000 Kentuckians burned Pekowi to the ground. The warriors tried to defend the village, but they had no answer to the Big Knives' six-pounder. The Shawnee built another village along the Great Miami River but it, too, was destroyed in the early winter of 1782. When peace was finally declared in 1783, Tecumseh was living at the northern end of the Mad River. Since 1775 the Big Knives had forced him to flee on five occasions, and more than once, over his shoulder he saw his village in flames. He was fortunate to escape these turbulent years with his life, but many Shawnee did not share his fortune. The battles of the 1770s and 1780s had cost them much. While it was true that the Big Knives had lost more men than the Natives during those years, the Shawnee had lost control of their traditional territories south of Ohio. It proved far easier for the Big Knives to endure their losses than it did for the Shawnee to recover theirs.

With the Treaty of Paris and the end of the American Revolution in 1783, Cheeseekau was freed from the warpath and able to devote more time to his younger brother. He taught Tecumseh the ways of the forest and of the animals that called it home so that the boy might hone his hunting skills. Tecumseh listened well and became a great hunter. Cheeseekau ensured that Tecumseh took his daily dip in a nearby cold stream to develop the fortitude and self-control necessary in a warrior, which would serve him well in later life. Of greatest importance, however, was Cheeseekau's influence on Tecumseh's emerging character. Stephen Ruddell remembered that Cheeseekau taught his younger brother "to look with contempt on everything that was mean," and sowed the seeds of "correct, manly and honorable principles" in him.

Perhaps Cheeseekau's teachings contributed to Tecumseh's popularity among his peers. He took the lead in many games, which were always more than mindless pastimes. His athletic skills were apparent in his prowess on the field during ball games. One popular game pitted 100 boys against 100 girls, with each side trying to kick the ball through the goalposts. Boys had to kick the ball up field. Girls could carry it, but if they did, they were fair game for tackling. Especially favorite contests were the mock battles. Ruddell noted that in such encounters Tecumseh "always distinguished himself by his activity, strength and skill."

When Tecumseh reached 14, however, it was time to put the games of childhood behind him. He was of the age when it was necessary to embark on a vision quest, the first in an important series of steps that would see him emerge as a man. The Shawnee practiced the vision quest somewhat differently than other Native groups did because it occurred over a lengthier period.

Little is known of Tecumseh's vision quest. It was a private matter that he chose to keep to himself, but it is likely that Cheeseekau supervised it. He blackened his younger brother's face and sent him into the woods to reflect and to fast. At first, Tecumseh's sojourns lasted little more than half a day. Over time, they were extended, with the final vision quest lasting several days. Others knew it was successful when Tecumseh washed the paint from his face.

Tecumseh's next steps towards manhood were taken in an atmosphere of renewed violence. After achieving its independence from Britain, the United States fixed its sights on the land east of the Great Miami River and south of the Ohio River. In 1783, the United States Congress annexed the territory, and as settlers arrived, Natives resumed raiding. Initially, the Iroquois and the Cherokee took the lead, attacking settlements in Kentucky. The Big Knives didn't differentiate among Native tribes, so the Shawnee along the Great Miami River found themselves subject to intense retaliation. Natives were killed and villages burned. By the mid-1780s, the Shawnee were at war again.

In 1786 Tecumseh killed his first buffalo. Usually such an occasion was cause for celebration, but less so during days of warfare. Tecumseh and a friend had accompanied a party of warriors, likely as servant-apprentices. The leader of the party had given specific instructions that prohibited the warriors from any action that might alert the American militiamen who were known to be in the vicinity. Nevertheless, the boys slipped away and took down a buffalo. When they returned to the war party with news of their kill, they were met with the chief's disapproval. The Big Knives were sure to notice the dead buffalo. He was so upset that he struck the boys across their shoulders with his ramrod as punishment. Tecumseh remained undeterred. The next day he set out with Stephen Ruddell, and they chose their targets more carefully this time. The boys joined a party of hunters authorized to find meat for the camp. Tecumseh hid in the branches of a tree and brought down 16 buffalo! It was an amazing feat by anyone's standards, and he was given a rifle as a reward.

A successful vision quest and a buffalo hunt were important in a youth's development, but to become a man among the Shawnee one had to prove his ability as a warrior. Expectations were undoubtedly high for Tecumseh when he took that final step. His Kispoko clan enjoyed a tradition among the Shawnee for producing prominent war chiefs, including his own father Pukeshinwau. Cheeseekau had already established an enviable reputation as a warrior. After his first experience on the warpath, however, Tecumseh wondered if he had the power to be ranked among their number.

In 1786, Tecumseh joined his brother and other warriors to defend Shawnee villages north of the Great Miami River. Intent on stopping Native's raids west of the Alleghenies, 800 Kentucky militiamen rode into Shawnee territory north of the Ohio River. Tecumseh and his party encountered the Big Knives on the Mad River. The battle was short-lived for the novice warrior. The unsettling noises of gunfire, the death cries, the smells of blood and gunpowder and the general confusion may have been overpowering. He may have even witnessed Cheeseekau being injured. Fearful, Tecumseh fled and remained hidden until the battle ended. It was a shameful act. Although Cheeseekau attempted to comfort him by noting that a single failure was unlikely to prevent him from becoming a warrior, Tecumseh took little relief. He would be ready when the next occasion called for courage.

The opportunity did not present itself along the Mad River. As was Shawnee practice, most bands abandoned their villages after the fighting and slipped deeper into the interior of present-day Ohio. By 1787 they had joined

with the Delaware and the Miami at the head of the
Maumee River. For a time, life was quiet. The Shawnee
had moved beyond the encroaching line of white settlers,
and, more importantly, their soldiers. They were closer to
their British allies, who had retained forts along the Great
Lakes and were able to access supplies more easily. Most
significantly, negotiations had tempered the frontier violence. The Mohawk chief Joseph Brant had convinced
other tribes to join in a confederacy that could more effectively respond to the United States' territorial expansion. It
was a political confederacy, founded on the idea of a united
Native front on treaty matters. It proved effective, especially
since the United States government did not wish to continue fighting costly Native wars. The government adopted
a policy of buying Native land rather than taking it by
force. Unfortunately, negotiations dragged along at a pace
that failed to match the enthusiasm of western-bound settlers. By 1787, warriors were raiding again.

The Ohio River, 120 miles south of the new Shawnee
villages, proved to be an ideal location for the Shawnee and
their Native allies to launch their attacks. Kentucky-bound
settlers found that the waterway was the easiest route to
their destination, and more than 12,000 traveled it between
October 1786 and June 1788. Many discovered that the
ease of travel was deceptive; the route held terrible dangers,
largely because of the settlers' mode of transportation.
Settlers used flatboats that were little more than small
barges and were difficult to maneuver. Warriors simply
took shelter along narrow passages and ambushed their
enemies. It was a profitable exercise because settlers usually
came with all their belongings. Those Big Knives who were
unfortunate enough to be attacked often lost more than
their possessions. Captives were sometimes killed, and many
died after being tortured.

In March 1788, Tecumseh redeemed himself after the disastrous experience of 1786. He was one of 100 warriors, including Cheeseekau and Stephen Ruddell, from several tribes, camped near the mouth of the Great Miami River. It was a good place for an ambush and the raiding party enjoyed success. In a week, they had taken 3 flatboats, 14 prisoners and considerable booty. Tecumseh played a significant role, as judged by Ruddell, who noted that the young Shawnee showed "great bravery and even left in the background some of the oldest and bravest warriors." Ruddell also claimed that it was "the first engagement in which he particularly distinguished himself." The ambushes were marred, however, by injuries to warriors and the escape of a few flatboats. A dark mood settled over the warriors. They scalped some prisoners and put five to death.

The torture of one particular settler revealed as much about Tecumseh as did his bravery in fighting. The prisoner was taken ashore, hands and feet bound, and thrown to the ground. He watched as the Natives cut down a sturdy oak sapling and drove it into the ground. Attached near its top was a long strip of rawhide, falling to the ground. The Natives stripped the captive, painted him black and then tied his hands to the rawhide rope. The prisoner watched, confused, as a large fire was lit nearby. It was only when he saw the warriors pull out sticks with glowing red tips that he realized what lay ahead. With shouts of triumph, the warriors set upon him. Each time the settler was jabbed with burning wood, he tried to jump free, only to be pulled back to the pole by the rawhide tether. Neither his pleas for mercy nor his suffering had any effect on the warriors. The torture continued throughout the night. Eventually, the captive was granted relief. His head slumped to his chest, and in the silence, Tecumseh heard only the crackles and pops of the fire.

Tecumseh had participated fully in the day's activities. He had cried the war whoop when boarding the flatboat and had helped to restrain the Big Knives and bring them ashore. He had returned to the vessel and rifled enthusiastically through the crates of supplies and equipment. But he only watched the torture. Although he knew that his people occasionally tortured their enemies, this was the first time he had witnessed it as a warrior. He remained silent throughout the ordeal, but he was not unaffected. Whether it was the rising bile in his throat or indignation firing his heart, he lashed out at his companions and the grisly tradition.

"What we have done is wrong! It is one thing to kill an enemy in battle. It is another to torture him when he is helpless. Victory for Shawnee and Iroquois, for Delaware, Cherokee and Wabash is not to be found at the end of a burning stick," he declared as he looked to the warriors from each of those tribes. "The Big Knives' suffering does not make us stronger. It does no justice to our cause. Let us fight like men and leave the dead on the field of battle."

Tecumseh had no right to interfere with the treatment of prisoners, especially those held by other tribes. He had no reason to believe that his passionate words would be persuasive. And yet, the warriors decided that they would no longer burn prisoners. Their decision must have been satisfying for Tecumseh, who not so long ago likely wondered if he would even be accepted among warriors, let alone influence their decisions. Tecumseh thereafter rejected torture, as Ruddell noted: "…when prisoners fell into his hands he always treated them with as much humanity as if they had been in the hands of civilized people—no burning, no torturing. Neither did he tolerate the practice of killing women and children."

By the fall of 1788, Tecumseh's family was on the move again. Joined by other Shawnee, Cheeseekau led his family west across the Mississippi River into present-day Missouri, which at the time was Spanish territory. Along the way, Tecumseh suffered a terrible accident while he was hunting for buffalo. He was thrown from his horse, and one of his thighbones shattered. Months later the break was still not healed. Tecumseh considered killing himself rather than endure a future of dependency but the thought was fleeting. The jagged bones never did mend properly, and Tecumseh thereafter walked with a limp. His new nickname became Broken Thigh. Few in Missouri got to know him well enough to use that name, however. When it was discovered that Big Knives were settled there and that more were expected to come, Cheeseekau decided to keep moving.

In early 1790, Tecumseh's Kispoko Shawnee were living with the Chickamauga Cherokee along the Tennessee River (near present-day Chattanooga). Tecumseh joined Cheeseekau in raids with the Chickamauga, who were considered to be among the fiercest of southern Native warriors. Tecumseh found a wife among the Chickamauga. It was the first of his many marriages, but unlike many Shawnee men, he was never married to more than one woman at a time. His wife's name is not known, but his relationship with her was the longest one he maintained. They had a daughter, and perhaps the two traveled with Tecumseh when he left Cheeseekau in the summer of 1791 and returned with his younger brothers to his home north of the Ohio River.

Tecumseh returned home as a minor war leader, with some 10 followers. Although only in his early 20s, he possessed a desirable reputation. The bravery and skill he demonstrated during raids along the Ohio River and his willingness to share the booty taken with his followers already had some

Shawnee referring to him as "the boldest warrior of the West." Undoubtedly his friends and relatives were pleased to see him because there was talk of war, and every warrior was needed. Since 1785, some 20,000 settlers had entered the Ohio Valley, and they had successfully pressured the United States government to send troops into the region for their protection. In 1790, President George Washington had persuaded Congress to establish a federal army, and most of its 1200 men were sent into the region. In addition, a force of 1500 militia was raised in Kentucky and Pennsylvania for frontier duty.

The commanding officer of the 2700 men, Arthur St. Clair (also the governor of the Northwest Territory and a Revolutionary War hero), first tried to negotiate a peace treaty with the Natives in the region. When he was rebuffed, he angrily set about the "humbling and chastising of some of the savage tribes." The Natives were aware of his intent, and the Shawnee, Miami, Wyandot and Ottawa tribes banded together with a force of 1000 warriors. In November, they encountered St. Clair's detachment, which was substantially reduced because of desertions, but still outnumbered the Natives. When the battle on the Wabash River ended, the army had lost almost 650 men and had another 271 wounded. Only 61 Natives were killed or wounded. It was the most one-sided defeat ever suffered by the American army.

Tecumseh missed the battle because he was hunting to support the many warriors. He nevertheless took a lesson from the Wabash River Battle. It demonstrated the power of his fellow Natives if they united.

A greater disappointment than missing the battle along the Wabash awaited the young Shawnee to the south. Throughout the summer of 1792, Cheeseekau and the Chickamauga raided many of the white settlements along the Cumberland River. Their success emboldened them to launch a major attack on Nashville in late September. Cheeseekau sent word to Tecumseh asking him to join in the offensive. Tecumseh arrived with his 10 warriors. While the reunion was undoubtedly a happy one, it was soon tempered by a revelation from Cheeseekau. As the warriors camped near Nashville, Cheeseekau addressed them.

"My brothers, I have had a dream. I have seen a morning attack on the Big Knives' fort. If we persevere, we will capture it. But when the sun is high in the sky, a bullet will strike me in the forehead," he explained. "I will not return."

While there is no indication that Cheeseekau had any special abilities to predict the future, the Shawnee and the other Natives viewed any dream seriously. His disclosure stunned the gathering to momentary silence. Here was a great warrior. Only days before he had revealed that he had killed over 300 men and that he expected to kill 300 more. Now he claimed that he would not live out the week.

"Turn back!" someone finally shouted.

"There is no dishonor in resting a war club when death is certain," suggested another.

Most agreed; Cheeseekau should not fight this battle. Tecumseh remained silent. He knew better than to try to persuade his brother to return to his village. He also knew how his brother would respond to the warriors' entreaties.

"There is honor in dying in battle," Cheeseekau replied. "I will die as my father did and not at home like an old woman. It is better that the birds should pick my bones."

The attack did not unfold as Cheeseekau had foreseen, perhaps because it was launched at night. It is possible that Cheeseekau changed the timing to avoid his demise. If so, he failed. The Shawnee war chief was the first to die. Before morning came, the warriors were in retreat, having failed in their mission.

Tecumseh never spoke of his feelings about his brother's death, but he was surely devastated. Not only had Cheeseekau been a father figure, he had served as Tecumseh's role model. The younger brother sought to be like Cheeseekau in action and attitude. Even in death, Cheeseekau taught Tecumseh about honor and courage. These were lessons not to be forgotten. Tecumseh had more pressing matters, however, than dwelling on the tragic events on the Cumberland. He had to avenge his brother's death, and that required the death of a Big Knife. During the fall and winter of 1792 he raided with the Chickamauga as the leader of the Shawnee contingent. They enjoyed success. With spring Tecumseh returned to Ohio.

Throughout 1793, there was renewed talk of peace with the Big Knives. Unfortunately, the United States government and the Native tribes could no more agree on treaty terms than they could a shared boundary. Shawnee leaders were incensed that the government representatives spoke to them of accepting terms. It was not the Natives who had been defeated on the Wabash River. The government was aware of its military weakness and tried to remedy it. In 1792, Congress authorized the recruitment of 5000 more soldiers. Even as the government talked of peace, troops under the command of Revolutionary War hero Anthony Wayne were pushing west. In the spring of 1793, they established headquarters at Fort Washington, near Cincinnati. Later that year, Wayne marched farther into Native territory. By the following summer, his 3000 soldiers and militia were at the Glaize, where they established Camp Defiance. Behind them lay a trail of burned villages and hastily constructed forts. Wayne's advance was one that did not envision retreat. The Shawnee and their allies were impressed. They gave Wayne the name Black Snake for his cunning in the field.

The Natives realized that they had to stop Black Snake. Led by the Miami chief Little Turtle, and with the urging of their British allies who promised support, they planned an ambush at Fallen Timbers. It seemed an ideal location. Some years earlier, a tornado had cut through the area, leaving a tangle of broken and uprooted trees in its wake. The Natives expected that it would be difficult terrain for the Big Knives. But two years training in the wilderness had done much to sharpen the skills of the soldiers and the militia. And most importantly, Wayne's scouts had advised him of his enemies' preparations. He waited until many of the warriors left Fallen Timbers for supplies. They numbered about 800 when Black Snake slipped into the trap. The Big Knives' line did not break as it made for their enemies' center; the Natives were forced into the fallen trees they had expected to use to their own advantage. Finding it difficult to fight under such conditions, the Natives retreated to the British Fort Miami, where, to their surprise, they were refused entrance. They fled to the woods.

Tecumseh took little solace from the determined efforts of his Shawnee warriors at the Battle of Fallen Timbers. They had fought at the forefront, and it was only their courage that allowed those in the rear to retreat unharmed. Unfortunately, among the 40 or so Natives who died there (Wayne lost a similar number) was his remaining older brother Sauawaseekau. After the Battle of Fallen Timbers, Tecumseh moved north with others of the Native alliance, eventually settling near the mouth of the Maumee River on the eastern shore of Lake Erie. The journey was surely a difficult one. As Tecumseh surveyed the ragged condition of the Natives—perhaps 2500 strong—forced to move yet again with little in the way of supplies or equipment, he reflected on the enormity of the recent Native defeat. The Big Knives had surprised the Natives with their discipline; their British allies had abandoned them; and the Natives were distancing themselves from their traditional homelands.

Tecumseh wasn't the only one thinking about the state of the Natives. Wayne realized that he had the upper hand, and in the summer of 1795, he sent soldiers to the Lake Erie camp with a message of peace. Still recovering from their defeat, many Native chiefs decided to listen. The Treaty of Greenville was signed in August 1795. It would prove to be one of the most significant agreements between the United States and the Natives, and it signaled the collapse of the Native confederacy of previous years. Most of Ohio and Indiana were ceded to the government and opened up for settlement. In return, the Natives received annuities and peace. They were also expected to settle near American forts. Ninety-one chiefs from 12 tribes in the Ohio Valley and lower Great Lakes put their mark on the treaty.

Tecumseh was not one of them. As a chief—only in his late 20s, his leadership had attracted a following of some 250 Kispoko—he had a right to be included. Tecumseh did not even attend the peace council in Greenville even though Wayne declared that any failure to participate was an unfriendly gesture. Tecumseh demonstrated his disdain for the proceedings by riding into southern Ohio and raiding white settlements, clearly in violation of the treaty. But they were acts that stood well in his own mind, acts that honored the memory of his father and brothers who had died in an effort to prevent what happened at Greenville.

Tecumseh settled his band on territory that the Natives had ceded in the Treaty of Greenville. Although his decision to slip back into Ohio ran counter to that made by most other chiefs, it was not a difficult one for Tecumseh to make. He wanted his band to continue living as the Shawnee had lived traditionally, and he knew that such a life would be impossible in the shadows of the American forts and the white settlements near the forts. There would be competition for game, and as the forests were hunted out, the Natives would inevitably become dependent on annuities and trade goods. Tecumseh realized that dependency would allow the Big Knives greater control over the Natives. How would his people be able to refuse more demands for land when refusal meant destitution? Treaty life seemed to be a trap every bit as effective as a well-planned ambush; once Natives fell into it, escape was difficult.

In the closing years of the 18th century, Tecumseh's band lived in south and central Ohio, seeking isolated locations where the women could grow crops and the men could hunt. Tecumseh took time for his personal life. Over three years, he took two more wives, with whom he had two sons. He had little time for his children, however, so he sent them to his sister to raise. His all-consuming consideration was the livelihood of the band. Since he wasn't raiding during this period, his efforts were devoted to bringing in game. No one did that as well as Tecumseh, who continued to demonstrate his prowess as a hunter. One story tells of how he was challenged to a competition by some of the younger warriors in his band. Among their number was his brother Lalawe'thika. They wagered that they could kill as many deer as Tecumseh could within a three-day period. Three days later Tecumseh's deer numbered 30. The most that any of the younger men had killed was 12. Tecumseh ensured that the meat went to others in his camp.

Whether it was game taken in a hunt or supplies stolen during a raid, Tecumseh rarely kept more than he needed. He was not interested in acquiring personal wealth, and as a result, his band benefited. Anthony Shane, a mixed-blood who was married to a relative of Tecumseh and who knew the Shawnee chief (although not as allies), elaborated on this aspect of Tecumseh's character.

"Tecumseh was remarkable for hospitality and generosity. His house was always supplied with the best provisions, and all persons were welcome and received with attention. He was particularly attentive to the aged and infirm, attending personally to the comfort of their houses when winter approached, presenting them with skins for moccasins and clothing, and upon his return from a hunting party, presented the old people of his neighborhood uniformly with the choicest game that was the result of his great skill as a hunter. This course of conduct was not confined to the rich, or those of influence and reputation...."

About this time, in the fall of 1799, Tecumseh first came to the notice of the Big Knives as a thoughtful speaker of some ability. The white settlers of southern Ohio were concerned by unexpected war preparations made by the Shawnee and their allies. Anticipating an attack, some of the settlers took the levelheaded approach of sending a letter to the chiefs at the Shawnee village of Wapakoneta requesting an explanation. At the subsequent meeting, attending Shawnee chiefs chose Tecumseh to speak for them. Tecumseh assured the settlers that his people were preparing for an invasion by southern Chickasaw, their long-time enemies. They did not intend to strike against the Big Knives. However, it was not so much what Tecumseh said as how he delivered it that most impressed those gathered. One witness reported that the speech was "much admired for its force and eloquence," despite the admission of the well-qualified translator who confessed that "it was difficult for him to interpret [Tecumseh's] lofty flights of eloquence." Reassured, the settlers departed and they spread word of the oratorical flair demonstrated by the young Shawnee chief.

Tecumseh was soon called on to use his speaking skills to use on a much grander stage. The 19th century brought great changes to Shawnee ancestral territory. In 1800, the Indiana Territory was created. It included land west to the Mississippi River and north to the British colonies. Some 6000 white settlers inhabited the region at the time, but the aggressive expansionist policies of Governor William Henry Harrison dramatically increased that number. Harrison was from a prominent American political family and a veteran of the Battle of Fallen Timbers.

At first, Harrison was sympathetic to the Native cause. "The Indian chiefs all profess, and I believe most of them feel, a friendship for the United States...but they have made heavy complaints of ill-treatment on the part of our Citizens," he noted. "They say that their people have been killed—lands settled on—their game wantonly destroyed and their young men made drunk and cheated of the peltries which formerly procured the necessary articles of clothing, arms and ammunition to hunt with. Of the truth of these charges I am well convinced."

As governor, Harrison's primary concern was not the welfare of the Natives, but the directive of his president. In 1800, France acquired the vast Louisiana Territory from Spain. Therefore, in an effort to limit French influence over the Natives, President Thomas Jefferson ordered Harrison to secure title to as much Native land as possible. The Treaty of Greenville stipulated that Natives had to sell their land when the Big Knives came knocking. By 1805, Harrison had negotiated seven treaties, acquiring territory in the present-day states of Indiana, Wisconsin, Missouri and Illinois for the United States. Harrison was a shrewd and ruthless operator. Rather than negotiate with Native tribes as a unified whole (as had been the case at Greenville in 1795), he divided and conquered. When a tract of land was wanted, he would meet with representatives of the band that used it, and with bribes, threats and liquor, he would acquire it. By 1806, he had secured 70 million acres of Native land west of the Treaty of Greenville line, paying at *most* two cents an acre.

The Shawnee ceded little land during these years, primarily because Governor Harrison was not yet interested in it. Tecumseh was well aware of the large transactions, however. His band was camped in Delaware territory and that tribe had made treaty. It's also likely that Tecumseh attended the first of the treaty meetings, at Fort Wayne in June 1803. Eight tribes ceded more than one million acres for an annuity of 150 bushels of salt. The Shawnee present tried to block the transfer by walking out of the council, but not before agreeing to sell their rights to an Illinois salt spring in return for the annuity. A few years later, other Shawnee ceded some land east of the Sandusky River. Although these were insignificant land cessions, it's unlikely that Tecumseh agreed to either. He did not want the Big Knives troubling Natives west of the Treaty of Greenville line.

As disturbing as American expansion was, it may not have been the most significant matter in Tecumseh's life during these years. His younger brother Lalawe'thika, whose life to this point showed nothing of the prominence he was to achieve, underwent a profound transformation. A childhood accident during a game had blinded one eye and deformed the right side of his face. The clumsiness that caused the accident was seen as a bad omen, one born out in the failures of Lalawe'thika's youth. He fell short in most things the Shawnee considered important. He was without a war record, too lazy to hunt and often drunk. Anthony Shane suggested that he was "a talkative, blustering, noisy fellow, full of deceit," a description many others accepted. He was a healer in Tecumseh's village on the White River, a calling that had been revealed when he was a young man, likely on a vision quest. In this he enjoyed some success, and he was able to support two wives and several children.

Throughout the spring and summer of 1805, Native communities along the White River were overcome by influenza. Confusion led to panic. Was *Waashaa Monetoo* (the Great Spirit) angry with the people? Was it the power of the Big Knives' spirits? Was *Motshee Monetoo* (the Bad Spirit) exercising influence through witches? No one could be certain, and more powerful healers than Lalawe'thika had no answers. But at least the disease had not affected him, suggesting something of his power. In November, a message arrived from the Shawnee village of Wapakoneta. Would he come and help? Lalawe'thika went there and ministered to the sick. Seeing the dying and believing that their condition was a result of his personal inadequacies, Lalawe'thika's thoughts turned to his own failings. He prayed to *Waashaa Monetoo* to show him how he might be saved.

Later, when he was asleep, he was granted a vision. Lalawe'thika found himself on the trail traveled by the souls of the dead. Before him the trail forked. The right-hand road led to Heaven, but few Natives traveled it. The left-hand road was crowded with those walking to Eternity. He saw two houses along the left-hand road from which extended paths that led back to the right-hand road. The houses offered opportunities to change one's ways and repent. Most Natives chose to walk past them. The third and final house along the left-hand trail over-flowed with suffering souls, where each was punished according to his sins. Lalawe'thika described the house as "roaring like the falls of a river." He saw a drunkard drinking molten metal, a vision of his own future.

When Lalawe'thika awoke, he decided to tell others of the fork and of what awaited them if they chose the wrong path. Other visions clarified the message. The proper choice was to reject not only the vices of the Big Knives but all white influences. The change in Lalawe'thika was dramatic. The man known before the vision disappeared. He adopted the name Tenskwatawa ("The Open Door"), but as his message became increasingly popular with Natives in the northeastern woodlands, he became known as the Prophet.

What did Tecumseh make of his brother, the Prophet? It's uncertain. Some suggest that he put Lalawe'thika up to it, that the vision was Tecumseh's creation, to be used by Tenskwatawa to foster a message that might aid Tecumseh's own emerging political vision of a Native confederacy. Those who witnessed the Prophet's emotional commitment to his cause suggested that there was nothing forced about it. There is no doubt, however, that Tenskwatawa's religious message and Tecumseh's political goals were mutually supportive. The Shawnee chief adopted practices in line with his brother's vision. Tecumseh dressed in Native styles that had been obsolete for half a century and included nothing of the Big Knives' apparel, although he kept his silver-mounted tomahawk, knives and muskets. The Prophet had declared that the musket was appropriate to use if fighting Big Knives. He gave up alcohol and rejected foods that he considered foreign.

Tecumseh's efforts to purge the white influence from his life were first noted when he took his band back to Greenville, Ohio, in 1805. Returning there brought him closer to the lands of his childhood, but the move was motivated by more than memory. Greenville was a symbol of much that had gone wrong for the Shawnee and their Native allies in the previous decade. It had been the site of

An 1835 lithograph of Tecumseh's brother Tenskwatawa
(1768–1837) made from a James Lewis 1824 painting.

Anthony Wayne's headquarters and had served as the location for the signing of the Treaty of Greenville. By 1805,
it was well within American territory and supposedly off
limits to Natives. Tecumseh's move was a statement of defiance, one more resounding than any words could convey.

Governor Harrison understood the message. As reports
indicating Tenskwatawa's growing influence among the
Native tribes of Ohio piled on his desk at his office in

Vincennes, Harrison took action to undermine Tenskwatawa
by questioning his power before other Natives.

"Who is this pretended prophet who dares speak in the
name of the Great Creator?" he mocked. "Make him prove he
is God's messenger. If he really is a prophet, ask him to cause
the sun to stand still or the dead to rise from their graves."

Harrison should have reconsidered his challenge. In the
closing days of spring 1806, Tenskwatawa sent word to his
followers that he would make the sun stand still and turn
day into night. They gathered on June 16. Tenskwatawa
stood alone in a field, surrounded by anxious Natives. They
held their breath as the Prophet raised his arms to the sky.
The sun disappeared and night fell!

The governor cried foul. It was merely an eclipse, and
Tenskwatawa likely learned of it from a farmer's almanac. His
protests fell on deaf ears. The Prophet had performed a mira-
cle on demand. Soon the Shawnee village at Greenville
overflowed with newcomers. So many came that Tecumseh
had to turn them away, promising that the Prophet would
have more to say during the harvest when there would be
food enough to feed them all. United States government
officials were also worried. They viewed the gathering
Natives as a military threat, and they sent word to Tecumseh
that his settlement showed disrespect for the United States.

"It must be vacated," they added.

Tecumseh's reply was equally direct. "*Waashaa Monetoo*
has appointed this place for us to light our fires, and here
we will remain."

The government need not have worried about a military
threat. It is true that Tecumseh and Tenskwatawa wanted to
reduce the white influence among their people, but they
envisioned doing it through self-imposed isolation and sepa-
ration, not with violence. Perhaps American fear was understandable with the rumors of an emerging Native alliance

farther west, accurate rumors of support for armed resistance. The placement of the Shawnee village also suggested aggression. But, had officials considered the situation carefully, they would have realized that the Greenville location precluded violence. Because it was in American territory, the only way it could survive was if the Shawnee maintained good relations with the Big Knives. Tecumseh spent many nights in the Big Knives' communities trying to reassure them of his peoples' peaceful intent. His calming influence proved effective and the settlers' worries dissipated.

But they did not disappear, and the settlers' concerns waited only for an opportunity to resurface. That opportunity came on June 22, 1807, many miles away on the Atlantic Ocean, when the British ship *Leopard* fired upon the United States frigate the *Chesapeake*. The *Leopard* was searching for naval deserters. The issue had long been a thorn in the side of British-American relations. Britain was at war with Napoleonic France and had employed a coastal blockade of Europe as part of its tactics. The blockade interfered with American-European trade, which was bad enough, but it had greater implications. The manpower necessary to maintain an effective blockade was staggering, and Britain had been forced to press men into service to fill its ships. These men often deserted and found employment on neutral American vessels, where conditions and pay were better. British ships stopped and searched American ships at every turn, a bullying action that brought howls of protest. Crying "Free Trade and Sailors' Rights," many Americans were prepared to go to war over the matter. The possibility brought back memories of the American Revolution and of the Natives' support for Britain during that war. Americans began to wonder whether the British were fomenting unrest among the Natives in preparation for yet another war.

When news of the speculations of war reached the frontier, colorful rumors blossomed that the British were behind
the whole Greenville affair. The murder of a settler less than
a month before the *Leopard–Chesapeake* encounter did little to
help the situation. The settler had been struck with a tomahawk and scalped. Tecumseh himself met with settlers to deny
Shawnee involvement. Government officials in Greenville,
most notably the local Indian agent, pressed Washington to
intervene. The Prophet—clearly a British agent, he argued—
must be removed as a threat to national security. While no
evidence could be found that Tenskwatawa was counseling
rebellion, to American eyes he was exercising undue influence on the Natives. Increasingly, Natives were unwilling to
cede land, and they pointed to the Shawnee brothers in
Greenville as having shaped their decisions. In August,
President Thomas Jefferson ordered frontier governors to
make preparations for war against the Natives. That he didn't
attack at this time was likely a result of his fear of an imminent war with Britain.

Tecumseh, meanwhile, was active on two fronts. He was
shaping his brother's religious message into a political one,
and he was working to bridge divisions among the
Shawnee. He also visited the Wyandot to the north in early
September. There he sought advice on a course of action
should the British and Americans go to war. He invited
tribal delegates to Greenville to discuss a unified approach
to dealing with the Big Knives. Undoubtedly he sought to
revive the old notion of a dish with one spoon, the idea
that Native lands were held jointly and could be ceded
only with the agreement of all. Not everyone who listened
was receptive. Although few disagreed that Native lands
should be protected, for many the memories of intertribal
warfare remained too strong. They would have nothing of
Native unity.

Just as important were Tecumseh's dealings with the Big Knives. In September, a delegation from Thomas Kirker, acting governor of Ohio, arrived in Greenville seeking first-hand information about the Shawnee's intent. When Stephen Ruddell was identified as the interpreter, the party was well received. The American delegates pointed out that the British had been poor friends since the American Revolution. They added that the Great Father was busy organizing an army of 100,000 men to march north. If they found that the Natives were conspiring with the British, they would attack. Tecumseh felt that the most effective way to deal with the rumors was to return with the delegation to Chillicothe, where he could address the governor in person. What he said has not been recorded, but an eyewitness to his speech later described the effect of his words.

"When Tecumseh rose to speak, as he cast his gaze over the vast multitude which the interesting occasion collected together, he appeared one of the most dignified men I ever beheld. While this orator of nature was speaking, the vast crowd preserved the most profound silence. He spoke confidently of the Indians' intention to adhere to the treaty and live in peace and friendship with their white brethren, and by doing so, he dispelled as if by magic the apprehension of the whites. The settlers immediately returned to their farms, and the active hum of business was resumed in every direction."

Tecumseh returned to Greenville, but he did not remain there long. Despite the message of *Waashaa Monetoo*, the location of the village was proving inadequate. Game was insufficient to feed the many who came to see Tenskwataw, the Prophet. In the autumn of 1807 Main Poc, an important Potawatomi chief from Illinois, visited Greenville. He opposed the land sales and a Native alliance, but he invited Tecumseh to move his band to Potawatomi territory, where access to food was good. In the spring of 1809, the Shawnee moved close to the fork of the Wabash and Tippecanoe rivers. There they built the village of Prophetstown on the northwest bank of the Tippecanoe River, 200 miles north of the governor's headquarters at Vincennes.

Tecumseh and Tenskwatawa were not long in Prophetstown before the British came calling. Although British officials did not think highly of Tenskwatawa, they saw his influence among the Natives. His anti-American stance was undeniable, and the British sensed that an alliance with him might be valuable if war erupted with the United States. James Craig, the governor general of the Canadas, instructed his subordinates to avoid openly inciting the Natives, but to make it clear to them that Britain would look favorably upon their assistance. Deputy Superintendent-General of Indian Affairs William Claus followed up on Craig's directive in late May. He sent word to Prophetstown requesting that the Prophet and his tribal allies visit Fort Malden, where they could discuss mutual interests.

Tecumseh, however, had a different task for Tenskwatawa. The building of Prophetstown had been so time-consuming that there had not been an opportunity to plant sufficient crops or to hunt. As Natives continued to arrive, the food situation grew serious. Tenskwatawa was dispatched to Vincennes, where he pleaded with Governor Harrison for corn. The Prophet spoke about more than his band's hunger. Probably at the Tecumseh's command, Tenskwatawa honey-coated his request by noting his efforts to reform the Natives so that they would live in peace with the Big Knives. Harrison left the meeting convinced that Tenskwatawa could be a force for good on the frontier. He readily issued food and equipment, including ammunition for hunting.

Meanwhile, in June, the British received an unexpected answer to their request for a meeting when Tecumseh

arrived at Fort Malden, on the northwestern shores of
Lake Erie in Upper Canada. The British likely didn't
know much about the Shawnee chief, but they were
immediately impressed with his frank attitude. Tecumseh
explained to Claus that he was forging a multi-tribal settlement on the Tippecanoe and that, while he would fight
the Big Knives if necessary, he had no desire to do so at
present. He also reminded Claus that several chiefs had
died when they discovered that the gates to Fort Miami
were barred following the Battle of Fallen Timbers.
Grasping quickly that Tecumseh was no mere chief, Claus
gave him presents to curry favor. He asked that Tecumseh
remain until Francis Gore, lieutenant-governor of Upper
Canada, arrived. That Gore was already en route was an
indication of the importance that the British placed on
a renewed Native alliance.

Tecumseh had business that needed his attention so was
not about to cool his heels at Fort Malden, but he promised to return. He first traveled south to Michigan
Territory and met with Wyandot, Shawnee and Mohawk
leaders to spread his idea of a Native confederacy. In mid-
July, Tecumseh and 1000 warriors were back at Fort
Malden, where they found Gore waiting. Once the ceremonies were completed, the lieutenant-governor addressed
the gathering. While he avoided reference to war with the
United States, he gave clear signals that war was expected
and that Native support would be both welcomed and
rewarded. He advised the Natives to keep their warrior
skills sharp and to remember that it was the Red Coats
who had fought by their side in the past. His counsel
surely gave Tecumseh pause to reflect, but it was Gore's
reference to the United States' expansionist policies that
likely gave Tecumseh the greatest satisfaction. Gore stated
that the British king did not recognize the United States'

purchase of northwestern lands. Could it be that Ohio might belong to the Natives once again? The lieutenant-governor concluded his speech by presenting a belt of wampum to the Natives. Everyone recognized the belt as a symbol of friendship.

The Wyandot representative delivered the response to Gore's speech, as was the tribe's traditional right, following a consultation with the other Natives. Although Tecumseh did not speak before the council, his influence and importance was nonetheless recognized when his Native brothers gave him custody of the wampum belt. The Shawnee chief also impressed Gore. He called Tecumseh "a very shrewd intelligent man." The assessment hardly did him justice. In just a few months, Tecumseh had successfully courted the Red Coats and convinced the Big Knives that he posed no threat, all the while openly admitting that he was building a Native confederacy.

Despite the supplies from Harrison, the winter of 1809 proved difficult for Prophetstown because of hunger, disease and hardship. Some Natives questioned the Prophet's power, and finding it wanting, returned to their home communities. Harrison seized the opportunity provided by the dissension and by Tecumseh's absence to negotiate the Fort Wayne Treaty of 1809. The Delaware, Miami and Potawatomi Natives ceded three million acres of land. When Tecumseh learned of it, he was incensed. The treaty undermined his efforts, and he declared it invalid because it was not agreed to by all Natives. He threatened to kill both the chiefs who made treaty and any Big Knives who tried to settle on the ceded territory.

After the signing of the Fort Wayne Treaty, many Natives came to realize that the only way they could protect their ancestral lands was to join together in the alliance suggested by Tecumseh. It was all too clear that unless all Natives considered their territory a dish with one spoon, the Big Knives would simply continue their successful expansionist strategy of dealing with one or two tribes at a time. Harrison became concerned when he heard that the tribes were lining up behind Tecumseh and Tenskwatawa, so he proposed a meeting to find out about the brothers' intentions. Tecumseh arrived at Vincennes in the late summer of 1811. Although he outlined his plans for a peaceful Native alliance in a most impressive manner, Harrison was worried about how Tecumseh was calling on Natives to fill the ceded territory. When Tecumseh informed Harrison that he would be traveling south after the council, the governor made plans to attack Tecumseh's village.

While Tecumseh hoped that Harrison would not resort to violence in his absence, he anticipated it. Before leaving Prophetstown for the Vincennes council, he left specific instructions with Tenskwatawa not to engage soldiers. If the soldiers attacked, Tenskwatawa and all others were to leave the village. In September 1811, a combined force of army and militia marched on Prophetstown. By early November, 1000 soldiers were camped a mile from the village. Rather than flee before the imminent attack, Tenskwatawa ordered an ambush. The 400 warriors in the village responded to his command when he told them that *Waashaa Monetoo* had revealed victory. The battle did not go as Tenskwatawa hoped. Although more soldiers died than did warriors, the Natives were forced to flee Prophetstown and watch it burn from a distance.

Prophetstown was not the only thing razed at the Battle of Tippecanoe. Tenskwatawa's reputation was also destroyed because his medicine had failed. Many angry Natives returned to their villages, but no one was as upset as Tecumseh. When he came back to Prophetstown, his first act was to swear revenge against the Big Knives. Then he dealt with his brother, who in a day had broadsided his efforts of the past decade. Tecumseh put his knife to Tenskwatawa's throat, but before he made the bloody cut, declared that death was too good for him. All was not lost, however. As Tecumseh reflected on his broken confederacy, he recalled the inroads he had made with the southern tribes. In every village he called on, councils were organized and he was permitted to speak. Although he did not always win the support of chiefs and elders, he found that warriors were always ready to join his cause.

An eyewitness left a record of Tecumseh's visit to the Osage (in present-day Missouri). He noted how Tecumseh forcefully described all Natives as one family, who would be destroyed separately if they failed to stand together.

"Brothers, we must be united; we must smoke the same pipe; we must fight each other's battles; and more than that, we must love the Great Spirit. He is for us. He will destroy our enemies and make all his red children happy."

Tecumseh emphasized that the Natives would not have to fight the battle themselves. He revealed that the British would help them. With humility, the eyewitness continued on, illustrating the power of the Shawnee's oratorical ability.

> *I wish it were in my power to do justice to the eloquence of this distinguished man, but it is utterly impossible. The richest colors, shaded with a master's pencil, would fall infinitely short of the glowing finish of the original. The occasion and subject were peculiarly adapted to call into action all the powers of genuine patriotism; and such language, such gestures and such feelings of fullness of soul contending for utterance, were exhibited by this untutored native of the forest in the central wilds of America, as no audience, I am persuaded, either in ancient or modern times ever before witnessed.*

My readers may think some qualification due to this opinion, but none is necessary. The unlettered Te-cum-seh gave extemporaneous utterance only to what he felt. It was a simple but vehement narrative of the wrongs imposed by the white people on the Indians, and an exhortation of the latter to resist them.... This discourse made an impression on my mind which, I think, will last as long as I live.

The Battle of Tippecanoe was followed by renewed attempts at peace. Although the United States government had strong proponents of aggressive westward expansion within, Harrison was directed to make treaty with the Natives. Tecumseh thought negotiations were a good idea. He even declared that he was prepared to visit the president, as he had pledged the previous fall. Perhaps Tecumseh believed that something good might come out of a meeting with the Great Father, but it is more likely that he was buying time to rebuild his confederacy. Indeed, before the winter snow had melted, Tecumseh had runners visit other tribes to shore up support. Tecumseh himself may have traveled south with that purpose again in March. Whatever measures he took, they were successful and by spring the confederacy was stable. Tecumseh did not have time for a sigh of relief before its stability was rocked again.

Throughout the late winter and spring of 1812, the frontier was thrown into chaos by raiding warriors, who were angered by the attack on Prophetstown and American Native policy in general. Neither Tecumseh nor the chiefs who supported him could rein them in. The situation was serious enough that an intertribal council was held in May to address it. Tecumseh attended although he found as many adversaries there as allies. Skilled at shaping the mood of such gatherings, Tecumseh won the favor, if not the support,

of some critics by appealing to shared rallying points: the
injustice of the Big Knives and a desire for peace.

> *Governor Harrison made war on my people in my*
> *absence. It was the will of Waashaa Monetoo that he*
> *should do so. We hope it will please Waashaa Monetoo*
> *that the white people may let us live in peace. We will not*
> *disturb them, neither have we done it, except when they*
> *have come to our village with the intention of destroying*
> *it....And I further state that had I been at home there*
> *would have been no blood shed at that time.*

But Tecumseh was as blunt a speaker as he was artful,
and he continued on to accuse the Potawatomi for the
raids. The Potawatomi chiefs who were present agreed, but
they blamed the action of their warriors on the counsel of
Tenskwatawa, whom they called a "pretended prophet."

> *It is true we have endeavored to give all our brothers*
> *good advice, and if they have not listened to it, we are sorry*
> *for it. We defy a living creature to say we ever advised any-*
> *one, directly or indirectly, to make war on our white brothers.*
> *It has constantly been our misfortune to have our views*
> *misrepresented to our white brothers. This has been done by*
> *pretended chiefs of the Potawatomies and others that have*
> *been in the habit of selling land that did not belong to them*
> *to the white people.*

Blunt, but with a sharp edge! Tecumseh's words were sufficiently compelling to draw warriors from those tribes that
had made treaty with the United States. Over the weeks
that followed, they joined him by the hundreds. But the
council concluded on a dark note. Before Tecumseh left, an
emissary of the British government approached him bearing

unfortunate news. The British would no longer offer their support for fear of American accusations that they were inciting Native unrest. Such claims might well be enough to send Britain and the United States to war. Undeterred, Tecumseh was determined to act without them. He made his way west to shore up his support. By June, he could claim that the confederacy included some 3500 warriors from at least 10 different tribes north of Shawnee territory. It was a confederacy to match any in recent Native history. And there was no telling how many more might join. Tecumseh would find out soon enough. On June 18, the United States declared war on Britain.

Tecumseh was at Fort Wayne, still reassuring officials that his followers were not responsible for frontier violence, when the declaration was made. He left to travel north to meet with Natives in his continuing efforts to bring them into his peaceful confederacy. While there, he also planned on visiting Fort Malden. He was correct in assuming that, with hostilities imminent, the British might be more inclined towards alliance and sharing supplies. The Red Coats were ready to do so because they feared that if Tecumseh didn't ally with them, he would side with the Americans. It was a mark of Tecumseh's ability that he was able to keep both the Americans and the British guessing as to his intent until the War of 1812 finally forced his hand. Brigadier General William Hull, governor of Michigan Territory and commander of the Army of the Northwest, was the first to feel the blow of Tecumseh's fist.

When Tecumseh arrived at Fort Malden in late June, he found a community in despair. The situation seemed bleak. The population of the American territories that surrounded Upper Canada was nearly 10 times greater. The new lieutenant-governor, Major-General Isaac Brock, had under his command only 1600 soldiers. An additional

11,000 militia—volunteers from local settlements—were mostly recent American arrivals whose loyalty to Britain and commitment to fighting was in no way assured. Even as Tecumseh rode north, reports indicated that Hull was on his way to Fort Malden with 2200 men. The British redoubled its efforts to attract more Natives to its side. However, save for Tecumseh's followers, few were willing to join what so clearly appeared to be the losing side.

Even Brock was dubious about the outcome. He wrote to his superiors that the mood in York (Toronto) was "that this province must inevitably succumb...." He continued on to observe that "most of the people have lost all confidence. I, however, speak loud and look big."

Tecumseh also began rallying his troops because he realized that here was the long-awaited opportunity that could see the Big Knives driven from the Native homelands for good.

When the call came, Tecumseh was ready, as he declared to a group of pro-American Natives who asked him to consider supporting the Americans. "No! I have taken sides with the king, my father, and I will suffer my bones to lay and bleach...before I will...join in any council of neutrality."

On July 16, Hull's forces took a bridge on the Aux Canard, a river five miles north of Fort Malden, with little opposition. Many thought that Fort Malden would fall as easily. Unexpectedly, the Americans pulled back the next day. Hull had been informed of the large number of Natives at Fort Malden, and he feared he could not take the position. He decided to wait in the hope that more British militia would desert. He also tried to speed the desertions by issuing public orders that any white man fighting with a Native would be put to death. Events, however, were to change the fighting landscape before his strategy could take effect.

On June 17, the American Fort Mackinac fell to a combined force of British soldiers, Native warriors and fur trappers. The fort's commander had been taken unawares, since Hull had neglected to inform him of the declaration of war. The victory did much to boost morale on the British-Native side, morale that was further strengthened by successful efforts to keep the Americans from retaking Aux Canard. The American failure was largely attributed to Tecumseh and his allies, who kept the Americans at bay with a steady downpour of arrows and bullets. Hull retreated to Fort Detroit. Sensing a turn in the fortunes of war, many heretofore reluctant Natives decided to join Tecumseh. The number soon increased dramatically. In early August, Tecumseh led a combined force of 24 warriors and 40 soldiers on a mission to intercept a 150-man detachment sent from Fort Detroit to meet a supply convoy. Although Tecumseh was wounded in the battle, his men killed or injured nearly 40 Big Knives and forced their retreat. The Shawnee chief returned to Fort Malden a hero and hundreds more warriors rode north to join him.

At Fort Malden, Tecumseh met Brock, who had arrived with some 300 men to direct military operations. Brock wasted no time in assuming command. Before a gathering of soldiers and warriors, Brock announced that Fort Detroit would be attacked. It was a bold move because the American contingent there outnumbered what Brock could muster. But he had seen enough of Hull's actions to believe in the effectiveness of a bluff. Tecumseh heard the news with enthusiasm.

When Brock finished speaking, Tecumseh turned to the Natives and declared, "Hoo-yee! This is a man!"

In mid-August, Brock and Tecumseh led their men (700 soldiers and 600 Natives respectively) to a point across the river from Fort Detroit.

Brock sent word to Hull. "Surrender. Should there be fighting, the numerous body of Indians who have attached

Isaac Brock (1769–1812), commander of British troops in Upper Canada. He called Tecumseh "the Wellington of the Natives."

themselves to my troops will be beyond control the moment the contest commences."

It was a bloody threat, one that Hull must have fretted over, since he knew that the Natives fought with abandon. Nevertheless, Hull refused to surrender, and that night Brock set his battery upon the fort. The Americans responded in kind. The next day, Brock pressed the assault. But it was not his approaching column that won the day. Tecumseh led his warriors across an opening in the woods near the fort three

times in rapid succession. Believing that the fort was surrounded by thousands of Natives, Hull raised the white flag
of surrender. The Northwestern Army, nearly 2200 men,
walked out of the fort. Its contents, including great amounts
of munitions and supplies, slipped easily into British hands.
Although he won great praise for the victory at Detroit,
Brock was quick to credit his Native collaborators, especially
Tecumseh, whom he called "the Wellington of the Natives."
Brock even gave Tecumseh his red sash as a token of his
appreciation. Tecumseh gave the sash to one of his fellow
chiefs, noting that he was an older and more able warrior
than himself. As for Hull, he was subsequently court-
martialed for cowardice and sentenced to death. President
Madison commuted the punishment because of his service
during the American Revolution.

By summer's end, the British–Native alliance had taken
every American post on the Great Lakes west of Cleveland.
The success was in no small measure attributed to
Tecumseh and his Native confederacy. Brock wrote to Lord
Liverpool, the British prime minister, suggesting as much.

> *Among the Indians whom I met at* [Fort Malden]…
> *I found some extraordinary characters. He who attracted*
> *most of my attention was a Shawnee chief,*
> *Tecumseh…who for the last two years has carried on, con-*
> *trary to our remonstrances, an active warfare against the*
> *United States. A more sagacious or a more gallant warrior*
> *does not, I believe, exist. He has the admiration of every-*
> *one who conversed with him.*

Here was recognition both of Tecumseh's ability and the
independent efforts of the Natives to secure their lost territory. Brock was convinced that Tecumseh and his allies
would not stop until they had taken the Ohio River, an

outcome Brock considered just because he believed that the Americans had taken the land fraudulently. The general advised that the Natives be given the territory in any future peace negotiation.

Increasingly confident and with a shared objective, Brock and Tecumseh made plans to launch a southern offensive against Forts Harrison and Wayne. Victories there would all but realize Tecumseh's dream of control of the ceded lands in Ohio. Unfortunately, Brock was called to Niagara before the southern attacks were launched because the Americans were threatening. Colonel Henry Procter, commander of Fort Malden and lauded for his victory at the recent Battle of Raisin River, became the leading British official in the region. On orders from Britain, where officials hoped diplomacy might bring an end to the war, Procter delayed the southern attacks. In early September, when word arrived that diplomacy had failed, Tecumseh hurried south with some 800 warriors and 250 regulars and militia. The delay was costly, however. It had given time for William Henry Harrison, who had resigned his governorship in favor of the rank of major-general in the Kentucky militia, to arrive with 2000 men. The attack on Fort Wayne was quickly abandoned. Tecumseh turned to Fort Harrison, which his brother had placed under siege at Tecumseh's command. Although the warriors had the fort at their mercy, they were unable to breach its defenses and were forced to abandon the attack when Colonel William Russell arrived with supplies and nearly 1400 men.

Tecumseh returned to Fort Malden where terrible news awaited him. Isaac Brock had been killed at the Battle of Queenston Heights while defending the Niagara River peninsula. Although Tecumseh was interested in British success only as it furthered his own objectives, he was shaken by the news. Brock had proven his worth as both a man and an ally. Procter, who was elevated in rank to brigadier general and placed in command of Britain's western military operations, had yet to demonstrate that he was either. Tecumseh would not count on him. The United States galvanized its resolve and gave it life in the Second Northwestern Army under the command of Harrison. Tecumseh returned to Prophetstown, where he sought to assemble his warriors in a defense both of Upper Canada and the dreams he held for his people. Although he was ill, which limited his ability to travel, some 700 warriors answered his call.

By spring he confidently boasted, "I have everything accomplished and all the nations of the north are standing at my word."

Tecumseh headed north to Fort Malden in April 1813. He had been in contact with Procter, who informed him that Harrison was busy building Fort Meigs (near present-day Maumee, Ohio). Tecumseh's own scouts had so informed him. As Fort Meigs was close to Fort Malden, the British rightly assumed it was be used as the launching point for an invasion into Upper Canada. Procter advised Tecumseh that he was going to attack before the fort was completed, and Tecumseh was supportive. He would join in the attack, and if it failed, he would lead his followers against Fort Wayne. Tecumseh arrived at the mouth of the Maumee River with some 1200 warriors, many of whom had come down from Fort Malden. Some 800 British soldiers and militia joined them. The British artillery laid siege to Fort Meigs on April 28. But they could not penetrate the fort's walls, and Harrison would not be drawn out to fight, despite Tecumseh's challenge that he stop hiding "in the earth like a groundhog."

Harrison, however, was merely biding his time. On May 5, 1400 Kentucky troops under the command of Brigadier General Green Clay arrived as reinforcements. Suddenly,

Harrison enjoyed numerical superiority, and he took the offensive. He dispatched 350 men to take the British guns, anticipating that they would be joined by 800 of the reinforcements. Tecumseh's warriors killed or wounded a third of the smaller detachment and forced the remainder back into the fort. Then he turned on the 800 men led by Colonel William Dudley. Dudley's men had successfully taken the British guns, and they confidently pursued Tecumseh's warriors into the nearby woods. The warriors led the aggressive soldiers deeper into the forest, where they abruptly turned on them. Forced to flee, Dudley's men met an unexpected British counterattack. Dudley was killed, and those of his charge who lived were taken to Fort Miami. Praise for the victory went to Tecumseh.

John Richardson, serving with the British army, noted "Never did Tecumseh shine more truly than on this occasion."

Unfortunately, some of his Native allies were less luminous. They began to massacre the prisoners and stopped only when Tecumseh intervened with his tomahawk raised, defying anyone to kill another Big Knife.

After the victory, most of the Natives left Fort Meigs, and Procter abandoned the fight on May 8 without actually taking the fort. Otherwise, the results were favorable. The British had lost less than 100 men to death, injury and capture; the Americans had lost nearly 1000. It is not known how the Natives fared.

Tecumseh would try a second time in July to take the fort, but it proved impenetrable again. He enjoyed no greater success in a subsequent attack on Fort Stephenson, on the Sandusky River. Although his Native forces outnumbered those defending the forts, the warriors were far better suited to open air battles than to taking fortified positions. What made the situation worse was the growing

Second Northwestern Army. Constantly renewed by volunteers, it numbered 8000 by late summer. The British-Native alliance could boast only 2500.

Events took a decisive turn in September, when American Lieutenant Oliver Perry defeated British Commander Robert Barclay in a key naval battle. Control of Lake Erie, which had been in British hands, passed to the Americans. Procter was suddenly faced with attack from both Harrison and Perry, and he panicked. He ordered the evacuation of Fort Malden. Tecumseh learned of it only when Native runners arrived from the fort. The Shawnee chief was astonished, then incensed. His relationship with Procter had become strained over the past months, mostly because the general would not share his battle strategy. Here Procter was set to flee, leaving the Natives to fend for themselves against the Americans. Tecumseh could see his Native homeland slipping away. He would not let it end that way and demanded a council with Procter. Procter agreed, perhaps under pressure from his own men. His second in command, Lieutenant-Colonel Augustus Warburton, was just as astonished at the evacuation as was Tecumseh. Procter and Tecumseh met at Fort Malden on September 18. Tecumseh took the offensive, reminding Procter of past promises.

> *Listen! When war was declared, our Father [Procter] stood up and gave us the tomahawk and told us he was now ready to strike the Americans; that he wanted our assistance; and that he certainly would get us our lands back which the Americans had taken from us. Listen! You told us at that time to bring forward our families to this place. We did so, and you promised to take care of them, and that they should want for nothing while the men would go to fight the enemy.*

Tecumseh then turned his words against Procter's course of action. He did not know that the fleet had been defeated.

> *Father, listen! Our fleet has gone out. We know they have fought. Our ships have gone one way and we are much astonished to see our Father…preparing to run the other, without letting his red children know what his intentions are. You always told us to remain here and take care of our lands. It made our hearts glad to hear that was your wish. You always told us you would never draw your foot off British soil. But now, Father, we see you are drawing back, and we are sorry to see our Father doing so without seeing the enemy. We must compare our Father's conduct to a fat animal that arrives with its tail upon its back, but when affrighted, it drops between its legs and runs off. Listen, Father! The Americans have not yet defeated us by land; neither are we sure they have done so by water. We, therefore, wish to remain here, and fight our enemy should they make their appearance. If they defeat us, we will retreat with our Father.…*

Tecumseh pitched one final appeal, in case his previous words had not been persuasive.

> *You have got the arms and ammunition which our Great White Father* [the King] *sent for his red children. If you have an idea of going away, give them to us and you may go and welcome from us. Our lives are in the hands of the Great Spirit. We are determined to defend our lands, and if it is his will, we wish to leave our bones upon them.*

The Natives exploded in thunderous support, and only when they fell silent did Procter reveal that Britain's navy on Lake Erie had been defeated. He then asked Tecumseh for two days so that he could consider a reply to his demands. Procter used the time to flee from the fort. Tecumseh and his followers discovered the general's answer only when they saw goods being transported from Fort Malden a few days later. However, Procter was not abandoning the fight. A subordinate explained Procter's strategy to Tecumseh. He planned to fortify the lower Thames River at Chatham 60 miles east of Detroit, a position inaccessible to the American fleet. There he would make his stand. Tecumseh was reassured, but he met with the other Native chiefs before committing to Procter's plan. They were satisfied, and in late September, the Natives and the British set fire to Fort Malden. Tecumseh turned his back on the burning ruins and led his 1200 warriors south, still hopeful that the Natives might have their homeland in the Northwest.

The Shawnee chief was staggered by what he found in Chatham. Although Procter had the better part of three weeks to fortify the position, it was deserted. Tecumseh had no way of knowing that Procter had retreated farther up the Thames River to Moraviantown, and he likely thought that the general had quit the fight. When word of Procter's changed plans reached Tecumseh, he again held council to determine the mood of his followers. Tecumseh never considered abandoning the British because he knew that the future success of his confederacy rested upon their support, but he was uncertain if others in his alliance were of the same opinion. They agreed to continue to Moraviantown, although all knew it would not be an easy journey. Spies had reported that Harrison was marching 3000 troops north and that they were within striking distance. Tecumseh sent out warriors to harass Harrison from the rear, and hopefully delay his arrival until the warriors arrived at Procter's location. The action was

An 1833 lithograph of the Battle of the Thames (October 1813). Tecumseh was killed as he rode among his warriors.

not as successful as anticipated. Tecumseh was injured when a bullet struck his arm. Sensing defeat, warriors melted away and Tecumseh was left with only 500 braves. They arrived at Moraviantown on the Thames River in early October.

As Tecumseh prepared for the inevitable encounter, he was troubled by what he saw of the British soldiers. Few remained and these were poorly positioned for battle. Nevertheless, he set out to raise their spirits by riding along the British line, shaking hands and offering words of encouragement. Finally, he reached Procter.

"Father, tell your men to be firm, and all will be well," implored Tecumseh. "Father, have a brave heart!"

Tecumseh's reassuring words belied his fading confidence. Before the battle, he prepared for his death. He gave his sword to his followers and directed them to give it to his son Paukeesa should he ever become a warrior. When Harrison appeared in mid-afternoon with his 3500 men, at least three times the number of the British-Native alliance, it appeared that Tecumseh's preparations were well taken. On October 5, Harrison launched the attack. He directed his men towards the British soldiers and militia, expecting the Natives to flee if he broke their line. Procter quickly pulled his men back and left the Natives to do the fighting.

Tecumseh would not retreat. Indeed, he rode among the warriors, urging them to be brave. He was seen leading a Native charge when a bullet hit him in the chest. He fell from his horse and lay still on the ground, the British medal around his neck darkened by blood seeping from the wound. Tecumseh was dead. The Natives lost heart and retreated. The Americans won a decisive victory, and with it, ownership of the Northwest.

An American officer who saw the Shawnee chief's dead body noted: "he did not seem to me so large a man as he was represented—I did not suppose his height exceeded five feet ten or eleven inches...." It was a revealing statement. During his own lifetime and among the enemy as well as his allies, Tecumseh's stature had achieved mythical proportions. His body was given to the Canadians, and to this day, its burial site remains a secret.

CHAPTER TWO

Crazy Horse

~~~

Oglala Sioux, 1840–1877

IN LATE SUMMER 1875, Young Man Afraid of His Horses, a chief and head of the Red Cloud Agency Indian police, set out from his reserve on the White River for the Powder River country. The small party that accompanied him had many pack horses loaded with trade goods to be given as gifts to the Sioux and Cheyenne who lived in the northern territory. Young Man Afraid of His Horses was glad to have the gifts because he would need every advantage if his mission was to be successful.

The United States government wanted to buy *Paha Sapa*, the Black Hills, which had been marked as Sioux territory by the Fort Laramie Treaty of 1868. Young Man Afraid of His Horses had the responsibility of delivering the offer to purchase to Crazy Horse and Sitting Bull, two of the most important chiefs in Powder River country. Even as he rode north, Young Man Afraid of His Horses was not hopeful that

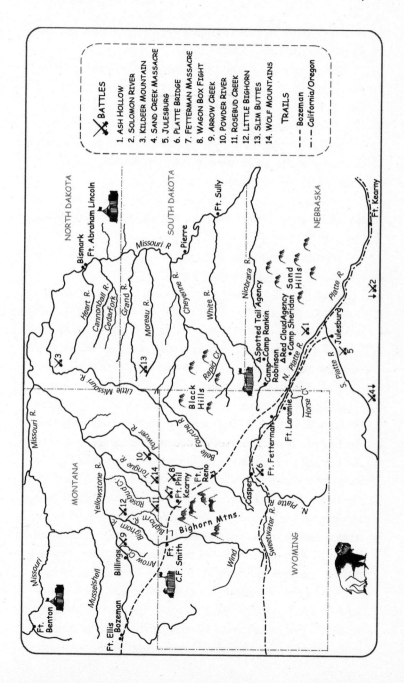

BATTLES

1. ASH HOLLOW
2. SOLOMON RIVER
3. KILDEER MOUNTAIN
4. SAND CREEK MASSACRE
5. JULESBURG
6. PLATTE BRIDGE
7. FETTERMAN MASSACRE
8. WAGON BOX FIGHT
9. ARROW CREEK
10. POWDER RIVER
11. ROSEBUD CREEK
12. LITTLE BIGHORN
13. SLIM BUTTES
14. WOLF MOUNTAINS

TRAILS

— — — Bozeman
— · — · California/Oregon

the two would return to the Red Cloud Agency and discuss terms with the treaty commissioners.

The party first reached the Tongue River, where they discovered 2000 lodges, mostly Sioux and Cheyenne and all followers of Crazy Horse. They held that the Wasichus (white men) had no right to be in Powder River country. If they ventured there, war would result. The villagers grumbled at the appearance of the party, but they let Young Man Afraid of His Horses go to their chief's tipi.

"Crazy Horse, will you come south to discuss *Paha Sapa?*" he asked. "It is important that the voice of all Sioux be heard."

"I have nothing to say," replied Crazy Horse. "My arrows, my bullets speak for me."

"And they have spoken well. But it is time for words. You know that I do not wish to sell *Paha Sapa*. But it cannot be kept by going on the warpath. If we speak to the Great Father [the president] as one, perhaps he will respect our wishes."

"Ha!" laughed Crazy Horse. "The Wasichus have shown what they think of our wishes. The Sioux no longer speak as one. Red Cloud and Spotted Tail and their Hang-Around-the-Fort people have become dependent on what the Great Father gives them. They would sell *Paha Sapa* to keep their master happy," he growled.

"They have made treaty and they do not want. It is more than can be said for your followers," suggested Young Man Afraid of His Horses, who had observed that the hunt had not been successful. "Your influence is best used to provide for your followers."

"I will provide for them in my own way, as the Sioux have always done, as Wakan Tanka [the Great Mystery] wishes," continued Crazy Horse. "What influence I have will be used to keep the Wasichus far from us."

Crazy Horse bent over and took a pinch of dirt from the ground.

"I will not sell, not even as much as this," he declared as he let the dirt fall from his fingers. "One does not sell the dirt upon which the people walk."

Sitting Bull agreed with Crazy Horse, and Young Man Afraid of His Horses had to return south without their support. Their voices, however, were not needed at the negotiations. Red Cloud, head chief of the agency Oglala, demanded too much money, and the commissioners left with nothing.

When President Ulysses S. Grant learned of the commissioners' failure, he was livid. There was gold in the Black Hills and Americans wanted it. He was determined to satisfy their desires, and neither Sioux demands nor government treaty obligations to keep settlers out of the Great Sioux Reservation would stand in his way. Grant's government decided to take the Black Hills by stealth. Prospectors would be permitted into the region, and once enough were there, the government would force the sale. To prevent attacks by the Sioux, the Natives were ordered to surrender at the agencies. Any who refused would be declared hostiles—enemies of the United States—and would be attacked. In the new year, the deadline came and passed, and neither Crazy Horse nor Sitting Bull appeared.

Early in 1876 the army demonstrated that it was serious about carrying out the government's new policy. In mid-March, the cavalry stumbled upon Two Moons' Cheyenne camp along the Powder River just north of the Wyoming border. Frank Grouard, the head scout, believed that it was Crazy Horse's camp so six troops of cavalry attacked it. The Natives were forced to abandon their camp, which was then razed by the soldiers. The survivors took flight, and they staggered into Crazy Horse's camp near Pumpkin Creek cold and hungry. Upon their arrival the two chiefs met.

"We were not looking for a fight, but the Wasichus have brought the battle to us," said Two Moons. "Crazy Horse's stand against the invaders is well known. Now the Cheyenne stand with you."

"We welcome you with open arms. Let us go and see Sitting Bull," said Crazy Horse.

When the Oglala and Cheyenne arrived at the Hunkpapa camp, they were greeted enthusiastically and fed well. The mood turned black, however, when Sitting Bull learned of the unprovoked attack.

"Who are these Wasichus?" he shouted. "They agree that *Paha Sapa* are ours forever, and then they demand to own it. Money they will give us for food. I get my food from *Paha Sapa*, and do not need what the Wasichus offer. It is known that I accept no price. And when they learn of this? They attack! They are not to be trusted."

"My brothers, we are as islands in a lake of white men. If we continue to stand separately, they will destroy us all. We must unite," declared Sitting Bull. "For many moons I have raised my lance only in self-defense. I have been patient and put up with much. Well, now the Wasichus have come shooting; they have brought war. War they will have," he concluded.

Crazy Horse remained silent as the Hunkpapa chief spoke because silence was in his nature. But he also recognized Sitting Bull's leadership and, more importantly, Crazy Horse agreed with his words. Runners took messages to every Sioux, Cheyenne and Arapaho camp west of the Missouri River asking them to join in one great battle against the Wasichus along the Rosebud Creek. The spring of 1876 saw the trails leading to Sitting Bull's camp thick

A shirt that belonged to Crazy Horse—hide with paint, scalp-locks and woodpecker feathers

with Natives. Soon nearly 1500 lodges were gathered, representing some 3000 warriors.

In late spring, Sitting Bull called a war council. The council selected him to lead the Sioux attack and Crazy Horse as his second in command. By early June, this uncommonly large gathering of Natives united by a single and monumental cause made their way towards the Rosebud Creek and the advancing United States Army.

≈≈≈

To the northeast of *Paha Sapa*, a steep hill rises unexpectedly from the flat, grassy plains. While its presence is
dramatic, there is little in *Mato Sapa's* (Bear Butte) appearance to suggest it is special, and unknowing eyes see a hill
little different from others. But the butte's significance
does not rest in its appearance. It is mysterious, and those
who know of its mystery consider it sacred, its caves the
home of powerful and benevolent spirits. The Sioux are
among that number.

Since long ago the Sioux had traveled to the butte, to
hold councils and perform rituals under the watchful eyes of
the spirits. So it was that a band of Oglala Sioux made its
way there in the fall of 1840. Among those in the band were
Crazy Horse (the father of the great warrior) and his wife
Rattle Blanket Woman. Crazy Horse was an Oglala, well
respected among his people as a *wichasha wakan* (holy man).
Rattle Blanket Woman was a Miniconjou Sioux and she
counted among her family leaders of that tribe. They had
been married for a few years, and Rattle Blanket Woman was
heavy with the couple's second child. They were not long
camped when she slipped away to give birth to a boy.

The elderly woman who assisted her delivery gasped
when she saw the infant. Rattle Blanket Woman understood the old woman's distress when her son was placed in
her arms. She swaddled the child in soft doeskin and
secured him in a cradleboard that she slipped onto her
back. Then she returned to her lodge, where she found an
anxious Crazy Horse waiting.

Crazy Horse could see by the look on his wife's face
that something was wrong. He waited for Rattle Blanket
Woman to lift the cradleboard from her back and remove
the infant. Crazy Horse took the boy in his hands and held

him before the lodge fire. Uncertain that the flickering of the fire was deceiving him, he stepped from the lodge into the sunlight.

"His skin is the light color of the Wasichu!" he muttered in disbelief. "His hair, too. It is not dark and straight, but sandy and curly."

"What can this mean, husband?" asked Rattle Blanket Woman, who had followed him outside.

"I do not know," he replied as he shook his head gently. "But perhaps I can find out."

Later that night Crazy Horse climbed *Mato Sapa* in search of the special prophetic vision brought to *wichasha wakans* by their spirit helpers. Reaching the flat summit, he performed secret rituals, sang and smoked his pipe, hoping that his prayers for guidance would be carried to Wakan Tanka, the Great Mystery, in the rising smoke. He continued performing the rituals until the sun woke. Somber faced, he returned to the camp below.

He sent word to the chiefs and headmen of the gathered bands that he wanted a council. Such a request from a *wichasha wakan* brought an immediate response, and that night many gathered in the council lodge. News of Crazy Horse's son had spread throughout the camp and everyone wondered whether his words would explain the infant's strange appearance.

After they shared a ceremonial pipe, Crazy Horse spoke. "Last night Wakan Tanka appeared to me in the form of a bear. He bestowed upon me powers to conquer all earthly beings, including the Wasichus who are coming into our land. They are not yet here in great numbers, but I have seen them darken the Plains as the buffalo do. But I am not a warrior, so I wondered, *Was this gift meant for me? No,* I concluded. The gift was given to me, but I am not the one to use it. I give the gift to my son, who will grow strong.

He will use the gift of the bear spirit to become a greater leader of our people."

Crazy Horse's words were met with silence. None dreamed that there could ever be so many Wasichus and it seemed unlikely that an infant who looked so much like the strangers would be the one who would offer protection from them. There was much to think about, and even as the bands went their separate ways some weeks later, most were still contemplating the odd-looking boy, Crazy Horse's vision and the mysterious powers of *Mato Sapa*.

The boy who was named Light Hair, but called Curly by all (and eventually Crazy Horse), knew nothing of his father's vision and was raised the same as other Sioux boys. He learned that he was a Lakota, known popularly as Sioux (an Ojibway term meaning "enemy"). His tribe, the Oglala ("to scatter one's own") was the largest of the seven Teton Sioux tribes, which, in turn, was the largest of the seven divisions of the Sioux. Over many decades, Curly's people had migrated from the northeast, and by the time of his birth, the Powder River country (present-day South Dakota) had not long been their home.

Curly enjoyed the carefree, unrestrained life of a Sioux boy. For a time, boys were content to sit and mimic the domestic activities of adults, but soon they could not contain their energy and they ran through the camp, chasing dogs and each other in turn. By the age of six or seven, Curly was playing the war games that dominated lives of young boys. "Throw the Mud" required the boys to divide into sides and attack each other with mud balls propelled from the end of springy willow sticks. "Fighting the Bee Tribe" involved an attack on a bee's nest, imagined to be a band of enemy Crow. Curly sensed, however, that the Bee tribe was unlike any enemy because they were always prepared.

Eventually, direction was introduced into the activities of childhood. Little is known of Curly's experiences during this time of his life, but the educational responsibilities of a boy were usually shouldered by an uncle, and it was likely no different for Curly. His uncle told him entertaining and informative stories about the Sioux and about his own experiences as a hunter and a warrior. He also gave Curly his first set of bow and arrows and perhaps some cursory instruction, but it was up to Curly to master its use with long and determined practice. Encouragement was rarely needed because boys knew that a man's reputation rested on his ability to hunt and raid, both of which required skill with the bow and arrow.

Raiding was the business of warriors, but Sioux boys were given opportunities to hone their skills by making serious practice raids against their own people. On one occasion Curly and some other boys were comparing their arrows when one shouted,

"Look! The women return with the meat."

Making its way slowly towards the camp was a line of hunting ponies, each laden with buffalo meat. The boys made for the edge of the camp, where they prepared to do battle against the band. They built grass tipis and waited for their adviser. The full moon was out and the noise of the camp's merriment rolled across the plains, when an older Oglala arrived to aid the boys in planning their raiding strategy.

"Listen to them feasting. It is not right that we should sit here while they celebrate. Let us take their meat, so that we may also feast," declared the adviser. He held out a stick. "Each take a bite. The bigger the piece that you split off, the bigger the piece of meat that you must steal."

Curly waited impatiently for his turn. Finally, he clenched the stick between his teeth and snapped it in half.

"We will eat well tonight," laughed the adviser, "if Curly's cunning is any match for his mouth."

Taking no chances, he crawled on his belly well beyond the camp. At the drying racks, Curly snatched a long strip of buffalo meat and made his way back to the boys. He was greeted with a cheer. Eventually, all the boys returned, some without meat, their heads low.

Curly's childhood was difficult. He was quiet, even shy. His appearance often brought teasing and he felt uncomfortable around most of his peers. His self-confidence wasn't helped by the loss of his mother when he was four. She took her own life when her brother-in-law died during a raid. His father remarried the sisters of the important Oglala chief Spotted Tail, but apparently Crazy Horse did not have a close relationship with them. As with most young Oglala, he had one close friend, a *kola*, with whom he partnered in all activities and to whom he pledged to share his takings on raids and in hunts—High Backbone, known as Hump. Although Hump was a few years older than Curly, they would share a long, intimate friendship. Later, Lone Bear and Curly's brother Little Hawk would expand the intimate group to four.

Over the years, Curly honed the skills necessary to be a warrior. He knew from his uncle that the warrior's path was a long and difficult one. While most Sioux boys aspired to travel the path, his uncle explained to him that it was one not easily taken. A warrior must possess the four great virtues of the Sioux—bravery, generosity, fortitude and wisdom—learned over a lifetime. Curly was determined to be prepared, so that when opportunities appeared on his path he would be able to make the choices that led to warriorhood.

Curly became a warrior in a rapidly changing world. In the mid-1830s, Fort Laramie was built along the as yet unnamed California/Oregon Trail. The route hugged the

southern banks of the North Platte River. The trail was just
south of traditional Oglala territory, and it was close enough
for them to see the Wasichus journey west. Throughout
the early 1840s, not many white settlers ventured west, but
the promise of good land in Oregon and the discovery of
gold at Sutter's Mill in California brought them in unimag-
inable numbers. By the early 1850s, tens of thousands overlanders had passed through Fort Laramie. Curly was pleased
to see them continue west.

Not much violence occurred during the early years of
white expansion westward, but as migration increased, so
did problems. The wagons frightened the buffalo, which
were fewer in number as cattle and horses devoured the
grass that once drew them into the region. The Sioux
found the buffalo increasingly difficult to hunt. The overlanders were witnesses to increased violence as the Sioux
moved into non-traditional hunting territories and fought
Native enemies for the right to hunt.

In 1851, an American government anxious to reduce
the problems opened treaty negotiations with the Plains
Natives along the California/Oregon Trail. In the late fall
of that year, some 10,000 Natives, likely including Curly,
flooded the territory around Fort Laramie. The treaty
council was held at nearby Horse Creek. Although it was
not the Sioux way, the commissioners insisted that they
choose one chief to represent their entire nation. When the
Sioux proved reluctant to obey the odd request, the commissioners chose Conquering Bear, a Brulé Sioux. The
Sioux agreed, perhaps because Conquering Bear was well
respected among them, but they never took seriously the
notion that the "paper chief" was their supreme leader.

The Fort Laramie Treaty of September 17, 1851 was
the first major agreement with the Plains Natives and it
established a pattern. The Sioux agreed to cease intertribal

hostilities, to make restitution to settlers who suffered losses at their hands and to allow the government to establish roads and military posts in their territories. They also accepted a boundary for their territory—the area encircled by the Missouri River (east), the North Platte River (south), the western foothills of the Black Hills (west) and the Heart River (north). In return the Sioux were protected against depredations of white settlers and were promised an annual annuity for 50 years. When the Senate ratified the treaty, they reduced the annuity payments to 10 years but failed to inform the Sioux.

Curly was worried about the treaty. Like most Sioux he didn't understand all its details, but he heard rumors that it prohibited fighting the Crow and other traditional enemies. He wondered how a boy might become a warrior if he could not prove himself against the enemy. Curly discussed the matter with Hump, who assured him that the words were meant to please the Wasichus and would be soon forgotten. Curly was not so sure and he asked his father about it.

"Treaty is serious and the promises are made to be kept," said Crazy Horse. "But I do not think that the ways of a people will change so quickly. A boy might still become a warrior," he smiled.

Curly sighed in relief.

Then his father asked unexpectedly, "Curly, you have a fast pony?"

"Yes, father," he replied.

"You have a stout bow and quick arrows?"

"Always, father."

"Then let us go shoot tipis."

Curly's face lit up in a smile that was rarely seen. Finally, he was going to hunt buffalo!

Curly killed a strong bull. He was a hunter and suddenly everything seemed possible. Upon his return to camp, Curly

scouted out Hump to share his triumph. Curly found him in
a group of boys. He made a motion to draw Hump away
from the others. Hump knew something was up.

"You look like the fox who has eaten a meal he did not
catch," said Hump.

"No. I killed my meal, brother," replied Curly.

"A rabbit's not much of a meal," suggested Hump.

"And it's not just my meal. Today my arrow brought
down a buffalo!"

Hump put his arm around Curly's shoulders.

"The rabbits are safe then!" he laughed. Curly smiled.

"Some of the older boys are riding to capture wild
ponies. Join us," suggested Hump.

Curly did not think twice about the invitation. He
would do anything to be with the older boys.

The Sioux maintained their pony herds by raiding.
While warriors stole ponies, boys tried to capture the wild
ones. Few succeeded, however, because the free-spirited
animals challenged even the most skilled of men. They
found a herd near the Sand Hills and the boys pursued the
ponies until the animals tired. Curly acted quickly and captured the first pony. It was a proud moment because none
of his friends had yet broken a wild pony. His father
thought Curly's accomplishment to be particularly
important and gave Curly a new name, bestowed to mark
a special achievement as was traditional among the Sioux.
He was called His Horse Looking. Most in the village,
however, continued to call him Curly.

In 1854, when Curly's band was again camped near Fort
Laramie, an event occurred that led to Curly's vision quest.
Matters between the Sioux and Wasichus had been mostly
quiet since the Horse Creek Treaty (1851 Fort Laramie
Treaty), but in August of that year a Miniconjou named
High Forehead killed a cow that belonged to a Mormon

immigrant. When Conquering Bear learned of the incident, he went to Fort Laramie and offered a pony as compensation. Lieutenant Hugh Fleming, the post commander,
demanded instead that High Forehead be brought in to
face charges, but Conquering Bear could not do that
because the man belonged to another band. Negotiations
proved fruitless, and Lieutenant Fleming ordered High
Forehead's arrest.

Second Lieutenant John Grattan was placed in charge
of the detachment, hardly an appropriate choice for such
a mission. He had often bragged that he could wipe out
the entire Sioux nation with 20 men and a fieldpiece. He
must have been confident when he left with 29 men and
two Howitzers. Nearing the Oglala camp, Grattan met
with Conquering Bear to demand that High Forehead be
turned over to him. Conquering Bear agreed to speak to
High Forehead, but the Miniconjou would not meet
with Grattan. Instead, the Sioux leaders returned with
a more generous offer of compensation. Grattan, however, wanted his man so he attacked the Oglala camp.
When the fight was over, Grattan and his entire command were dead. No Sioux died, although Conquering
Bear received a mortal wound.

The Sioux broke camp and made their way north after
the incident. Curly's family traveled with Conquering
Bear's band. A curious Curly caught sight of the dying
chief lying in his lodge. Angry, he ran to the outskirts of
the camp. It was not Conquering Bear's inevitable death
that upset him; he knew that even important chiefs died.
But few died at the Wasichus' treacherous hands.
Conquering Bear did not want to fight, but the Wasichus
attacked. It was not right! Soon Curly heard the wails
from the camp. He did not need to be told that they were
for the dead chief.

Curly's thoughts turned to revenge because it was only with revenge that justice could be achieved. But what could he do, a boy not yet a warrior? Nothing. And that was not good enough. Looking across the golden prairie, he decided that he would take the next step to becoming a man. Curly would go on his vision quest and hope that Wakan Tanka might send a spirit helper to assist him on his life path.

Traditionally, careful preparation accompanied the vision quest, but Curly, who already harbored distaste for ritual and ceremony, departed from camp early the next morning without telling anyone of his intent. He headed east to the Sand Hills, his pony cantering along no trail, a mountain peak in the distance serving as his guide. Curly knew that the vision quest was a time of humility and fasting, so he was dressed only in his breechcloth and an old buffalo robe, his hair was loose around his shoulders and he carried no food. When he reached the mountain, he circled to its eastern slope, so that he would be truly alone. He hobbled his pony beside a lake and he climbed up the mountain's side. At a suitable outcropping, he settled in to pray, chant and cry to Wakan Tanka, beseeching that a vision be granted.

By the second night, Curly had taken to lying on sharp rocks and placing jagged pebbles between his toes so that he might stay awake. He greeted the sun as it emerged from its lodge, but it was not a happy sight because there had still been no vision. Discouraged, Curly slipped down the mountain. When he reached his pony, he fainted and entered a mystical world.

A man on horseback appeared suddenly from the lake. He changed colors as he approached, but otherwise there was nothing striking about him. He wore plain leggings and an unadorned shirt. His face bore no paint, but the eagle feather above his long brown hair identified him as a warrior. A small brown rock was tied behind one ear. His pony traveled above the water and when he reached the land, the animal still did not touch the ground. Although his lips did not move, Curly heard the warrior speak.

"Never wear a war bonnet. Do not tie up your pony's tail [as was the Sioux practice], for the animal needs it to jump streams and to brush away the flies in summer. Before you go to battle, rub dirt over your hair and body."

Curly watched as the rider fought off a shadowy enemy. Arrows and bullets disappeared as they approached the man. Occasionally his progress was impeded, as his own people clutched his arms and made his riding difficult. As the man approached, Curly could see lightning appear on his cheeks and hailstones on his body. Curly continued to hear his words.

"Know that you will not be killed by a bullet or an enemy. Never take anything for yourself."

Finally, the rider could not resist the pull of his people, and he stood still. A screeching hawk flew overhead, and the vision slipped away.

Curly's father was upset to learn that his son had sought a vision quest without the proper preparation. Even Hump's kind words did not lessen the pain Curly felt at his father's anger. Pain and anger, however, were mostly forgotten with the events of the following year.

In June 1855, Curly participated in his first raid. He had ridden with warriors before, but always as an apprentice, whose role it was to run errands, to observe and to suffer jokes. On this occasion he rode as a warrior. The party planned to steal ponies from the Omaha, traditional enemies of the Sioux. Curly and 500 more warriors headed south to the lower Platte country. Curly killed his first enemy, an Omaha woman. There was no disgrace in killing a woman but Curly did not know that he had done so until he saw the body. Shocked, he vowed never to kill a woman again. The night of the battle, he listened to warriors joke and sing of his refusal to scalp the woman. They were not the songs of bravery and respect that he had heard in his dreams.

Meanwhile, the United States government had finally organized a response to the Grattan debacle. In September 1855 Brigadier General William S. Harney (known to the Sioux as the Hornet) and his 1200 men attacked Little Thunder's band of Brulé. The band had not participated in the bloodshed at Fort Laramie, but that meant nothing to Harney. He was charged with teaching the Sioux a lesson and was anxious to do so. The Battle of Ash Hollow was a massacre. Almost 100 Natives were killed and another 70 were captured.

Curly was living with Little Thunder's band at the time, but he was away hunting during the attack. He returned to the sight of his razed village, but he managed to save the life of a Cheyenne woman, who was the niece of a powerful medicine man. It was the beginning of a long and close relationship Curly shared with that southern tribe.

After his victory over the Brulé, Harney led his troops north through Sioux country. The visible warning to keep the peace proved persuasive, and the immigrants who traveled the California/Oregon Trail did so with less fear. Still, the Sioux carried out some isolated attacks. When a mail train was robbed, Harney demanded that those responsible surrender or the bands would feel his Hornet's sting. Spotted Tail, who had participated in the raid, surrendered and was transported to Fort Leavenworth, Kansas. While there he saw many Wasichus and he became convinced that resisting them would be futile. When President Franklin Pierce pardoned him in January 1856, Spotted Tail returned to his people and became an advocate of peace.

Brulé Sioux chief Spotted Tail (1823–1881), Crazy Horse's uncle and chief of the agency Sioux.

Harney's efforts were followed by army offensives to the south. Colonel Edwin Sumner and 400 cavalry attacked a Cheyenne band southwest of Fort Kearny, Nebraska, in July 1857. Curly, then living with the Cheyenne, was probably a participant in the Battle of the Solomon River that resulted in the destruction of the Cheyenne camp. After the battle, he rode north to *Mato Sapa*, where the Sioux planned a Sun

Dance and a war council to address the problem of the Wasichus. At council the tribes pledged to band together and agreed that any Wasichus who entered their lands would be turned back. Fewer were seen, however, because most Americans were soon preoccupied with their Civil War.

The summer of 1858 found Curly's band camped in the Powder River county. Despite the lull in fighting with the Wasichus, the Oglala did not want for enemies, so they turned to their traditional Native foes. Curly was still a teenager when he fought the battle that earned him the name Crazy Horse.

Curly joined Little Hawk and Lone Bear in a small raiding party led by Hump. When they headed west in August, Curly rode with great confidence. His father had given him a medicine bundle that held, among other sacred objects, a powder of dried eagle brain and aster flowers. Crazy Horse had advised him to sprinkle it over his tongue. In final preparation, Curly threw some dirt over his pony, just as the warrior in his dream had done.

The raiding party rode for many days, past the White Mountains (Bighorn Mountains), until they were in a strange territory (present-day central Wyoming). The Natives they first encountered were unfamiliar to them—the Shoshone. Shoshone scouts saw the Oglala approach and they warned a nearby village. The Natives scattered onto a rocky hillside before the approaching enemy warriors arrived. The Oglala made several attempts to climb the hill, but with little shelter to provide cover, they were easily repulsed.

Rather than rush into the fray, Curly held back, watching for an opportunity. He saw one as the skirmish came to a standstill. With a great whoop, he urged his pony up the gradual slope of the hill towards the enemy. Recklessly, he refused to hold his head tight against his pony's neck and so provided the Shoshone with a good target. However, their bullets and arrows failed to find their mark, and he counted three coups before he retreated to the base of the hill. He listened as the Oglala shouted his name, his heart thundering in rhythm with their cries, and he charged up the hillside again. He let loose an arrow at one enemy and stabbed another. Curly slipped from his horse to scalp his victims, but as he tore the second lock free an arrow pierced his leg. In great pain, he mounted his pony and rode to safety. Then he looked at the scalps and remembered his vision. He was not to take anything from his enemy. He tossed the scalps away in disgust.

Hump finally called an end to the raid. Coups had been counted, ponies taken and no Oglala had died. Their effort was deemed a success. When the raiding party returned to the camp along the Powder River, there was a great victory celebration. Women danced and sang and warriors told of their exploits. Curly was pushed into the great circle to tell his story, and although he had every right to so speak, he chose to remain silent. He was not comfortable speaking before his people, particularly when speaking of himself. That night he drifted off into a restless sleep, his injured leg painful and throbbing. He awoke the next morning to his father's song just outside his tipi.

> My son has been against the people of unknown tongue.
> He has done a brave thing;
> For this I give him a new name, the name of his father,
> and of many fathers before him—
> I give him a great name
> I call him Crazy Horse.

Curly limped from his resting place and lifted the buffalo hide that covered the opening of his tipi. Outside stood his father in his ceremonial robe. Behind him were the people of his village.

"Long ago, my father, Makes The Song, told me of a dream. He saw that one day my son would have the spirit of a wild horse, powerful and untamable," called Crazy Horse. "That time has come to pass. From this day I will be known as Worm. Behold the warrior Crazy Horse!"

The people looked at the young man, perhaps 18. In so many ways, he was different—the fine sandy hair, the pale complexion, the long, thin, straight nose. And yet, was there any doubt of his bravery? They sang and shouted their approval, and Curly became Crazy Horse.

Throughout the late 1850s and early 1860s, Crazy Horse's reputation as a warrior grew, and soon his name was on the lips of all who spoke of courage in battle. From the first, it was clear that he was not a follower in battle. Veteran warriors considered him little more than a boy when he met the Pawnee and charged their braves in an effort to take first coup. In a subsequent skirmish with the Shoshone, Crazy Horse's pony was shot out from under him. Rather than retreat, he ran forward, killed an enemy, mounted the dead man's pony and rode home. Strangely, Crazy Horse was more comfortable fighting dismounted (he had his pony shot from under him eight times in battle, although he was never injured seriously).

His friend He Dog, who rode at his side in many battles, remembered, "[I]n critical moments of the fight, Crazy Horse would jump off his pony to fire. He is the only Indian I ever knew who did that often. He wanted to be sure that he hit what he aimed at." Rarely would he miss, for he always rode into the heart of the enemy's forces before taking aim.

Although his approach suggests that Crazy Horse fought with unreasonable abandon, that was not the case. His first battles were infused with the rashness of youth, but as he matured, he considered his attack and did not fight without a good plan and the confidence that he would win.

He Dog noted, "He always used judgment and played safe....That is the kind of fighter he was."

His careful approach included personal preparations that closely followed the directions received in his vision. Eagle Elk, a cousin who also fought with him, described the measures Crazy Horse took.

"Just before the start of battle, when they were ready to go into it, he got off his pony and got a little dirt from a molehill and put it between the ears of his horse, and then on the hips of the horse and then he took some and got in front of the horse and threw it towards the tail, and then he got around behind the horse and threw some of it over towards his head. Then he went up to the horse and brushed it off and rubbed it on. Then he rubbed a little dirt on his hand and over his head. Then he took a spotted eagle feather and put it upside down on the back of his head instead of standing up, as most did. He wore moccasins. He generally wore just a shirt and breech cloth, taking off his leggings."

Under his left arm hung a pierced white stone. He also painted his face, but not as most warriors did traditionally. Sometimes he had a zigzag streak stretching from his forehead, along his nose, to the base of his chin. Occasionally, he dabbed his face with white spots. Both designs were for protection in battle. The feather he wore was from the middle of an eagle's tail. Crazy Horse enjoyed success on raids, and he found that he did not want for warriors to ride with him. Those who did discovered something of his generosity. The number of coups counted suggested a warrior's courage. On any enemy, four coups (striking of the enemy) could be taken. First coup was most highly prized, while fourth coup ranked least. Crazy Horse, although always first in battle, let other braves count first coup.

His was odd behavior, but, as Eagle Elk thought, "He had such a reputation that he did not have to get more of that."

During the early 1860s, when word of the exploits of the young Oglala was spreading throughout the Sioux nation, the United States was continuing its slow westward push. In 1863 the Bozeman Trail was scratched out from Julesburg north to Virginia City on the Yellowstone River, providing easier access to the Montana gold fields. The Bozeman Trail cut through Oglala hunting territory in the Platte and the Powder River countries and this worried the Natives. The route would disrupt the buffalo hunts, as had happened along the California/Oregon Trail early in the 1850s. Added to this were renewed efforts by the United States cavalry to subdue the hostile Natives. In July 1864, at Kildeer Mountain, General Alfred Sully and a 2220-strong army contingent defeated the Santee Sioux, who had gone on the warpath in Minnesota. The location was on the Little Missouri River north of the Black Hills, not far from Crazy Horse's home along the Powder River.

The Battle of Kildeer Mountain was followed in November by what has become known as the Sand Creek Massacre in Colorado. Colonel J.M. Chivington directed 700 men to attack Black Kettle's band of Cheyenne. Chivington's men knew that Black Kettle believed his band to be under the protection of the army. But Chivington ignored their protests, declaring that he had "come to kill Indians." The Cheyenne suffered 163 deaths, many of them women and children.

When the survivors of Black Kettle's band limped into another Cheyenne camp, a war council was held. Everyone was incensed by the news, including Americans (faced with a court-martial, Chivington resigned). By December 1000 Sioux, Cheyenne and Arapaho warriors gathered for revenge. The result was the Cheyenne-Arapaho War. On January 7, 1865, they raided Camp Rankin and a stage-coach station on the Bozeman Trail at Julesberg, Colorado.

The Natives hoped to draw the soldiers out of the post, but the younger warriors charged too soon and alerted the soldiers to the ambush. Still, the Natives left with a great store of supplies.

Crazy Horse and his friend Little Big Man were among those that joined the war party after the attack on Julesberg, and they raided along the South Platte River. In a second raid on Julesberg in February, Crazy Horse led a party of braves to Camp Rankin in an effort to engage the Wasichus while others attacked Julesberg. The decoy wasn't necessary, because the soldiers suspected an ambush and wouldn't be drawn from the post to fight. Throughout the spring, warriors continued to raid along the South Platte until the territory was under Native control. By summer, with little more to accomplish, the bands dispersed.

Pleased with the great blow dealt to the newcomers, Crazy Horse traveled across the Bighorn Mountains to his Oglala camp south of Powder River country. When he arrived, he was informed that the Big Bellies, a small group of elder warriors, had called for a ceremony to install new shirt-wearers. The position was a critical one within the rather simple and effective system of Sioux governance. Tribal chiefs and their councils made decisions on camping positions, warfare and hunting, which usually reflected a consensus of opinion. Their decisions were implemented by the shirt-wearers, who directed the *akicita* (a police-like force). To be a shirt-wearer was to enjoy great prominence in the tribe. The role also endowed one with great duties and obligations.

The ceremony began with a group of warriors, all dressed in their finest apparel, riding around the camp. They made the three circuits, each time calling the name of a chosen brave. Young Man Afraid of His Horses, Sword and American Horse were chosen, each one a relative of the Big Bellies. The warriors made a fourth pass and selected Crazy Horse, which was something of a surprise since he had no powerful relative in the tribe. Crazy Horse knew that he had been chosen because of his ability and his prominence as a warrior.

When the shirt-wearers gathered near the center lodge, one of the Big Bellies rose and spoke to them of their duties. "You will lead the warriors, both in camp and on the march. You will see that order is preserved and that there is no violence. You must ensure that all Oglala have their rights respected. Be wise, kind and firm in all things. Counsel, advise and then command if necessary. Those who are deaf to your words will rightly feel your strength. But they will know that you act out of justice and for the betterment of your people."

The four warriors were given their shirts, which were colorful and decorated with quills and locks of hair, each representing a courageous act of the warrior who had given it. Crazy Horse had over 240 locks on his shirt.

An elder rose and addressed the shirt-wearers. "Today you are no longer important. You must always think of others first. Look out for the poor, the orphaned, the widowed. If someone harms you, it must be ignored, as is the dog that lifts its leg at your tipi. It will not be easy, but you have been chosen because you are great-hearted, generous, strong and brave. I know that you will do your duty gladly and with a big heart."

With that, the celebration began. Crazy Horse avoided the emotional and high-spirited affair and took time to reflect alone. His new position did not bring him material gain, which was inconsequential to Crazy Horse. He was content with his pony and weapons of war. But it did mark him as one of the greatest of Oglala warriors. It was a matter of some satisfaction, and as Crazy Horse reflected, a matter of great responsibility.

A war council followed the investiture ceremony. Many remained angry about the attack at Kildeer Mountain and the Massacre at Sand Creek, and the council decided to go to war. Crazy Horse joined some other 3000 Sioux, Cheyenne and Arapaho warriors (including Red Cloud and Young Man Afraid of His Horses) at the Battle of Platte Bridge in July 1865. The Platte Bridge (at present-day Casper, Wyoming) allowed the California/Oregon Trail to cross the Platte River, and the presence of a military detachment demonstrated its importance.

Crazy Horse had the important responsibility of leading a 10-warrior decoy party to the bridge, but they were unable to draw the soldiers into the planned ambush. The next day the warriors attacked a detachment that rode out to offer protection to a supply train. Only one of the 25 soldiers escaped and, although Native losses exceeded those of the military, the Natives took the bridge. As was their usual practice following a major engagement, the tribes dispersed, and Crazy Horse went back to the Powder River country.

On this occasion, they were not allowed to slip back into their traditional ways. The American Civil War had ended and troops were finally available to fight on the plains. The Powder River Expedition led by General Patrick Connor was launched against the Cheyenne, but it was an expensive failure. American officials adopted a new strategy. Many politicians and religious organizations believed that assimilating the Plains Natives would be a more appropriate policy, so the government established the Northwest Treaty Commission. As a result, commissioners negotiated the Fort Sully treaties with nine Sioux bands along the upper Missouri River in October 1865.

For the most part, the Natives who signed these treaties were the Hang-Around-the-Fort people who were already dependent on American trading posts. The independent northern bands, including Crazy Horse's Oglala, would not "touch the pen." Throughout the fall of 1865 and winter of

1866, the Oglala continued to raid in the Platte and Powder river countries. The government renewed its efforts to bring treaty to them, and in June 1866, prominent Oglala (likely including Crazy Horse) agreed to meet with treaty commissioners at Fort Laramie.

Red Cloud, who had assumed leadership of the Oglala, demanded that chief negotiator E.B. Taylor explain the treaty to them in detail. The Natives said little until Taylor reached a clause addressing the construction of roads through the Powder River country. Red Cloud declared that the Oglala would never consent to the invasion. A few days later, the Oglala learned that the Wasichus were already marching to the Powder River to build forts and to guard the Bozeman Trail. Colonel Henry B. Carrington, commander of the Department of the Platte, and an army battalion of 700 soldiers, had been ordered to oversee the Bozeman Trail's development and to protect those who traveled on it.

The Oglala were incensed, and Taylor could only argue feebly that his government did not want the right to additional territory, but only wanted to safeguard settlers.

Red Cloud leapt from the stage and shouted, "In this and Wakan Tanka I trust for the right."

He walked from the council arena and sat on the floor, wrapped in his blanket. Taylor tried to explain his government's position, but Red Cloud ignored him.

Finally, the Oglala chief shouted over him, "The Great Father sends us presents and wants us to sell him the road, but White Chief goes with Wasichus to steal it before the Indians say yes or no. I will take no gifts. You treat us as children, pretending to negotiate for a country you have already taken by force. My people called these plains home," stretching his arm from beneath his blanket and making an arc with it. "You have forced us north. We are crowded around the Powder

River. There is not enough buffalo to feed us. Our women and children starve."

Then Red Cloud turned to the Sioux. "It is better to fight. What else is there? To starve? To die in a land no longer ours? We should fight and we will win."

Red Cloud left Fort Laramie with Crazy Horse and his supporters. While Spotted Tail and others made treaty, the commission was in a shambles. Ironically, the United States Senate subsequently rejected the treaty, but the Natives were not informed of this.

Red Cloud headed for the Powder River country, and along the way warriors raided Wasichus on the Bozeman Trail. On July 17, 1866 they attacked the site chosen for Fort Phil Kearny, at the forks of the Big Piney and Little Piney creeks, less than 50 miles from the Powder River. The raid marked the beginning of what became known as Red Cloud's War. A week later Natives attacked three wagon trains bound for Montana. Carrington sent out soldiers to assist the migrants, but Red Cloud attacked them as well.

Carrington sought a peace council with Red Cloud, but Red Cloud was not interested in peace unless the Wasichus closed the Bozeman Trail. Only then would Sioux hunting territory be safe, and with that, their traditional way of life. Carrington couldn't insure that, and it appeared to the Oglala that the Wasichus were more determined than ever to control the Bozeman Trail. In August, they began construction of Fort C.F. Smith on the Bighorn River. Including Fort Reno, three forts had been established along the Bozeman Trail, three too many for the Oglala.

Crazy Horse and other warriors continued to raid throughout the late summer. Meanwhile, the Oglala held a Sun Dance along the Tongue River. They decided to send the war pipe to neighboring tribes. Many smoked it, and by November, some 3000 Sioux, Cheyenne and Arapaho had gathered in Red Cloud's camp. Warriors rode out to harass Fort Phil Kearny, which by November was under a state of constant siege. And there was more trouble all along the Bozeman Trail. Between August and December, more than 150 soldiers and travelers were killed and over 700 animals were stolen. Sioux confidence grew with the success of their raids. They talked of taking the fort. Crazy Horse discussed the matter with Red Cloud, Hump and other shirt-wearers.

They agreed to try to take Fort Phil Kearny by stealth. The Oglala knew that the fort depended on woodcutters to bring in firewood. They expected that a small band of warriors could pin down the wood train, which would then require the fort commander to send out Wasichus to rescue it. The great body of warriors would remain hidden until the detachment arrived, and then they would attack. It was an old Native war strategy, effective because most of their many raids never included any more than one or two dozen warriors.

Crazy Horse remained with the ambush party, watching from a bluff as the plan was put into action on December 6, 1866. As anticipated, the decoy party that pinned down the woodcutters drew out a detachment of some 40 soldiers. A second detachment, led by Carrington himself, was sent out to attack the Oglala, whom they expected to flee as they usually did. The situation quickly deteriorated. The decoy closed too quickly on the first detachment, and the ambushers charged the second detachment before the soldiers were close enough to attack effectively. Carrington realized what was happening and ordered a hasty retreat. The Oglala took only two lives, and the attack was a failure. Crazy Horse was enraged.

"We cannot expect victory if the warriors cannot hold their places until it is time to attack! The warriors want to be brave and to count coup, but that will not remove the Wasichus," he declared to Hump. Crazy Horse's anger over

the incident was understandable, but he could hardly hold
the warriors responsible. They had fought as they were
taught, with courage, responsible for their own actions.
With the failure of the raid, Crazy Horse realized that
fighting the Wasichus required a new approach.

Red Cloud was anxious to attack again, so he was open
to Crazy Horse's advice. Perhaps Crazy Horse's new standing among the Oglala also influenced Red Cloud.

He Dog remembers "The older, more responsible men of
the tribe conferred another kind of chieftainship on Crazy
Horse. He was made war chief of the whole Oglala tribe."

They decided to try the same ambush strategy as used
on December 6. This time, however, Red Cloud wanted
there to be no escape for the Wasichus, and the ambush
party was increased from 300 to 2000 warriors. Crazy
Horse led the decoy party, while Hump was responsible for
the ambush party, which was well hidden in a ravine along
Peno Creek, some miles from the fort.

The next day fortune—or perhaps Wakan Tanka—
smiled on the Oglala. Carrington dispatched Captain
William Fetterman to relieve the woodcutters. Fetterman
was another braggart, ignorant of the strength and ability of
the Sioux. He'd often declared that all he needed was
a company of cavalry to wipe out 1000 Sioux. When he
approached the woodcutters with his command of 80 men,
the Oglala decoy party led by Crazy Horse fell back.
Although Fetterman was under orders from Carrington
not to pursue for fear of ambush, Fetterman believed
retreat to be both unnecessary and cowardly. As he watched
the Sioux scamper back to the Lodge Trail Ridge, he
pushed his men after them and smiled. Victory would be
his, and promotion was sure to follow.

Crazy Horse was smiling as well. Hump and the *akicita*
had managed to hold the warriors to their positions and

remain concealed. When the decoy party reached the ravine, 2000 warriors suddenly appeared. Fetterman had no opportunity to retreat. The short battle was chaotic, and Fetterman's detachment was wiped out. Americans came to know the battle as the Fetterman Massacre, but the Sioux called it the Fight of 100 Killed (they believed that they had killed 100 Wasichus). Under either name, it was the greatest defeat yet suffered by the cavalry.

The battle was also tragic for Crazy Horse. After the victory he joined Hump in a search for their old friend Lone Bear, who had disappeared during the fight. They found him so badly wounded that he could not move. He died in Crazy Horse's arms.

By the summer of 1867, the Native attacks along the Bozeman Trail forced the United States government's hand. Settlers were increasingly reluctant to go West, and those en route complained about Sioux harassment. Railroad expansion was threatened, and an increasingly loud chorus in the East held that the Native problems reflected official intolerance. To appease everyone, additional troops were dispatched to Fort Phil Kearny and a peace commission was sent to Fort Laramie. In the summer of 1867, word reached the Oglala that the government wanted to make treaty.

The Natives held a council to discuss their response, and the council agreed that Old Man Afraid of His Horses would go to Fort Laramie to hear the Wasichus' proposal. But at the insistence of Red Cloud, Crazy Horse and his fellow shirt-wearers, he was not allowed to sign anything until the Wasichus abandoned the forts along the Bozeman Trail. Old Man Afraid of His Horses arrived at Fort Laramie in June but left without a peace agreement.

Crazy Horse, for one, was neither surprised at nor disappointed with the outcome of the mission. He joined other warriors in harassing wagon trains and soldiers on the

Bozeman Trail, but it brought little satisfaction. Migrants had all but abandoned the trail, and the soldiers were increasingly cautious about venturing from the safety of their forts. In mid-summer 1867 the bands held a council and decided to launch a major attack against the Wasichus, but they disagreed about the target. The Cheyenne decided to attack Fort C.F. Smith, while the Sioux chose Fort Phil Kearny.

In discussion with Crazy Horse and Hump, the Sioux made plans to bring the fort to its knees by attacking the 26-man detachment that was protecting the woodcutters near the Bighorn Mountains. On August 2, Crazy Horse and Hump led the decoy against the woodcutters working about a mile away from the cavalry camp. They were to draw out the soldiers, who would then be ambushed by the 800 hidden Sioux. But when a soldier fired on Crazy Horse, the hidden Sioux broke ranks. With the element of surprise lost, Crazy Horse modified his plans. He had his braves surround the wagons, anticipating that they would draw fire from the Wasichus until their ammunition was depleted. However, there seemed to be no end to the bullets, and the Sioux arrows were unable to do more than lodge in the wooden wagon boxes, which had been placed in a protective circle. Six Sioux died before Crazy Horse called a retreat. They had killed 10 Wasichus and taken many ponies, but could not claim victory. The Wagon Box Fight taught Crazy Horse an important lesson, and he would never again attack white men when they enjoyed a fortified position.

As the weeks passed, it seemed likely that Crazy Horse would no longer need to trouble himself over battle strategy. The Sioux and their allies had proven to be more worthy adversaries than the United States government had expected. Despite great financial expenditures, the army was making little headway in bringing the northern Plains Natives under control. Because the cost of waging war was too great, the government sent commissioners back to Fort Laramie in the fall of 1867 to negotiate peace. By the following spring, they had agreed to Red Cloud's every demand. The Fort Laramie Treaty of 1868 pledged that the Bozeman Trail would be closed and the forts along it abandoned. The treaty also established the Great Sioux Reservation, which included much of northern Wyoming and the Black Hills. Access was forbidden, except to officials on government business. It was an amazing victory for the Sioux and their allies, and they celebrated by burning down the empty forts C.F. Smith and Reno.

Crazy Horse was not at the peace council in November when Red Cloud "touched the pen." He had no reason to be. As a warrior, his job was done; others could negotiate terms. Throughout 1869 and 1870, he led the occasional raid on the Crow, but there was little fighting during this period.

In the fall of 1870, Crazy Horse joined with Hump in a raid against the Shoshone. They made camp at the Wind River, and while the pair rode out to scout the enemy camp, the cold rain that had dogged their journey turned to snow. Crazy Horse, ever cautious, felt that conditions were not right for fighting.

"I wonder if we can make it back to Cone Creek. I doubt if our horses can stand a fight in this slush. They sink in over their ankles," observed Crazy Horse. "It is best to head back to camp."

Hump would have none of it.

"You called off a fight here before and when we got back to camp they laughed at us. You and I have our good names to think about," Hump reminded him. "If you don't care about it, you can go back. But I am going to stay here and fight."

"All right, we fight," sighed Crazy Horse. "But I think we're going to take a beating. You have a good gun and I have a good gun, but none of our men have good guns!

Most have only bows and arrows. It's a bad place for a fight, a bad day for it and the enemy are 12 to our one."

The fight that followed quickly deteriorated for the Oglala. Sensing defeat, most of the warriors withdrew leaving only Crazy Horse, Hump and Good Weasel to fight. They were having a hard time, but they knew nothing of retreat. Amid the rifle fire, Crazy Horse looked over to Hump and saw he was in trouble.

"We're done for now," shouted Hump. "My horse has a leg wound."

"I know it," replied Crazy Horse.

Crazy Horse called his war cry, echoed quickly by Hump. Both charged the Shoshone. When Crazy Horse looked back, he saw Hump's pony and the enemy swarming over the body of his *kola*. Hump was dead.

Distraught, Crazy Horse returned to Powder River country, where there was soon more bad news. His brother Little Hawk had been killed while on a war expedition south of the Platte River. Crazy Horse was close to his brother and had watched him grow as a man and a warrior with satisfaction. It was hard to accept that he would watch him no more.

Within months, Crazy Horse had lost two of his closest friends. Surely he felt more alone than ever. Perhaps this is why his thoughts turned to marriage. At the age of 30, Crazy Horse remained single, an odd situation for a Sioux man of his position and status. He might have been expected to have several wives. Ironically, however, to reach his lofty status as a warrior Crazy Horse may well have seen it necessary to avoid women, because Sioux culture considered that sexual relations depleted a man's strength. Or perhaps his marital status simply reflected his reserved nature.

The Oglala mystic Black Elk, who was a cousin of Crazy Horse, said of him, "...I was a little afraid of him....Everybody felt that way about him, for he was a queer man and would go about the village without noticing people or saying anything. In his own teepee he would joke, and when he was on the warpath with a small party, he would joke to make his warriors feel good. But around the village he hardly ever noticed anybody, except little children. All the Lakota like to dance and sing; but he never joined a dance and they say nobody ever heard him sing….He was a queer man…" though, added Black Elk, "everybody liked him…."

Crazy Horse wanted to marry Red Cloud's niece Black Buffalo Woman, a woman he had known since childhood. But Black Buffalo Woman was married to No Water. It is said that Red Cloud pushed his niece to marry No Water despite Crazy Horse's feelings towards her, thus sowing a rivalry between the two leaders. Black Buffalo Woman's marriage was no great obstacle, since Sioux women could divorce their husbands simply by leaving them. So sometime in 1870, while her husband was away, she left her children with friends and rode off with Crazy Horse on a raid.

When No Water returned and learned of his wife's desertion, he was furious. He borrowed a revolver and set off in pursuit of Crazy Horse. No Water found him camped along the Powder River. With the revolver raised, he stormed into Crazy Horse's lodge and shot him. The bullet hit Crazy Horse just below the left nostril, fracturing his jaw. No Water burst from the tipi, declaring that he had killed Crazy Horse. He hadn't.

Crazy Horse's friends sought revenge, and for a time it appeared as if the band might be torn apart. Violence was forestalled when Black Buffalo Woman returned to No Water on the condition, demanded by Crazy Horse, that she not be punished. It was not the end of the affair for Crazy Horse. Band leaders decided that his actions did not reflect what was expected of a shirt-wearer and he was stripped of his position. Crazy Horse must have been greatly humbled. He had been recognized as the greatest of Sioux warriors. He had counted many coups and had been a member of the Brave Hearts (an elite warrior organization) and a lance bearer (one who led warriors into battle and pledged not to retreat until victory or death). The loss of position must have been difficult to accept. Crazy Horse did finally marry a year later. His wife, Black Shawl, bore him a daughter, who died from cholera around 1872.

By 1872, it was clear to the Sioux that the United States government was not going to abide by the terms of the 1868 Fort Laramie Treaty. The California/Oregon Trail became popular again and American railroads were pushing west. By late summer, surveyors and their large cavalry escort approached the Yellowstone River, along the northern edge of Teton Sioux territory. Many Sioux tribes and some Cheyenne allies had gathered in the region to participate in a Sun Dance. They had planned to follow up the ceremony with an attack on the Crow, but when they learned of the Wasichus' presence, they reconsidered. Sitting Bull, a *wichasha wakan* and leader of many Teton Sioux, argued in favor of fighting the Wasichus and Crazy Horse likely supported him. But the consensus was for a parley and it was so agreed.

In mid-August, 500 warriors rode to the mouth of Arrow Creek at the Yellowstone River, where the Wasichus were camped. Anxious young warriors attacked before Sitting Bull had the opportunity to parley. In the dark hours before sunrise on August 13, the warriors and soldiers exchanged distant shots but few were injured.

Morning found Crazy Horse and Sitting Bull atop a bluff overlooking the battlefield. Sitting Bull observed that some warriors were recklessly running the daring line (the open space between two opposing forces). He thought that they should stop but Crazy Horse was not so sure.

Oglala Sioux mystic and medicine man Black Elk (1863–1950), age 73. He held his cousin Crazy Horse in high regard.

He knew the importance of the daring line. He had ridden it himself earlier that morning and wasn't about to tell warriors what they should or should not do. So he remained on the bluff as Sitting Bull mounted his pony and rode down the gentle slope of the bluff to the Sioux line of the fight. He could not hear what was said when Sitting Bull reached the warriors, but he could see that there was shouting and, he suspected, angry words. Surely the warriors objected to Sitting Bull's interference.

What happened next took Crazy Horse by surprise.

Sitting Bull dismounted, took his pipe and tobacco from a pouch on his pony and, with his weapons in hand, walked to the open space between the opposing forces. Crazy Horse watched him sit and signal to the warriors to join him. It was a challenge as much as an invitation. Soon four others joined him, two Sioux and two Cheyenne. Crazy Horse noticed that their journey was taken on shaky legs. When they arrived, Sitting Bull prepared his pipe, lit it and contentedly took a few long, deep drags. He passed it to his companions, whose trembling hands and short quick puffs suggested that they were more aware than was Sitting Bull of the small clouds of earth kicked up around them by enemy bullets. Once the ball of tobacco was spent, Sitting Bull cleaned his pipe and placed it back in his pouch. The Hunkpapa chief rose and walked slowly back to the admiring Sioux line, his limp emphasized for effect. He had taken only a few steps when the others rushed past him, deterred neither by courage nor disability. Crazy Horse chuckled when he saw that one left in such haste that he forgot his weapons.

Crazy Horse did not chuckle long because he knew that he had witnessed a singular act of bravery. To willingly risk his life in the face of such great danger! Sitting Bull's performance was unsurpassed and Crazy Horse could not let it go unanswered. He charged his pony down the slope and rode the daring line. His pony was killed, but Crazy Horse made it back safely to the Sioux line. It was a courageous act, but even Crazy Horse knew that it did not match Sitting Bull' actions.

With Crazy Horse's return to the warriors, Sitting Bull broke the silence.

"It is enough. Today's fighting is over."

None questioned his decision, and the warriors pulled back. The Battle of Arrow Creek was inconclusive; neither side could claim clear victory. The fighting, however, had deepened the surveyors' fears. They refused to go south of the Yellowstone and made hurried measurements near the northerly Musselshell River before hastily retreating to Fort Ellis. The Sioux's first blow against the Northern Pacific Railroad and everything it stood for was a successful one.

The Americans, however, were set on western expansion and determined to build railroads. The government dispatched additional troops to protect ongoing construction. The Sioux mostly ignored the troops because they were occupied with raiding the Crow throughout 1873 and 1874. By this time, Crazy Horse was leader of his own band. He wasn't a chief in the traditional sense; he didn't assume leadership of an existing band. Rather he led those Oglala and some other Sioux and Cheyenne—about 100 lodges, with some 300 warriors—who shared his views of a traditional life apart from, and independent of, the Wasichus.

But in the summer of 1874 Crazy Horse and his band were drawn back into the fight against the Wasichus. At the center of the matter was *Paha Sapa*, the Black Hills. *Paha Sapa* was considered sacred to the Sioux, and the Fort Laramie Treaty of 1868 had guaranteed that *Paha Sapa* would be theirs forever. Rumors of gold, however, cast the pledge in doubt. By the mid-1870s, the government had sent a number of military expeditions into the region to validate the rumors. The Sioux had forced each one into retreat, but not before they found conclusive evidence of the precious metal. Prospectors slowly began to arrive. For awhile the United States government tried to keep its treaty obligation by restraining efforts of Dakotan businesses to exploit the resources of the Black Hills, but prospectors continued to arrive and pressure mounted.

The Sioux attacked the newcomers, who were in violation of the 1868 Fort Laramie Treaty. Sioux depredations
were used as an excuse to send in the army to explore the
Black Hills and establish a local post. General George
Armstrong Custer was authorized to lead the Seventh
Cavalry into the Black Hills. When the expedition set out
on July 2, 1874, Custer had under his command 951 soldiers and teamsters and a good collection of civilian aides,
including reporters, miners and scientists.

Custer found gold, although he was cautious in his
judgment about how much there might be. The reporters
who accompanied him, however, were less reserved in their
assessments. William Eleroy of the *Chicago Inter-Ocean*
wrote, "From the grassroots down it was pay dirt." Stories
of valleys awash with the yellow ore soon filled American
newspapers. Despite warnings from army officials that the
territory was in the possession of some of the most fearsome warriors on the Plains, fortune seekers stampeded to
the new Eldorado. The army continued to make half-
hearted efforts to protect the Black Hills, but it was clear
that the sheer numbers and determination of the prospectors would make even that impossible. Sensing the
inevitable and anxious to avoid a costly war, the government tried to purchase *Paha Sapa*.

Those Sioux who were inclined to sell were mostly the
Hang-Around-the-Fort people led by Red Cloud. Crazy
Horse and Sitting Bull rigidly opposed the sale and they
were not swayed by the appearance, arguments or gifts of
Young Man Afraid of His Horses. When negotiations collapsed because Red Cloud's price was too high ($70 million),
President Ulysses S. Grant's government adopted a new policy: they would let prospectors into the region and simply
take it by right of possession. To protect the prospectors, the
government directed all Sioux onto reservations. Those who

didn't go, including Crazy Horse, were labeled hostiles—enemies of the United States.

General George Crook (known to the Sioux as Three Stars because of the insignia of his rank) was charged with reining in the hostiles in Powder River country. His first target was Crazy Horse, but his troops mistakenly attacked a band of peaceful Cheyenne. The Native survivors fled to Crazy Horse's village. Crazy Horse must have wondered whether these Wasichus would ever let his people live in peace. He couldn't afford to wait for such a time, and he traveled to Sitting Bull's village to discuss strategy. Crazy Horse supported Sitting Bull's decision to call a great war council.

By spring, 3000 warriors were in the camp. Sitting Bull was chosen to lead the Sioux, and Crazy Horse did not object because the Hunkpapa chief's medicine was strong and his words, songs and actions inspirational. Crazy Horse was not present at the Sun Dance when Sitting Bull had the vision that revealed an attack by the Wasichus and a Native victory, but when he learned of it, he was surely pleased. Wakan Tanka's revelations were not to be doubted. When the decision was made to go on the warpath in the spring of 1876, Crazy Horse was ready.

The army was also ready. By the spring of 1876, soldiers were marching to enforce President Grant's order to rein in the hostile Sioux. General Philip Sheridan, commander of the Department of the Missouri (known by many for his comment, "The only good Indian is a dead Indian."), was charged with organizing the campaign. Sheridan assigned General Alfred Terry to command the offensive against the northern Sioux. Terry was one of the commissioners who had agreed to close the Bozeman Trail back in 1868, and he was still rankled by that defeat.

Terry mustered the largest force ever to ride against the Sioux. Crook and 1200 troops marched from Fort Fetterman southeast of the Bighorn Mountains. General John Gibbon and 450 troops marched east from Fort Ellis along the Yellowstone River. Custer and 2700 troops marched west from Fort Abraham Lincoln, following the Yellowstone River to the mouth of the Powder River. Terry, who had no experience fighting on the Plains, rode with Custer. The plan required the three columns to converge on the Sioux in the Powder River country. As they were searching for the Sioux, the Natives discovered Crook and his men at Rosebud Creek.

Learning of the Wasichus' presence, Crazy Horse took quick action to organize the warriors. He directed 1500 warriors to remain in the camp to protect the women, children and elderly. Another 1500 rode with him against Crook. Crazy Horse, ever mindful of the impulsiveness of young warriors, gave strict orders to the *akicita* to ensure that no one broke from the war party. He didn't want Three Stars to have even the smallest sign that warriors were approaching.

Crazy Horse arrived at the valley of the Rosebud Creek on the morning of June 17. He and his scouts climbed a hill that overlooked the valley for a quick reconnaissance. The Wasichus were camped along the river to the east. Crazy Horse observed the surroundings and noted that the valley narrowed to the north, forming a canyon. Crazy Horse thought that the location held promise as a place for an ambush.

"Crow!" called one of the scouts. "They've seen us!"

When Crazy Horse realized that his force had been discovered, he called to the *akicita* to let the warriors go. The element of surprise was lost and there was no need to hold them back. Indeed, Crazy Horse realized that the best strategy was a fast strike made before the Wasichus could organize a defense. The Sioux swept around the base of the hill. The warriors might have rolled through the camp had the 250 Crow and Shoshone warriors scouting for the army not fought so bravely. Their determination gave the soldiers valuable time to prepare a defense.

Crook barked orders for a counterattack, and under pressure from the advancing soldiers, the Sioux fell back. Suddenly Crazy Horse and four other experienced warriors rushed the Wasichus, bringing them to a jarring halt.

Colonel Anson Mills, who was in the battle, described Crazy Horse's attack. The warriors were "charging boldly and rapidly through the soldiers, knocking them from their horses with lances and knives, dismounting and killing them...."

Crook then made a series of decisions that almost resulted in the decimation of his command. Believing that Crazy Horse's camp was downstream, he dispatched Mills and eight troops of cavalry to find and capture it. Then, worried about the warriors' effectiveness in pinning down his men, he divided his command into two groups, hoping that the columns might provide mutual support.

Crazy Horse surely smiled as he watched the Wasichus carry out their orders. Mills' men marched towards the canyon. Crazy Horse directed some warriors there to wait in ambush and others to fall behind Crook's two newly formed groups and attack the weak points along the flanks and from the rear. When scouts informed Crook that the troops were being surrounded, he sent a hurried message to Mills to return. Mills pulled back with some relief. He had seen the canyon and he was uncertain about venturing into it. Doubling back, his men approached the warriors from the rear. The warriors weren't expecting the maneuver and they broke off the attack. Crook's men were tired from marching and fighting, and he did not order them to pursue.

The Battle of the Rosebud was a stalemate—28 soldiers and 36 Natives killed. Both sides, however, claimed victory. Crook's was confident in victory because the Sioux and

Cheyenne were the first to retreat. Those who fought with Crazy Horse believed that he used good judgment in the battle.

Black Elk said, "Crazy Horse whipped Three Stars on the Rosebud that day, and I think he could have rubbed the soldiers out there. He could have called many more warriors from the villages and he could have rubbed the soldiers out...."

Perhaps it was so. But the real measure of Crazy Horse's victory was that he neutralized Three Stars, who retreated south to his camp at Goose Creek, where he remained for the next six weeks, oblivious to events along the Little Bighorn River.

The Natives packed up their camp and moved on in their ongoing search for buffalo. Warriors rode with their weapons close at hand. Everyone knew that there would be more fighting because Sitting Bull's vision had revealed that the Wasichus would attack the Native camp, which had not happened on the Rosebud. A week following the Battle of the Rosebud, they made camp in the wooded valley of the Greasy Grass, south of the fork of the Bighorn and Little Bighorn rivers.

Meanwhile, Generals Gibbon, Terry and Custer and their troops had arrived at the mouth of the Rosebud Creek. Scouts reported many Sioux tracks leading to the Little Bighorn River, and they declared that a Sioux camp was in the region. The generals decided to divide the 2700 troops and move on the camp. Custer marched his men south along the west bank of the Rosebud. Gibbon's troops also headed south, but they followed the east bank of the Little Bighorn. Terry's troops took up the rear. They believed that Crook was still approaching the Rosebud from the south. Their goal was to surround the hostiles and cut off any escape.

Strategically, the plan was sound enough, but Custer saw a problem with timing. The attack was set for the morning of June 26, but Custer thought that the Natives might well be gone by then. Custer wanted desperately to engage the hostiles because he believed that a victory could propel him to the presidency of the United States. He was not to be deterred even when his Native scouts told him that the enemy outnumbered his troops.

On June 24, Custer and his two senior officers, Major Marcus Reno and Captain Frederick Benteen, reviewed their strategy. Reno's 130 troops were to attack the upper end of the camp. Benteen's 250 men would support him. Custer held 220 men under his command, and he planned to attack the lower end of the camp. The offensive was planned for the next day. It was an odd strategy, taken without the usual reconnaissance. It was also planned for the day before the attack date set by Terry.

Reno's battalion led the attack on the afternoon of June 25, advancing on the Hunkpapa camp. Reno must have sensed that something was not quite right because the warriors did not scatter under the troops' fire. After the initial confusion the Hunkpapa rallied, and under the direction of Sitting Bull and Gall, mounted a counterattack. Reno's men had all they could handle, but he took heart when he saw Custer and his troops on the east side of the river. Custer's attack on the Cheyenne at the northern end of the camp was to remove the pressure from Reno's men. Victory seemed only a matter of time.

But victory did not come. Even as the warriors were holding their own, a cry gave them greater courage.

"Crazy Horse is coming! Crazy Horse is coming!"

Crazy Horse had gathered his warriors and was riding hard from the northwest. They came in a great cloud of dust, like a "big wind roaring," their "eagle bones scream-ing" yelling, "Hoka hey!"

As increasingly large numbers of Oglala and Cheyenne joined the Hunkpapa, Reno's confidence melted away. Led by Crazy Horse, the warriors charged the Wasichus. Their line broke quickly, and the soldiers fled for the trees. Crazy Horse then pointed to the northeast.

"There's a good fight coming over the hill!" he barked as he saw Custer and his men, although he did not know that it was Long Hair (the Sioux name for Custer). "That's where the big fight will be! We'll not miss that one!" shouted Crazy Horse.

Crazy Horse left the fight against Reno, who was pinned down waiting for the Benteen's reinforcements. Crazy Horse rushed through the camp, shouting words of encouragement, blowing his eagle bone whistle and collecting warriors.

When Crazy Horse finally rode out of the north end of the camp, he led 1000 warriors. They splashed across the Little Bighorn and settled in a ravine, where they harassed Custer's flank. Gall, who had also left the Reno fight, and his few hundred warriors kept Custer occupied from the front, while Two Moons and his Cheyenne attacked from behind. For a time, the battle was reduced to an exchange of gunfire from well-protected positions, but such fighting did not satisfy the younger warriors who longed to demonstrate their courage. White Bull ran the daring line and challenged Crazy Horse to do the same. Crazy Horse gave a sharp blow on his eagle bone whistle and charged out of the ravine. The warriors took his action as a signal to attack, and they poured out of the ravine and charged the hill.

Some soldiers fled, while others held their positions. But as their ammunition ran low and the warriors continued to press, the tide turned. The soldiers were forced to fight hand-to-hand, and they didn't have a chance against the more experienced Natives. Before sundown Custer and his 220 troops were dead.

Crazy Horse deserved much of the credit for the rout. As one of the warriors noted, "[He] was the bravest man I ever saw. He rode close to the soldiers, yelling to his warriors. All the Wasichus were shooting at him, but he was never hit."

With Custer's force decimated, the Natives turned back on Reno's battalion, which had been strengthened by Benteen's arrival. Perhaps Crazy Horse joined them. When night fell, the Natives halted their attack, but with sunrise they began again with renewed vigor. When the guns were finally silenced, Reno and Benteen had lost 50 men. More might have died had Sitting Bull not called an end to the fighting. There had been enough bloodshed.

With the battle over, the Natives counted 30 warriors dead, but they had killed more than half of Custer's force. They did not know that Long Hair was dead because no Wasichu had the telltale flowing reddish yellow locks. Unknown to the Sioux, Custer had shorn his hair before leaving Fort Lincoln.

Crazy Horse probably did not attend the victory celebrations. Sitting Bull did, but he could not enjoy them. When he was asked about his reluctance to participate, he replied with a heavy heart.

"The young braves have taken the spoils of victory. They have taken the Wasichus' guns, clothing and horses. From this time on they will covet his goods. They will be at his mercy; they will starve at his hands. The soldiers will crush them."

The outcome of the battle had been foretold in his vision. The truth of Sitting Bull's observation would soon enough be clear in the army's response. It was all too anxious to satisfy American demands for revenge and bring an end to the problem of the Sioux.

After the Battle of the Greasy Grass, as the Sioux called the fight, the bands dispersed in search of game. Sitting Bull went north, and Crazy Horse and his band went south, continuing to raid in *Paha Sapa*. His role in the battles of the Rosebud and the Little Bighorn had gained him notoriety in the Plains' newspapers, and perhaps his growing reputation among whites contributed to the army's determined efforts to catch him.

Black Elk remembered, "[W]herever we went, the soldiers came to kill us...."

Crook finally caught up to American Horse's band of Sioux in early September 1876. Few casualties occurred in the Battle of Slim Buttes (in South Dakota), but American Horse was fatally wounded. Crazy Horse was nearby with about 700 warriors, and when he heard of the attack, his warriors rode in support of American Horse's band. Crook's soldiers managed to hold off the Sioux and, after a couple of days of fighting, they made for the Black Hills. The Sioux nipped at their flanks during the retreat, but broke off when Crook finally reached a supply column.

Crazy Horse led his band west to the Tongue River. He was there when news arrived in November that the Black Hills had been sold. The transaction was neither legal nor ethical. The United States government withheld rations from the agency Natives until they signed. When it was pointed out that the 1868 Fort Laramie Treaty required the signatures of three-quarters of the adult male Sioux population, the government declared that the number did not include the hostile Sioux. The *Paha Sapa* were gone, and the attacks continued. In late November, survivors of a cavalry attack on Dull Knife's Cheyenne band limped into Crazy Horse's camp. They were given what few supplies could be spared, but there was not enough food to go around and spirits were low.

One of a series of drawings by Crazy Horse's cousin, Amos Bad
Heart Buffalo (1869–1913), depicting the Battle of the Little
Bighorn (June 1876). Surrounded by warriors are Crazy Horse
(seated on the roan and spotted with paint that represented
the hailstones in his vision) and Sitting Bull. Between 1891
and 1913 Bad Heart Bull, a scout in the United States Army,
drew more than 400 pictures illustrating the history of his
Oglala tribe. Bad Heart Bull drew on a Sioux tradition of
depicting important events in pictographs, but his work was
richer in both detail and content than most earlier picture-
writing. Bad Heart Bull based his drawing of Crazy Horse on
oral descriptions because there is no fully authenticated
picture of the Oglala leader. Reports suggest that Crazy Horse
refused to have his picture taken. In accordance with tribal
custom, Bad Heart Bull's original drawings were buried with
his sister when she died in 1947.

Black Elk described the effects of these events on Crazy Horse. "After that the people noticed that Crazy Horse was queerer than ever. He hardly ever stayed in the camp. People would find him out alone in the cold, and they would ask him to come home with them. He would not come, but sometimes he would tell the people what to do. People wondered if he ate anything at all. Once my father found him out like that, and he said to my father: 'Uncle, you have noticed me the way I act. But do not worry; there are caves and holes for me to live in, and out here the spirits may help me. I am making plans for the good of my people.' He was always a queer man, but that winter he was queerer than ever. Maybe he had seen that he would soon be dead and was thinking how to help us when he would not be with us anymore."

For a good chief, the responsibility of leadership weighed heavily. And a life on the run without supplies was enough to make any man queer. Faced with an unrelenting government, its single-minded soldiers and the reality of a plains empty of buffalo, Crazy Horse realized the end was near. The Wasichus sent messengers with promises of food and peace. Many in his band thought surrender was the best option, and Crazy Horse had lost the will to argue. In mid-December the band held a council to discuss what should be done.

"We should accept the offer brought by the runners," sighed one of the Sioux.

"But they want our ponies and guns," replied He Dog. "How can we give them up?"

"What good are they to us? There is nothing left to hunt. Where can we ride on the reservation?"

"They say the Wasichus have promised not to punish us," added another.

"What punishment is greater than riding into the agency?" asked Crazy Horse. "The band will live, but not as Sioux."

All fell silent for a moment at the words of their chief.

"Better to live," suggested one.

"Then make plans to live," said Crazy Horse, who, despite his misgivings, knew that he was responsible for the well-being of the band. His personal desires no longer mattered. His people needed food, shelter and rest, and these could no longer be found in the Powder River country, especially while being chased by Wasichus.

On December 16, a small delegation of 25 Sioux and Cheyenne left the village and rode to Fort Keogh to meet with Colonel Nelson Miles (called Bear Coat by the Sioux). He considered Crazy Horse "the personification of savage ferocity." Crazy Horse was not with the delegation.

As they approached Bear Coat's camp, the army's Crow scouts attacked the delegation and killed everyone. Miles was incensed because he had given specific orders that the Crow do nothing of the sort. Crazy Horse sent word to Bear Coat that they had not started this fight, but that they were prepared to see it out to its end.

With Dull Knife and the Cheyenne at his side, Crazy Horse led 700 warriors on the warpath. Throughout late December and early January a series of skirmishes occurred, culminating in the Battle of Wolf Mountains on January 8, 1877. On that day, Miles and his 450 troops had the upper hand. The Natives were the first to withdraw, abandoning their few supplies.

There was increased pressure on Crazy Horse to surrender because it seemed that the war was lost. But hearts were lifted in late January, when Sitting Bull arrived in the camp. He informed them that he was going to the land of the Grandmother (Canada). Crazy Horse looked to his people and saw that they were already cold and hungry. They would not survive the winter in Canada. And he was confident that Bear Coat would not attack until the snows were gone. Perhaps then there might be more buffalo to hunt. He did not join Sitting Bull on the journey north.

In late winter, the Brulé chief Spotted Tail, Crazy Horse's uncle and head chief of the agency Oglala, arrived at Crazy Horse's camp to encourage surrender. He was there at the urging of General Crook, who anticipated that Crazy Horse's surrender would enhance his own prestige. Spotted Tail told his nephew that Three Stars promised Crazy Horse his own agency on the Powder River. Crazy Horse needed no such promise. His people could no longer survive on the plains that had nourished them so long. In the spring, Crazy Horse led his people south. On April 27 the weakening band was met by Red Cloud, who hoped his own prestige might be enhanced by leading the hostiles into the agency. Crazy Horse spread his blanket for his old ally to sit on and then gave Red Cloud his shirt. Everyone understood the meaning of the actions. Crazy Horse had surrendered.

On May 6, Lieutenant William Clark, military commander of the Red Cloud Agency, met Crazy Horse about two miles north of Camp Robinson. Crazy Horse gathered his headmen, and they sat in a row before Clark. The Oglala chief then moved to Clark and took the officer's hand in his own left hand.

"Friend, I shake with this hand because my heart is on this side," he explained. "The right hand does all manner of wickedness; I want this peace to last forever."

Crazy Horse then motioned to He Dog, who stepped forward and presented Clark with his war bonnet. It was the traditional act of surrender, one that Crazy Horse could not make because he never wore a war bonnet.

The formalities complete, the Oglala marched on to Camp Robinson. To those who watched, they appeared as anything but a defeated people. Crazy Horse and He Dog led warriors painted and dressed for war. As they entered the White River valley, Camp Robinson came into view but was quickly obscured by thousands of agency Natives who poured out to greet them. Those who rode with Crazy Horse were singing and onlookers soon joined them. They sang words of praise and respect for Crazy Horse.

An army onlooker declared, "By God, this is a triumphal march, not a surrender."

Crazy Horse wasn't long at his camp outside the Red Cloud Agency when Crook began pressuring him to go to Washington to meet with the president. Prominent Natives often traveled to Washington, usually in order to demonstrate America's might to wide-eyed easterners. Crook thought that Crazy Horse's appearance would be a handsome feather in his cap. Crazy Horse was reluctant to go. He was negotiating for an agency in the Powder River country, and he feared that the trip was designed to remove him from the region so that his people might instead be forced to an undesirable agency north of the Missouri River. Despite his appointment as a noncommissioned officer in the United States Indian Scouts and hints that his participation would ensure he was made chief of all the Sioux, Crazy Horse would not go.

"You have my horses and my guns," declared Crazy Horse. "I have only my tent and my will. You got me to come here and you can keep me here by force if you choose, but you cannot make me go anywhere that I refuse to go."

The Sioux, meanwhile, held a Sun Dance to honor Crazy Horse. Spotted Tail and Red Cloud were worried about the show of respect for Crazy Horse. They had also heard the rumors that Crazy Horse might be named the head chief of the Sioux. They knew it would be a popular choice among agency Natives, one that would erode their own influence. So they began to spread rumors about Crazy Horse, that he planned to escape and return to the Powder River country, where he would fight the Wasichus.

In response to the rumors, soldiers were posted in Crazy Horse's camp and ordered to watch his every move. Crook, however, remained hopeful that Crazy Horse could be used for his own benefit. In early August, he sent Lieutenant Clark to Crazy Horse with a proposal that he assist the army in defeating Chief Joseph and his renegade band of Nez Perce in the west. Frank Grouard translated Crazy Horse's response.

"When I came in from the north and met with the officers and others on Hat Creek, I presented the pipe of peace to Wakan Tanka," said Crazy Horse. "I said that I wanted peace, that I wanted no more war. I promised that I would not fight against any nation anymore. I want to be at peace now. I have been asked to go out and fight the Nez Perce. But I do not want to do that. I remember my promise to Wakan Tanka not to fight anymore."

"But I will do it," he declared finally. "I will go north and fight until not a Wasichu is left."

Clark stiffened when he heard the words. Crazy Horse *did* want to return to the warpath! His own words revealed the truth.

But they were not his own words. Others who were present claimed that Grouard's translation was inaccurate. Grouard denied the accusation, but he had long harbored a grudge against Crazy Horse. Word of Crazy Horse's desire to return to the warpath spread like wildfire through the agencies, where Red Cloud and Spotted Tail fanned the flames. By mid-August, the troubling rumors reached General Sheridan, who ordered Crook to investigate the matter. Crook called for a council at White Clay Creek in early September.

Crazy Horse's band held their own council to discuss whether or not they would participate. For the most part, the council decided to follow He Dog, who supported meeting with Three Stars. Crazy Horse was not convinced that it was a good idea. He was probably not even at the council and, while his absence was not unusual, many in his band were frustrated with his stubbornness. In the minds of some, Crazy Horse had a responsibility to lead in council just as he had on the warpath.

Crazy Horse, however, had his reasons. Wasichus had visited him, and he thought their gifts of a knife and a cigar and their behavior were a bad omen. He discussed the matter with He Dog, who thought his concerns were unwarranted.

"Does this mean that you will be my enemy if I move across the creek to the council?" asked He Dog.

Crazy Horse laughed.

"I am no Wasichu! They are the only people that make rules for other people and say, 'If you stay on one side of this line it is peace, but if you go on the other side I will kill you all.' I don't hold with timetables. There is plenty of room. Camp where you please."

Crook, meanwhile, was en route to the council and not aware of Crazy Horse's refusal to participate, but he was no longer sure that he could trust the Oglala chief. Nevertheless, Crook was an honorable man and was determined to give Crazy Horse a final opportunity to explain himself.

As his party approached the council grounds, it was met by Woman's Dress, a long-time enemy of Crazy Horse. The soldiers knew Woman's Dress because he had lived and worked as a scout at Camp Robinson. He advised them to be wary of Crazy Horse.

"When you hold this council at White Clay, Crazy Horse is going to come in there with 60 warriors and catch

Three Stars by the hand like he is going to shake hands, and he will hold on to him. Those 60 warriors will kill Three Stars and whoever he has with him."

There has never been any evidence that Crazy Horse planned to do this, but assured that Woman's Dress was an honest man, Crook concluded that Crazy Horse was out to cause trouble. He decided to avoid the council. When the chiefs at the council were informed that Three Stars had been recalled to Camp Robinson, they set out for that post. Included in the group were Red Cloud, Young Man Afraid of His Horses and No Water. Crook met with them and spoke of Crazy Horse's malicious influence among the Natives.

"You are being led astray by Crazy Horse's folly. You must preserve order in your own ranks. Crazy Horse must be arrested," declared Crook.

The chiefs took some time to discuss this and finally gave Crook their answer.

"Crazy Horse is such a desperate man that it will be necessary to kill him."

"That would be murder and I cannot sanction it," replied Crook. "There is enough force at or near the two agencies to round up Crazy Horse and his whole band. More troops will be sent if necessary. But I count upon you, who have demonstrated your loyalty, to arrest him. It will prove to your people that you are not in sympathy with the non-progressive elements of your tribe."

On September 3, 400 agency Natives and eight companies of cavalry from Camp Robinson set out to arrest Crazy Horse so that he could be transported to Fort Jefferson, south of Key West, Florida. But when they arrived at his camp, he was gone. Crazy Horse had departed for the Spotted Tail Agency so that he could avoid the bad talk about him at the Red Cloud Agency.

From Amos Bad Heart Bull's pictorial history of the Oglala. The caption reads, "In the season of 1877 Crazy Horse was killed."

⊰◈⊱

Once there, Crazy Horse traveled to nearby Camp Sheridan to inform the commander, Captain Daniel Burke, of his relocation. Burke demanded that he return to Camp Robinson. Crazy Horse hesitated, fearful that his life was in danger. When Burke assured him that the government did not intend to hurt him, Crazy Horse relented. On September 6, he set out for Camp Robinson. Upon arrival, he was directed to the office of the post commander Colonel Luther Bradley. Bradley ordered him arrested and placed in the guardhouse.

White Calf, a member of Red Cloud's band and a scout at the fort, described the events. "I was right there at the time when Crazy Horse was killed....When they got to the jail, all the Indians cried out 'It's the jail!' and they would not go in with him. Only one went in with him. It was Little Big Man [an old friend of Crazy Horse and an agency policeman]....

"When Crazy Horse found out it was the jail, he turned back and brought out his butcher knife. He wanted to hurt somebody. Little Big Man caught his hands behind his back. Crazy Horse dragged him through the door, out onto the parade ground. He cut Little Big Man in the wrists. The soldier who was walking up and down outside the jail stabbed Crazy Horse from behind with his bayonet. Crazy Horse fell, crouching."

Little Big Man and the soldier reached to pull him from the ground.

"Let me go, my friends. You have got me hurt enough," Crazy Horse whispered. He was taken to the officers' quarters, where he died about midnight, September 6, 1877.

His body was placed on a scaffold outside Camp Robinson. His father and one of his stepmothers put the body in a box, fastened it to a pony drag and rode northeast. They left alone.

"The old people would never tell where they put the body of their son," said Black Elk. "Nobody knows today where he lies...."

CHAPTER THREE

Geronimo

~~~

Chiricahua Apache, 1823–1909

IN A VALLEY BENEATH A HIGH SILVER MOON and a low reddish sun not yet gone to its lodge was a Mimbreno-Bedonkohe Apache camp. All of the band members were gathered around a large crackling fire. Closest to the fire sat Chief Mangas Coloradas. It was not often that everyone was invited to council, but the matter to be discussed affected the entire band. Great leader that he was, Chief Mangas Coloradas wanted to hear the words of any Apache who might speak. Against the backdrop of the Chiricahua Mountains in southeastern Arizona where high pockets of snow from the winter of 1863 were still visible, he stood and began to address those assembled. His imposing six-foot frame, his deep voice and the respect he commanded ensured that all eyes were drawn to him.

"I have met in council with the people of Apache Tejo," he told the council. Apache Tejo was a small settlement in New Mexico close to the traditional home of the

Mimbreno-Bedonkohe. "The scout they sent to tell us of their desire to make peace did not speak falsely. They pledge to be true to any treaty they would make. The Apache Tejo leaders told me that if I take my tribe to live near them, the government would issue provisions and other supplies. I told them that they would soon have an answer."

The council was silent as members considered the offer. Some were tired of war. The Apache had been fighting American soldiers for several years, and before that, Mexican soldiers. It would be good to return home and live in peace as Mangas Coloradas desired. But others wanted revenge.

"We have made treaty with these white men before and we know what comes of it," Geronimo finally said. He was no chief, but his words carried the authority of a warrior who had enjoyed success fighting Apache enemies. "Cochise thought he was at peace with the soldiers until they arrested him." Cochise was the chief of the neighboring Chiricahua Apache tribe. He had been taken hostage (and later escaped) while delivering supplies to a U.S. army camp. "Remember what happened to Mangas Coloradas the last time he tried to make peace." The chief had gone to the mining town of Pinos Altos where he was tied up and beaten. Geronimo looked to his chief. "Are your wounds yet healed? I do not think that the people of Apache Tejo will do as they say. I do not think we should go."

The discussion went on into the night, and it became clear that the band was divided on the issue. It was decided that half of the band would remain at the camp under the leadership of Geronimo. The rest would go with Mangas Coloradas to Apache Tejo. If the locals abided by the treaty, then everyone would follow and Apache Tejo would become their permanent home. Those headed for New Mexico, however, were not naive. They took with them the band's supply of ammunition so that they would be prepared for any surprises. It would not be enough to protect them.

Mangas Coloradas and his party weren't given a single night's peace at Apache Tejo. On their first night camped outside the town, Brigadier General Joseph West (who was responsible for putting the Apache on reservations) arrived with his soldiers. Mangas Coloradas knew he had been duped, and his great shoulders sagged as the soldiers led him to a guardhouse.

"This is my end," he groaned. "I shall never again hunt over the mountains and through the valleys of my people."

Mangas Coloradas was a man of peace, but as an Apache, his survival instincts were well honed. Later that evening, he tried to escape but was killed. The soldiers killed a dozen more Apache and destroyed their camp. As a final indignity to Mangas Coloradas, West ordered the army surgeon to severe his head. West then demanded that all the flesh be removed so that he might demonstrate "sci-entifically" what he considered to be the close relationship between animal and Native.

The Apache who remained in Arizona with Geronimo were unaware of these events. For many days they heard nothing from Mangas Coloradas and his party. Eventually, word of their fate came from other Natives. Geronimo later declared that the attack was, "perhaps the greatest wrong ever done to the Indians...."

Because they had few weapons and were afraid that sol-diers might hunt them, Geronimo led his people into the mountains near Apache Pass. Along the way, they stumbled upon four ranchers tending a herd of cattle. They killed the ranchers and butchered the cattle. While they were dressing the meat, the U.S. army, which had indeed been on their trail, attacked. It was bow, arrow and spear against repeating rifle and revolver. The Apache were forced to abandon horses and supplies to retreat. Leaving seven dead (including three children), they disappeared into the mountains with a skill and speed not before witnessed by the soldiers.

The fighting was not over. The army pursued and found them 10 days later. The Apache met the soldiers' bullets with rocks and clubs. Such weapons did little damage so the Apache retreated deeper into the mountains. Scouts remained to see what the soldiers would do, and the band was relieved to learn that the army had finally left the mountains.

Geronimo, age 64, likely at a photo studio in Fort Pickens, Florida, where he and his band were interred briefly in 1887.

For some time the Mimbreno-Bedonkohe waited, hoping that Mangas Coloradas would still return. Eventually a council was held, and his death was formally declared, so a new leader was needed. Often the Apache turned to the son of the previous leader, but Mangas Coloradas' son was unprepared to fill the position. Instead, wealth and ability became the sticks by which the band would measure their new leader. They looked to a man whose grandfather had been a chief (of the neighboring Nednai tribe) and a skilled warrior. He was a man of his people, meaning that he had come from good blood and had lived up to his ancestors' great deeds. This man was Geronimo.

Geronimo was a great warrior, whose greatness was enhanced by his special abilities as a war shaman. He held a special connection with the Power that flowed through everything. Ceremonies had been revealed to him, and when he performed those ceremonies, he foresaw the results of fighting before the battle. He could tell warriors where to go and what to avoid. He knew the ceremony that prevented an enemy's bullet from striking a mortal blow. There was no dissent when Geronimo was chosen chief of the Bedonkohe. He was just 40, and he was angry with the Americans.

In the early dusk of a late winter afternoon a young boy ran through a Bedonkohe Apache camp. Although he was only six, he already ran with skill, avoiding the obstacles that lay between him and his parents' tipi. His energy suggested that his name, Goyahlka, meaning "One Who Yawns" (Geronimo's name as a child), was an odd choice. He was oblivious to the tall mountains that rose to the north and south and heard nothing of the rippling river to the east. He was far too excited. He threw open the antelope robe that covered the tipi's entrance and darted inside.

"Mother," he cried, catching his breath. "Grandfather is telling stories tonight. Can we go and listen?"

Juana smiled. Her son's grandfather had died before he was born, but others in the band had been more than generous in allowing the young boy to visit and hear the stories of his people. She knew how much he enjoyed it.

"Yes, Goyahlka, we will go," she replied.

Later that evening, Goyahlka accompanied Juana, Taklishim (his father) and his sister to the lodge where the stories were to be told. Such occasions were common enough wintertime activities; the extended nights were often filled with lengthy stories. As the children huddled together under a deerskin blanket, an old man moved to the choicest location across from the tipi's entrance. He sat and tugged his feet towards his hips and then pulled some tobacco from a pouch around his waist. He rolled it in an oak leaf, put it into his mouth and lit the end with the glowing tip of a stick taken from the fire. He inhaled deeply and blew out a cloud of smoke. Satisfied, he began to speak.

"In the time after the birds defeated the beasts in the great battle to bring light to the world, there lived White Painted Woman and Killer of Enemies. They were the only humans that Usen, the creator of the universe, had brought to life. They had many children, but the beasts always took them. The wise and evil dragon was especially feared, for he would eat them. Eventually, the pair had a son named Child of the Water. White Painted Woman and Killer of Enemies sheltered the child deep in a cave. When the dragon came looking for food, they denied that any children remained. As Child of the Water grew, he was anxious to leave the cave and hunt. He was told of the dangers that waited outside of the cave, but he would not be stopped. He asked his father to make him a bow and arrows, and together they set out and killed a buck. As they dressed the deer, the dragon, which had discovered the pair's tracks, came upon them. He took the meat from the boy and sat beside it.

"'This is the child I have been seeking,' growled the dragon. 'Boy, you are nice and fat, so when I have eaten this venison I shall eat you.'

"'No. You shall not eat me or my meat,' replied Child of the Water, as he took the venison back.

"'I like your courage, boy, but you are foolish,' rumbled the dragon. 'What could you do?'

"'I can protect myself. Dragon, will you fight me?'

"The dragon gave a grisly smile. 'Yes. In whatever way you wish.'

"Child of the Water thought for a moment. 'I will stand 100 paces distant from you and you may have four shots at me with your bow and arrows. Then we will exchange places and you will allow me four shots at you.'

"'Agreed.' The dragon gripped his bow, which was made of a large pine tree. He notched the first arrow, a 20-foot long pine sapling. Just as he let the arrow loose, Child in the Water gave a cry and leapt into the air. The arrow was shattered and the boy stood atop a rainbow. The dragon had no success with any shots. Then it was Child of the Water's turn.

"The confident dragon roared, 'Your puny arrows cannot hurt me.'

"Child of the Water's aim was true, and as each arrow struck the dragon, a layer of thick skin fell away. The fourth arrow pierced the dragon's heart. The dragon fell into the canyon and died."

The old man was silent for a moment. Had his audience been adults, he would have left the story at that. But it was important that the children present understand its message.

"All Apache are like Child of the Water. We must protect ourselves from our enemies. We do it by becoming warriors. Learn to run fast and to shoot straight. Be brave in the face of danger."

Goyahlka listened to the other stories of the Mountain Spirits who lived in caves and offered protection and advice. He laughed as the old man told funny stories of Coyote. Other children drifted off to sleep. Sometimes their parents tickled them under their noses to waken them because it was important that they learn the stories and morals of their people. Juana never had to do that with Goyahlka. When it came to learning the ways of the Apache, Goyahlka was an ideal student.

The Bedonkohe were one of three Chiricahua Apache bands who lived in what was then northern Mexico. The Chiricahua were among the Eastern Apache; there was also a Western Apache division. Links between the bands, however, were not strong. It was more common to see small bands of extended families acting together, usually led by one with proven hunting and raiding abilities. The only exceptions were during times of celebration and crisis, either of which could unite the bands. They called themselves Dini, "the people." The term "Apache" was a Pueblo word meaning "enemy." The Apache had migrated from the northwest of the continent and along the way, acquired horses that enhanced their hunting skills. By the 18th century, they had reached Mexico. They did not get along well with the Spanish, the first lords of Mexico, who sought them as slaves. Later, after the Mexican revolution, the relationship deteriorated further. Mexicans sought to exterminate the Apache by offering bounties for their scalps. As a result, the Apache were involved in raids and battles for many years.

Goyahlka was born in 1823 north of the Gila River in what was then Mexico but is today southeastern Arizona. During his childhood, the Chiricahua enjoyed a period of peace. As a result, Goyahlka grew up in a stable setting. His people raised crops and lived in hide-covered tipis rather than thatched wickiups, since tipis were easier to move when it was necessary to flee. As a young boy, he helped his parents in the communal growing field. They ate melons and pumpkins in season, and ground corn and used it for bread or *tis-win*, an alcoholic drink.

Goyahlka did what he could in the field because it was the way of things and not because he enjoyed it. It was a different matter when it came to hunting. Goyahlka first joined the hunt when he was about 10, and he never considered it work. The skills of an effective hunter were honed in childhood activities, which included many arrow games designed to steady hands, improve accuracy and ensure judgment of distance. But they were never chores, and many days the sun would run its course before the boys tired of playing. About the time of his first hunt, the care-free days of boyhood were replaced with the rigorous training necessary to become an Apache warrior. Goyahlka's father, Taklishim, was his primary teacher.

It was midwinter and cold; the sun was still asleep. Taklishim was shaking Goyahlka's shoulder to wake him, as he had done for many days. When the boy was awake, they stepped from the tipi and Taklishim said the few words that Goyahlka had already learned by heart.

"My son, you come into this world alone. There is no one you can depend on. But your mind, your legs, your eyes, these can protect you. Make them strong and they will not fail you."

Goyahlka nodded.

"Before you begin your run, come back to me," advised Taklishim.

With that, Goyahlka stripped to his breechcloth and ran to the icy stream that flowed nearby. He plunged into the water. Some of the other boys pretended to immerse themselves by splashing water on their bodies. Not Goyahlka. His father said that it would make him strong and that was what he desired. He ran back to his father, not even stopping to rub his cold skin.

"Son, you have mastered the run to the mountains. You are fast; there is no doubt. Take a mouthful of water," directed Taklishim as he gave the boy a small vessel, "but do not swallow it. Run to the mountains and back. When you return, spit the water on the ground before me."

It was no short run, about four miles. As Goyahlka ran, his dry lips longed to be licked and his throat burned. He knew that the water in his mouth would douse that fire, so it took a great effort not to swallow it. When he returned to his father, he spat it on the ground. His father looked at him.

"You will do it again tomorrow. You will do it until even the hot sun of summer does not cause you to swallow."

Goyahlka learned the lessons of endurance and denial. They would be great assets when he became a warrior, which happened when he was about 15 after the death of his father. As his mother's eldest, he had new responsibilities. No longer would he hunt for the fun of it. He had to ensure that there was food for his family. When he felt confident, he took his family to visit a band of Nednai Apache, the village of his father's family (once married, Taklishim lived with his wife's family, as was usual with the Apache). There lived Goyahlka's good friend, Juh, leader of the Nednai. On arriving at the camp nestled in the Sierra Madre, they were greeted with a feast. Goyahlka's grandfather, Maco, had once been the Nednai chief, and it had not been forgotten. Goyahlka learned that Juh was planning to raid the Mexicans. He was excited and declared his desire to accompany the Nednai warriors. Such a declaration was enough; among the Apache, young men decided when they were ready to join in a raid.

Like most young Apache, Goyahlka had already ridden with raiding parties. Those raids served as his apprenticeship.

For the most part he had learned through observation, but he also had to demonstrate that he could care for himself and obey the rules deemed necessary for success. The war shaman provided much of the teaching during this period. He possessed special ability to find the enemy, plan the attack and protect the Apache warriors. Goyahlka enjoyed raiding because it demanded skill and cunning. The goal was to steal horses and supplies from the enemy and escape before they could retaliate. Goyahlka's experience had been against neighboring Native tribes but, when he rode with the Nednai, it was his first raid on the Mexicans. The Nednai hit pack trains and ranches and accumulated much, but they were not always successful. Occasionally, the Nednai had to kill a Mexican who tried to defend his property.

As exciting as a raid was, even more exciting was the status that came with being a warrior. Goyahlka was 17 when he was admitted to the council of warriors. With that came the freedom of manhood. Goyahlka could speak as he wished, travel where and when he desired and share in the spoils of the raid. He could even smoke, a pleasure reserved for men and married women. But, perhaps his greatest joy was that he could finally marry, and Goyahlka was anxious to do so.

In the few years before he became a warrior, Goyahlka enjoyed participating in the parties that were common affairs among the Bedonkohe. They were well-regulated affairs, with no *tis-win* and high standards. The parents of girls were particularly protective so there was little opportunity for intimate relationships to develop. It was probably at one of these parties where Goyahlka met Alope. He had been in love with her for some time before he was in a position to marry. When the time came, he went to her father's lodge as a warrior. Traditionally, it was an older man who made the offer of marriage and engaged in the necessary negotiations on behalf of the suitor. Perhaps because Goyahlka's father and grandfather were dead, he did this himself. Many horses were demanded for Alope's hand. Upon hearing the price, Goyahlka walked silently from the tipi. A few days later, he returned with the requested herd. He left with Alope, and the marriage ceremony was complete. Goyahlka and Alope set up their own lodge next to his mother's. She had never remarried, and Goyahlka accepted the responsibility of her upkeep.

Married life agreed with Goyahlka. "We followed the traditions of our fathers and were happy," he later declared.

Alope used her special talents to make beaded works and drawings to decorate the tipi. Goyahlka's own trophies, won during many hunts and raids, provided further adornment. But it was their three children who brought life to the place and smiles to the faces of the parents. They played and worked in the fields as had Goyahlka. None doubted that this was life as Usen had meant it to be. But in the early 1850s, it would all change; contentment would become a memory for Goyahlka.

The Bedonkohe and the Mimbreno (both shared a chief, Mangas Coloradas) were on their way to Casas Grandes, Mexico to trade. There was to be no raiding, so the women and children came as well. The Mexicans were as anxious to acquire Apache furs and hides as the Apaches were to get their knives and colored cloth. When they were close to their destination, they camped near Janos. The men went into the town to trade, leaving two men to guard the women, children, supplies and horses. As the traders returned from Janos one afternoon, they were surprised to be met by some of their women. Mexicans from another town had raided the camp and killed many. Immediately, the men separated; they would meet during the night at a predetermined place. After they had assembled, some of the men slipped into the ravaged camp. Goyahlka found his mother, wife and children, all dead.

Goyahlka was in shock. He walked to the edge of the camp and stared into the darkness. He finally moved when word came that the warriors were meeting in council. He was silent at the council, too numb to speak. When Mangas Coloradas decided that it was best to return to their home rather than seek revenge (the Apache had few weapons with them), Goyahlka followed the northern-bound band. He did so without purpose. All he could think of was his loved ones left on that bloody Mexican field and the meaning that had slipped from his life. For two days, Goyahlka said nothing because words could not describe his loss. And who would understand? No other warrior had lost so much. When he arrived home, he burned his tipi and all it held. He burned his mother's tipi and her belongings. Then he vowed vengeance on the Mexicans who had destroyed his happiness.

In the weeks that followed, Goyahlka spent much time away from camp. There, alone, the emotions that were frowned upon by the Apache were given free rein. On one occasion he sat on a rotting tree, his head in his hands, crying. Above the sobs he heard a voice call his name four times, a magical number. He held his breath and listened.

"No gun can ever kill you. I will take the bullets from the guns of the Mexicans, so they will have nothing but powder. And I will guide your arrows."

Although he had not heard the voice before, Goyahlka knew that it was Power that spoke to him, the voice of Usen. Power was Usen's way of helping the Apache. Power worked through selected individuals by giving them special abilities that could be used to benefit the tribe. Power would speak to Goyahlka on many occasions throughout his life, often in response to the ceremonies he created to call on it. Their relationship was so intimate that Goyahlka became a war shaman and medicine man. Rarely, however, did Power speak with the clarity of this morning. When Mangas Coloradas called a council to propose war against the Mexicans, Goyahlka was ready, as were all the Bedonkohe warriors. To reinforce their numbers, Goyahlka, who had lost so much, was selected to visit other Apache tribes and to solicit their participation.

He first called upon the Central Chiricahua Apaches. Their chief Cochise, an influential Apache leader whose star was still rising, greeted him. Cochise called a council to allow Goyahlka to speak directly to the warriors. Goyahlka waited patiently while the men smoked. Then he stood in the center, his slight five-foot eight-inch frame hardly imposing. Arranged around him were the warriors, the veterans closest and the neophytes in the wider circles. His impassioned words gave a hint his developing ability to both inspire and lead.

Kinsmen, you have heard what the Mexicans have recently done without cause. You are my relatives—uncles, cousins, brothers. We are men the same as Mexicans are; we can do to them what they have done to us. Let us go forward and trail them. I will lead you to their city. We will attack them in their homes. I will fight in the front of the battle. I only ask you to follow me to avenge this wrong done by these Mexicans. Will you come?

He nodded his head as he listened to the warriors' words of agreement.

It is well. You will all come. Remember the rule in war—men may return or they may be killed. If any of these young men are killed, I want no blame from their kinsmen, for they themselves have chosen to go. If I am killed, no one need mourn for me. My people have all been killed in that country and I, too, will die there if need be.

It was a revealing speech because it set out the philosophy
that would guide Goyahlka's attitude towards war for years to
come. He never forced men to go on the warpath with him.
And he always rode knowing that he might die. So be it. Let
the enemy attack; Goyahlka would trust his Power.

With the support of the Central Chiricahua, Goyahlka
continued on to the Nednai. He never doubted his old
friend Juh's support for his cause. Juh held the same opinion as Cochise and Mangas Coloradas: this was a war that
all Apache must fight.

A few months later, in 1851, the allied Apache met in
a secluded valley, well hidden from Mexican eyes. The warriors were ready. Their painted faces were capped by tight
war-bands across their brows. They were prepared to face
death as Goyahlka later described: "their long scalp-locks
ready for the hand and knife of the warrior who would
overcome them." They planned to attack the town of Arispe
in the Mexican state of Sonora, the home of those who had
wiped out the trading party. Leaving behind the women,
children and horses (the Apache commonly attacked on
foot, and on this occasion, it was believed that the animals
would attract too much attention), they made their way
south to the Sonora River. The absence of horses was no
limitation. Often traveling as many as 14 hours a day, they
covered as much in a day (45 miles) as would a dedicated
rider on horseback.

They camped near Arispe, close enough that the towns-
folk were aware of their presence. Eight Mexicans were sent
out to parley. The warriors had not come to talk, so gifts and
peaceful overtures would not change their minds. They
killed the small party and scalped them. The Apache thought
that the action would draw the soldiers from the fort, and
the following day, they came. There was no close fighting,
however, and once the Apache captured the Mexican supply

train, the soldiers returned to town. The warriors knew they would return so they made preparations for battle.

Never ones to leave anything to chance when it came to warfare, guards were posted around the camp. And although it was common to perform a war dance on the eve of an attack, the warriors knew that the battle would be draining and they wanted a good night's sleep. They were awake early the next morning and they gathered together for prayers. No one asked for victory because that was a man's responsibility. Instead, they prayed for health and to avoid enemy deception and ambush. Then Mangas Coloradas, Cochise and Juh called for Goyahlka.

"Goyahlka, these are the men who killed your family?" asked Mangas Coloradas.

"Yes," he replied. "I recognized them among the soldiers who attacked yesterday."

"Then you will direct the battle," declared Mangas Coloradas.

It was not uncommon for the Apache to give control of a war party to an aggrieved warrior, since these raids were usually undertaken only to avenge deaths. But war parties did not usually include three important Apache chiefs. Goyahlka considered the offer an honor, resolving to prove himself worthy. When scouts gave word that the soldiers were approaching, Goyahlka signaled the warriors to take the positions he had outlined earlier. The Apache formed themselves into an arc near the river, where trees provided some shelter. They were not hidden from the Mexicans. Perhaps the soldiers smiled when they took note that the Apache had forfeited retreat by arranging themselves next to the river. As soon as the soldiers opened fire, Goyahlka led a charge into the heart of their ranks. Simultaneously, some of the warriors slipped by the soldiers' flanks and attacked from the rear.

Goyahlka fought with a ferocious passion fueled by revenge. With each arrow unleashed, he thought of his murdered family. When his arrows were spent, he attacked with spear and knife. He was swept up in the fight, leaping from soldier to soldier. Before long, he was covered in blood, none of it his own. Legend has it that, certain they would die at the hands of this crazed fighter, the Mexicans called on St. Jerome to intervene. Their screams sounded like "Geronimo." And because they screamed when Goyahlka was about to attack, listeners believed that they were calling him Geronimo. After two hours, the battle was over. The ground was littered with the bodies of both soldiers and Apache, but mostly soldiers. The Apache were victorious. And they had a new hero, who was thereafter known by Apache, Mexicans and soon, Americans, as Geronimo.

The warriors left Arispe, and once they were certain that no one followed them, they returned to the camp where the women and children were hidden. Relatives of dead warriors were so informed, and they dealt with their pain individually. A great celebration then took place. A large fire was built; it served as the focal point for the dances over the following days. First, the warriors were feted. Singers called the name of each brave, and through song, detailed his exploits. When they called a brave's name, he stepped forward and danced around the fire, re-enacting what he did during the fight. The warriors' dance was followed by a series of communal dances. Interspersed among the dancing was feasting. After four days, the celebration was brought to a close and the bands returned to their northern homes.

Geronimo soon took two more wives, both from his own tribe, an indication of his growing status among the Apache. Although he was not yet 30, Geronimo was recognized as an important warrior who could provide for a large family. However, the demands of the warpath allowed little time for them.

Most Apache considered that the victory in Arispe had cleared the slate with the Mexicans, but not Geronimo. His desire for revenge was insatiable and he was anxious to continue waging war. As he later revealed, "I never ceased to plan for their punishment."

As was the usual practice, Geronimo sought out warriors who would attack with him. On his first raid after Arispe, he convinced two to join him. They entered Mexico on foot, following the Sierra de Antunez. At its southern extent, they found a small town and advanced on it. When the Mexicans spotted the Apache warriors, they opened fire. Geronimo managed to flee, but his two companions were killed. For two days the Mexicans pursued Geronimo and only his skills kept him safe. On returning to the camp, some of the Apache blamed him for the failed expedition. Geronimo did not defend himself, which would have been improper. Instead, he made more plans to attack.

Geronimo's poor fortune continued over the next year. In one encounter in the Sierra de Sahuaripa, he led 25 Apache against a troop of soldiers. Although he had managed a successful ambush, the soldiers were able to shelter themselves before the Apache could do much damage. Convinced that they could not dislodge the soldiers with arrows fired from a distance, Geronimo called the Apache war cry and led the charge. In the hand-to-hand combat that followed, he slipped and fell. A soldier knocked him senseless with a blow from the butt of his rifle. But the soldier was killed before he could finish the job. When the battle was over, Geronimo was found unconscious. Despite considerable blood loss and a throbbing head, he managed to walk back to Arizona. He would always wear the scar of the mishap, and he would again bear the burden of a failed attack (too many Apache had died).

His failures were giving Geronimo something of a bad reputation among his people. Although warriors always volunteered, he found himself blamed for the loss of Apache life. Even Mangas Coloradas (who was more peaceful in his outlook) disapproved of the raiding, although there was little he could do about it, since it was not the Apache way to tell a warrior how to conduct himself. But over the next few years, circumstances were to change, and many Apache would conclude that Geronimo's way was the best, if not the only, path.

Apache territory was in a state of flux during the years that Geronimo reasserted himself as a warrior. Historically, Spain controlled the land around the Gila River, and later, Mexico controlled it following the Mexican Revolution in 1821. In the 1840s, the United States turned its eyes to the region. James Polk was elected president on an expansionist platform, and in 1846 he made good on his promise to extend America's southern boundary. War raged for nearly two years, and in February 1848 the guns fell silent when the United States and Mexico signed the Treaty of Guadalupe Hidalgo. For $15 million, the victorious United States gained present-day California, Nevada, Utah and huge chunks of Colorado, New Mexico and Arizona.

It wasn't until 1851 that the United States and Mexico took on the task of mapping out the new international boundary. John Bartlett and General Pedro Conde led the Boundary Commission. Chief Mangas Coloradas met with the commissioners in June. Bartlett explained that the Apache were in American territory and that the government would protect them if they behaved. They were not, under any circumstances, to raid into Mexico because the Treaty of Guadalupe Hidalgo provided that American soldiers would have to stop them. Mangas Coloradas objected. His people had long raided in Mexico for supplies and prisoners; he would only agree to leave the commission unmolested.

The good relations did not last long. In late June, two older Mexican boys, who had been taken captive by the Apache, appealed to the commissioners to be returned to their people. Bartlett agreed and had Conde reunite them with their families. However, he knew nothing of traditional Apache practice when it came to adopting captives. The Apache were livid. Mangas Coloradas arrived at Bartlett's tent accompanied by some 200 warriors.

"Why did you take our captives from us? You came to our country. You were well received. Your lives, your property, your animals were safe. You passed...through our country; you went and came in peace. Your stray animals were always taken home to you again. Our wives, our children and our women came here and visited your houses. We were friends. We were brothers!" the chief declared. "Believing this, we came among you and brought our captives.... We believed your assurances of friendship and we trusted them. Why did you take our captives from us?"

"I have no doubt but that you have suffered much by the Mexicans. This is a question that is impossible to decide who is right or who is wrong," Bartlett conceded. "You and the Mexicans accuse each other of being the aggressors. Our duty is to fulfill our promise to both...to show to Mexico that we mean what we say; and when the time comes...to prove the good faith of our promises to you."

It was explained to Bartlett that the warrior who captured the boys did so at great risk and to avenge relatives killed by Mexicans. Apache justice demanded that they be returned. Bartlett did not want trouble with the Apache so he offered financial compensation to the wronged warrior. The warrior refused the offer. The boys had been with him for six years, and he considered them his sons. He eventually took $250 worth of supplies, but it did not soothe Apache anger. Soon after, a Mexican employed by the commission shot an Apache. He was arrested. Bartlett wanted him sent to Santa Fe for trial, but the Apache wanted him killed. The matter was resolved when the mother of the slain Apache was given the killer's wages. But, once again, the Apache were none too happy.

Relations worsened. The Apache raided commission supplies and horses. Bartlett called for military reinforcements. It was an ominous start to Apache-American relations. In 1852, in an effort to bring matters under control, American officials made treaty with Mangas Coloradas and other Apache leaders. The treaty promised the Apache gifts, fair treatment and punishment for Americans who harmed them. For their part, the Apache would allow Americans free passage through their territory. The treaty also stipulated that the Apache stop raiding in Mexico, but the Apache objected to this point and did not consider it binding.

Geronimo was in the south during these events and was not aware of the American presence. Around this time, he lost a wife and child during a surprise raid by Mexican soldiers who killed many Apache women and children. Desire for revenge invigorated Geronimo, and he set out on a series of raids that did much to rehabilitate his reputation as a warrior. He led eight men into the Sierra de Sahuaripa and returned with impressive booty. Mangas Coloradas was so pleased that he called for a feast and celebrations. The next year, Geronimo and three others raided a small village, where they stole enough supplies to last the tribe for a year. Geronimo considered it the greatest raid he ever made into Mexico.

In the early 1850s, Geronimo met some American surveyors, the first white people he had ever seen. He had no reason to be concerned by their presence, and both groups shook hands and promised "to be brothers," as Geronimo described it. Some years later he was to meet American soldiers "who were not as good as those who first came." But they were certainly much better than the next wave of newcomers.

In the late 1850s, gold was discovered in Mimbreno territory. Miners were not the most sensitive Americans, and they rarely let Native concerns stand in their way if they interfered with digging gold. One of the miners' first actions was to invite Mexicans into the region to farm, so that they might have easier access to food. The action angered the Apache and fomented hostility in the region. In an effort to negotiate a peace treaty with the miners, Mangas Coloradas decided to visit the mining town of Pinos Altos. Geronimo was opposed to the undertaking because he did not trust the miners. His intuition proved correct. The miners captured Mangas Coloradas, tied him to a tree and beat him with bullwhips. Humiliated, he staggered back to his camp. But the miners paid for their cruelty. When Mangas Coloradas recovered, he convinced neighboring Apache tribes to join him on the warpath, and they forced the miners from the region.

Other Apache leaders were also evaluating their relationships with the Americans. When western-bound settlers wanted to travel through Chiricahua territory, Cochise gave them access. He even allowed them to build a station at Apache Pass in the Chiricahua Mountains. However, matters turned sour in 1861 when a half-Mexican boy disappeared from his family's ranch. Certain that the Apache had taken the boy (they had not), his father went to the U.S. army and lodged a complaint. The army dispatched a cocky and inexperienced Second Lieutenant George Bascom and 54 soldiers to retrieve the boy.

Cochise knew nothing of the matter, and when he arrived with his family to deliver some wood to the military camp at

Apache Pass, he was surprised to be accused of kidnapping. Bascom arrested some of the Apache who traveled with Cochise and confined the Apache chief and his family to a tent. Certain that death awaited, Cochise slit the tent with his knife and escaped with his wife, child, brother and two nephews. The other Apache remained captive. Before he left Apache Pass, however, Cochise took three prisoners whom he offered to exchange for his people, but Bascom refused unless the boy was returned. Over the next few weeks, the Chiricahua and the soldiers engaged in several minor skirmishes, in which Geronimo participated (he had married a Chiricahua-Nednai woman and so was living with the band). Ultimately, all the hostages taken by both sides were killed.

The "Cut Through the Tent" affair, as the Apache called the episode, did much to turn Apache sentiment against the Americans. Geronimo later described its significance.

"After this trouble all of the Indians agreed not to be friendly with the white men anymore. There was no general engagement, but a long struggle followed. Sometimes we attacked the white men—sometimes they attacked us. First, a few Indians would be killed, then a few soldiers. I think the killing was about equal on each side. The number killed in these troubles did not amount to much, but this treachery on the part of the soldiers had angered the Indians and revived memories of other wrongs, so that we never again trusted the United States troops."

When General John Carleton arrived with 1800 soldiers in 1861, the Apache had even more reason to distrust the Americans. Carleton, who became commander of the Department of New Mexico, was determined to make the region safe for American settlers, many of whom had been forced to run for their lives in the early months of the 1860s. He first persuaded the Mescalero Apache and the Navajo to move onto a reserve, employing no-nonsense tactics. He informed his subordinates that their mission was "to punish [the Natives] for their treachery and their crimes." Officers were not to make peace, and soldiers were ordered to shoot male Natives unless they could be easily captured.

The Mimbreno-Bedonkohe and Chiricahua joined forces under Cochise to test the mettle of this new white man. Geronimo was among their number. With an unheard-of force of over 500 warriors, they waited for Carleton's troops at Apache Pass. The ambush started well for the Apache, and many soldiers fell. The warriors were so well hidden that the army's rifles couldn't even find a target. Then the soldiers brought out weapons that the Apache had never seen—howitzers. They were powerful enough to bring down a rain of shrapnel well up the side of the mountain. The Apache were forced to retreat. Scouts later reported that the soldiers were building a large stone building at Apache Pass. Called Fort Bowie, it gave the army a permanent presence in Chiricahua territory.

Throughout 1862, skirmishes between the Apache and the soldiers continued. However, when an opportunity for peace came, a peace that allowed the Mimbreno-Bedonkohe to return to more comfortable surroundings in New Mexico, Mangas Coloradas believed that it was worth investigating. He traveled to Apache Tejo, where town officials gave him assurances that his people could live there and be given provisions as well. But Geronimo no longer trusted the Americans, so the band decided that it was best to send only half of their members to New Mexico. The others would follow if the Americans were true to their word. The army, under General Joseph West's command (he shared General Carleton's views regarding Natives), had Mangas Coloradas and others of his party killed as soon as they arrived. Soldiers set out to find

the rest of the Mimbreno-Bedonkohe, but the Natives managed to escape by retreating deep into the Chiricahua
Mountains. When it was confirmed that Mangas Coloradas
was dead, the Bedonkohe chose Geronimo to be their chief.

Despite his reputation as a warrior, Geronimo was
involved in only minor raids throughout the rest of the
1860s. These raids were mostly against the settlers who were
arriving in greater numbers after the American Civil War. For
a time, the Bedonkohe lived with the Warm Springs Apache
band. Several prominent warriors led the band, but they were
not anxious to continue fighting. The warriors offered to
leave the settlers alone as long as the band was given their
homeland as a reservation; however, the government would
not cede land that settlers wanted. In 1869, Geronimo
returned to Cochise's Chiricahua band. While he was with
the Chiricahua, Geronimo deferred to the more prominent
leader Cochise, which was the natural way of the Apache and
no slight to the war shaman.

In the early 1870s, the American government finally
settled on a policy with regard to the Natives of the
Southwest. They sent in General George Crook, who was
charged with putting the Apache on reserves. Crook's superiors had great confidence in him because he had dealt
successfully with the Natives of the Pacific Northwest. He
was certainly sure of himself.

He wrote to his superiors, "If this entire Indian question
was left to me…I have not the slightest doubt of my ability
to conquer a peace with the Apache race in a compara-
tively short space of time."

He made changes to military practice. He got rid of large
supply trains that were easy targets for Apache raiders; he
made soldiers fight on foot ensuring greater mobility in the
mountain terrain; and he hired Apache scouts from among
those bands who had settled on reservations. Then he

ordered the rest of the Apache onto reservations, promising to punish those who declined. His troops were ready to move on the many resisting Apache, when word came from Washington that Brigadier General Oliver Howard was to arrive on a presidential peace mission. Crook was incensed. He didn't like Howard, and he thought force could bring about peace more effectively than could negotiations.

Howard met with Cochise and the leaders of his Chiricahua band in 1872. Cochise was blunt when he addressed the soldier.

"You Americans began the fight and now Americans and Mexicans kill an Apache on sight. I have retaliated with all my might. I have killed 10 white men for every Indian slain."

In the end, Howard made a good impression on the Apache so it was easier for Cochise, who was tired of fighting, to agree on peace terms. Geronimo participated in the council that set the terms of the treaty, finalized in October 1872. The Chiricahua agreed to confine themselves to a reservation of some 50 square miles in southeastern Arizona and to keep the peace. In return, they were given provisions. When the negotiations were complete, Geronimo rode with Howard (on the same horse) to inform the military of the treaty.

A good relationship developed between the two, as Geronimo later recalled.

"He always kept his word with us and treated us as brothers. We never had so good a friend among the United States officers as General Howard. We could have lived forever at peace with him."

Through to the mid-1870s, relations were mostly good between the Apache and Americans. All bands signed treaties and had reserves set aside. But among the Apache were renegades, who refused to live on reserves and continued to raid (Geronimo was not among them at this time).

These renegades were few in number, and Crook hunted them vigorously. Matters took a turn for the worse in 1875, when the government decided (against Crook's wishes) to consolidate the many Apache reserves at San Carlos, a mostly desert-like, barren chunk of land north of the Gila River and west of the Gila Mountains. The government believed that concentrating the Apache in one area would make them easier to control. Furthermore, the scattered reserves were on good land, increasingly coveted by settlers. The consolidation plan was fraught with problems from the start. Some bands did not want to live with other bands that were their traditional enemies. Others simply did not want to relocate. The result was violence and flight.

In June 1876, John Clum (the agent in charge of the San Carlos reservation) and Major General August Kautz (a replacement for Crook, who was sent north to deal with the Sioux) arrived at the Chiricahua reservation. Officials had an added reason to force the band onto a new reservation: intoxicated Apache had killed a local storeowner. Clum spoke with Taza, the son of Cochise (who had died in 1874) and the new leader of the Chiricahua. Geronimo was camped some 20 miles away, but he rode to the meeting when informed of it. When he heard the new policy explained, Geronimo agreed to go to San Carlos. He would return to the Bedonkohe and prepare them for the move. Clum let him go, but he was suspicious of Geronimo's intent and had him trailed. The soldiers later returned to say that Geronimo had fled. He took his band to the Warm Springs Apache on the Alamosa River, where they totaled some 135 warriors. Over the following months, they killed at least 20 whites and stole nearly 200 head of livestock.

Geronimo never considered himself bound to Clum's demands because he had given his word to General

Howard. Clum saw things differently, and he was livid once he learned of Geronimo's escape. He felt branded a fool. He began a campaign against Geronimo, labeling him a renegade. Clum blamed all Apache depredations on him, making Geronimo responsible for acts in which he did not participate. Clum told others that the Apache problem could have been prevented had Geronimo been hanged. He made it his personal mission to bring about that result. In the process, he created a legend out of the Apache leader.

In the spring of 1877, Washington ordered Clum to travel to the Warm Springs reservation and arrest the Apache renegades. He traveled with 100 Native police. When they arrived, he had most of them hide. Then he sent word to Geronimo requesting a meeting. Unaware of Clum's hatred for him, Geronimo agreed. He arrived with only six warriors and some women and children. He was wary when he saw the Native police because he had never before seen Apache in such uniforms.

"What do you want?" Geronimo asked Clum.

"I am here to charge you with murder and robbery," replied Clum. "You have broken the treaty made with General Howard. You lied to me when you pledged to go to the San Carlos Reservation. I have come to take you there."

"We are not going to San Carlos with you. And unless you are very careful, you and your Apache police will not go back to San Carlos either," Geronimo added. "Your bodies will stay here at Warm Springs to make food for coyotes."

Clum was ready for resistance. He gave a signal, and the hidden police spilled out of the agency office, surrounding the compound. Geronimo's finger slipped to the trigger of his rifle. He removed it when he saw the police level their weapons at him. The police took the rifles from Geronimo's warriors and escorted them to the blacksmith's

Here Natives are receiving their weekly rations at the San
Carlos Reservation in 1880. In 1875 the United States government consolidated numerous Apache reserves at San Carlos,
a barren chunk of land north of the Gila River. Officials
anticipated that concentrating the Apache in one area would
make them easier to control. They were wrong. Some bands
did not want to relocate, while others refused to live near their
traditional enemies. Geronimo agreed to move to the new
reservation, but changed his mind and led his warriors on the
warpath. He was captured in the spring of 1877 and escorted
to San Carlos. He was placed in the guardhouse, where he
remained a prisoner for four months as punishment for
depredations committed while on the warpath. After his
incarceration, Geronimo continued to live at San Carlos, but
he found it difficult because of disease and inadequate
supplies of poor quality food. Geronimo fled in early 1878.

shop. The officers locked iron shackles and chains to the captives' ankles and placed them in a guardhouse. Clum later had the rest of the Warm Springs Apache rounded up. In May, they were marched to San Carlos (those in irons, at least, rode in wagons).

Ironically, Clum's greatest triumph, seen by the Apache as yet another act of American treachery, marked the end of his tenure as the agent in charge of San Carlos. When Clum and his Native police returned to the reservation, a company of soldiers was waiting. The soldiers informed Clum that *they* would take charge of the prisoners. Clum was furious and resigned shortly thereafter. Geronimo was subsequently tried, although he wasn't present for it and only knew of it when he was released four months after he had been captured. But freedom on the reserve was little better than life in the guardhouse. The Indian agents were corrupt, so few of the supplies destined for the Apache actually reached them. Smallpox and malaria caused sickness and death, and the final insult was a reduction in the size of the reservation when prospectors discovered silver there. In late summer, some of the Apache escaped the reservation. Geronimo, however, remained. Perhaps it was because he had given his word to the new Indian agent.

Life at San Carlos proved to be increasingly demoralizing so the Apache turned to *tis-win* to deaden the pain. On one occasion, a drunken Geronimo scolded his nephew. Not only was it without cause, but it was an unusual act among the Apache. Geronimo later apologized, but the depressed young man committed suicide. Although Geronimo took it personally, he was convinced that reservation life was the underlying cause. When rumors came in early 1878 that authorities were planning to arrest the Apache leaders on the San Carlos Reservation, he left, taking with him those who wanted to go. Geronimo found his good friend Juh in Mexico, and together Bedonkohe and Nednai began raiding again.

Other Apache bands longed for reserves near their home territory, and when they were refused, they too went on the warpath leading to one of the most violent periods of Native warfare in the American Southwest and northern Mexico. Throughout 1879 and 1880, aggrieved Apache, most of whom had tried peace and found it wanting, killed every American and Mexican they came upon. The armies of the two countries were put under increasing pressure to rein in the renegades. Seeing that more soldiers than ever were in the Southwest, Geronimo decided that the wisest decision was to return to the safety of the reservation. In early 1880 he surrendered and was again placed on the San Carlos reservation.

For a time, Geronimo was content there. Even his old adversary Clum (who, as mayor of Tombstone, continued to comment on Apache affairs) conceded that he was behaving peaceably. However, matters began to deteriorate in 1881. An Apache prophet named Noch-ay-del-klinne gained popularity. He foresaw a time when the white men would be gone and the old order of his people restored. He claimed he could commune with the dead and even bring chiefs back to life. Geronimo knew of the prophet and perhaps even visited him, but there is no indication that he believed in the vision. Others did, however, including Apache police who abandoned their positions to follow the prophet. Worried reservation agents and army officials decided to end the matter, and Noch-ay-del-klinne was killed during an arrest attempt. Afraid that his death might bring unrest, all the soldiers from Arizona, New Mexico and California were sent to the San Carlos reservation. It was believed that their presence could also deter the renegade Apache raiding. Officials were concerned that the presence of the renegades would encourage those who were already on the reserve to flee and join up with them.

Geronimo eyed the growing numbers of soldiers with concern. He was afraid that they were being brought in to attack the reservation Apache in retribution for their past depredations. He was also increasingly disillusioned with the new reservation agent, whom he considered unduly restrictive and corrupt. In October 1881, Geronimo, Juh and some 70 Apache set out for Mexico. Pursued by soldiers, they raided and killed as they made their way through southern Arizona to the Sierra Madre. While living as fugitives in the mountains presented its challenges, the refugee Apache were happy. Geronimo and Juh joined with the Warm Springs Apache, led by Nana. Dances, ceremonies and the songs of the Apache echoed in the mountains as they had not for years. Practical jokes even had a place. On one occasion, Juh and Nana were relaxing in a canyon with some of their warriors when word came that Geronimo was approaching. They quickly extinguished their fires and hid. Geronimo rode right into their midst, and they finally emerged, laughing at him.

"I knew you were here all the time," Geronimo defiantly declared.

"You did not," replied Nana. "And you the sly fox of the Apache!"

Geronimo took it well; he had a good sense of humor.

The confidence of the Apache swelled during their time in Mexico. Soon, Geronimo was planning one of his greatest raids. At council he proposed that they return to San Carlos to rescue their friends and relatives from reservation life. But he was interested in more than reuniting families.

"My brothers, although we are safe here, the Mexican soldiers gather in great numbers near the foothills of the mountains. They are many more than us and we cannot hope to defeat them in battle. And surely battle will come. I am tired of running, of being chased," he conceded. "I want to be in one place. If we had enough warriors we would have to run no more. We need Loco's warriors."

Loco was the leader of the reservation Apache.

In mid-April 1882, the council decided that Geronimo would lead 60 warriors back to San Carlos. Geronimo was confident on this mission; he had good reason to be. He had taken time to sing four songs to his Power; it revealed that the mission would be successful. Always seeking an edge, Geronimo requested that his Power ensure the police were in a deep sleep when the warriors arrived at the reservation. He was careful as his warriors approached. He directed some to cut the telegraph wires to the agency headquarters. He had others seek out where the police were housed. With that information, the Apache slipped across the Gila River. The warriors quickly found Loco, only to discover that he did not want to go! Reservation life was difficult but at least, Loco argued, they were at peace. Geronimo was not willing to go back without the warriors he needed, and he forced Loco to gather his band. Travel proved difficult for Loco's followers. They were not used to the rigors of the trail, and Geronimo had to go slowly, which required additional supplies. They raided throughout southeastern Arizona, and soon 50 Americans were dead.

Geronimo had cause to use his Power as they drew near to Mexico. On one day near sunrise, his party, 300 of whom were women and children, found themselves at the northern side of the San Simon Valley that linked Arizona and Mexico. The valley was wide and provided no cover for those who crossed it. Geronimo wanted to spend no more time in the United States than necessary. He would much rather fight poorly trained Mexican soldiers than their well-armed American counterparts. He called on his Power to hold back the sun. Those who rode with him claim that the sun emerged three hours later that morning, allowing the Apache to cross safely in the darkness.

Despite Geronimo's view of Mexican soldiers, even they were effective using the element of surprise. They were waiting to ambush Geronimo's party. Two of his warriors had been captured in Mexico on the way to San Carlos, and in return for their lives, they revealed Geronimo's plans. The Apache were resting in a canyon when the Mexicans attacked, killing 14 Natives and wounding others. The Apache were forced to flee without their horses or supplies. Over the next day they made slow progress, the injured and exhausted women and children bringing up the rear. They were attacked by a second troop of Mexicans. Geronimo did his best to protect the women and children, but by the time they escaped under cover of fire, another 78 were dead. The Apache hid in the mountains, allowing the wounded to recover their strength and the able-bodied warriors to raid for food. Several months passed before they reached the Sierra Madre Mountains. When they arrived, Geronimo learned that Juh's wife Ishton (Geronimo's favorite cousin) had been killed during another Mexican attack.

Geronimo's blood was hot and he was anxious to go on the warpath to avenge Apache losses. Once the injured had sufficiently recuperated, the Apache put their plan in motion with 80 warriors. Some rode into Arizona and New Mexico in search of ammunition, while others, under the command of Geronimo, stayed in Mexico to raid for food supplies. Bold strikes and quick retreats into the mountains proved effective and soon the United States/Mexican border was in turmoil. But it wasn't until the Apache killed a United States federal judge and his wife that the government of the United States responded with force. They brought back General George Crook to deal with Geronimo once and for all.

Crook had an ace in the hole. Some months before, Geronimo had allowed one of his warriors, Tsoe, to return to San Carlos. Tsoe was upset with Geronimo, perhaps because he held the leader responsible for the death of his friend. Tsoe met with Crook and revealed the location of the Apache base camp. Crook asked for permission from Mexican officials to cross into their country. It came readily enough because the Mexicans realized that they could not fight the Apache effectively.

After a successful raid, Geronimo and his followers (some 36 at this point) were around a fire eating a meal. Geronimo unexpectedly dropped his knife. His Power had spoken to him.

"Men, our people that we left at the base camp are in the hands of U.S. soldiers. What should we do?"

There was no hesitation; all agreed to return. When they reached the camp, Geronimo was not surprised to see American soldiers everywhere. The army's journey, however, had not been an easy one. The hot sun, limited water and treacherous mountain trails were new experiences to most of the soldiers—that they even reached the Apache hideout was a testament to their dedication. Geronimo directed his men to take firing positions among the crevices and rocks of the mountainside. As he scanned the camp, he could see torn flour sacks attached to poles around the camp. They were a signal from the Apache in the valley that they wanted peace. Geronimo decided to send down two messengers to learn of Crook's intentions. If they did not return, he planned to attack. When he learned that Crook had pledged not to fire on the Apache, the warriors began to slip down from the mountains.

The soldiers were somewhat surprised to see the conditions and weapons of their enemies, as Second Lieutenant John Bourke later reported: "In muscular development, lung and heart power, they were, without exception, the finest body of human beings I had ever looked upon. Each was armed with a breech-loading Winchester; most had nickel-plated revolvers of the latest pattern and a few also had bows and lances."

Geronimo and some of his leading men did not come down. Aware that his mission would be a failure without Geronimo, Crook took a course of action that demonstrated some of his own courage. He left the camp alone telling others that he wanted to hunt, but in reality he went in search of Geronimo. The Apache leader found him soon enough, and he disarmed Crook. Geronimo allowed two interpreters to join them.

"Geronimo, I know that the Apache have not been treated well," said Crook. "The Mexicans will not stop hunting you until you are dead. Even now their soldiers are on the way here."

"They are treacherous," agreed Geronimo. "They make war on our women and children and then they run. But American hands are also bloody."

"Your people were ill-treated at San Carlos. The agents did not do their jobs properly. That your people kept the peace for as long as they did is a testament to their goodwill. But my government will not stop until you are taken back to the reserve."

"I cannot defeat American and Mexican soldiers if they are helped by Apache scouts," conceded Geronimo. "But if there is not peace, me and my warriors can fight for a long time in these mountains. We can fight until we are dead."

"That should not be necessary because the American government wants peace," replied Crook.

The discussion continued for about two hours and finally, Crook and the last of the Apache came into the camp. Geronimo agreed to follow Crook to San Carlos. It was eight months before there was any sign of the Apache leader. During the interval, Geronimo raided in Mexico, intent on building up a herd of cattle. Although Crook had promised that there would be no more dishonest agents at the reservation, Geronimo wanted to make sure he had enough to feed his people should that occur. He also took some time to grieve for his good friend Juh who had died from a heart attack while trading.

By November 1883, more than 400 Apache had arrived at San Carlos. Geronimo, who did not want to rush his cattle and have them lose weight, finally appeared with more Apache in late February 1884. In all, more than 100 warriors came. Geronimo met with Captain Emmet Crawford, who was in charge of the reservation. The Apache leader told of his meeting with Crook and of what the officer had promised him. He continued on, speaking with the consent of all Apache on the reservation.

> As soon as I saw Gray Wolf [the Apache name for Crook], I thought that I would leave the mountains and come to live in peace on the reservation....Now I am pleased to be here. It is a better place to live than in the rocks and thorns of the mountains.
>
> I want the past to be forgotten. I want everything to be done straight. All is made new so we can begin again. Before, in San Carlos, everything was wrong with the Indians and the people here. But now it is all being carried on straight and I want it to continue. I will never think again as I used to think before.
>
> Change for my people will not be easy. They are all here now like branch mules, which it is necessary to teach little by

little, until they are all tamed. I think we are to be treated well
until we are all living well. I am in a big hole and covered up
as far as my chest, while at San Carlos. I have surrendered
entirely. Any orders given I will obey without resisting.

Geronimo requested that his people be settled at Eagle
Creek, just outside the reserve, where the land was better.
However, Americans were living there, and while some
officials believed it was best to buy the land from the settlers and include it in the reservation, that was not to be.
All 521 Apache were moved to Turkey Creek and given
equipment to farm the poor quality land. Crook took
away the cattle because they had been stolen. The local
agent was more honest than most that the Apache had
dealt with, but he had policies that were not popular. He
paid spies to collect information about band members,
seeding distrust. He outlawed the fermentation of *tis-win*,
and he forbade the beating of women. For many generations, Apache men cut off the tips of the noses of unfaithful
wives. Crook had stopped this practice, so the men had
replaced it with beatings. If a man did nothing to an
unfaithful wife, he lost the band's respect. The rule emas-
culated the men, resulting in their frustration, desperation
and the occasional suicide.

Rumors began to circulate that Geronimo and Kaahteney
were planning an uprising. Since Kaahteney was long a troublemaker, the agent had him arrested and sent to a prison in
California. The Apache believed that Kaahteney was killed.
And although Geronimo was a model reservation Native, he
feared for his life. He demanded to communicate with
Crook. The agent promised to telegraph him, but word
failed to come from Crook (the telegraph line had been
cut). Geronimo grew impatient, and in May 1885 he left the
reservation. With him were 144 Apache, including 35 warriors.

His departure was news in the American Southwest, and newspapers made sure everyone was aware of it. "The Apaches Are Out!" was the bold headline, and settlers were quick to run to army posts when they read it. Geronimo led the Apache south to Mexico; on the way he killed those settlers who couldn't read or who didn't respond fast enough to the news.

General Crook returned again to deal with the situation, and knowing well that Geronimo would run for Mexico, he stationed troops at key routes along the border. One detachment met up with the Apache and in a costly battle most of the women and children were captured, including Geronimo's two wives. He was able to rescue one of them, but as the group continued to Mexico, they captured some Mescalero Apache women to serve as wives. Geronimo took a Mescalero Apache woman as a wife, and throughout the winter in the Sierra Madre, despite the stress the band was under, he began training her son (who was captured with her) in the ways of Apache manhood. To survive, the Apache raided.

In January 1886 the U.S. army finally caught up with Geronimo and his renegades near the Haros River in Mexico. The Apache sent a woman to relay a message from Geronimo; he wanted a conference. Eventually, the second in command of the detachment, Lieutenant Marion Maus, was escorted to a small council composed of Geronimo, 3 headmen and 14 others.

Geronimo looked to the fire and asked, "Why did you come down here?"

"I came to capture or destroy you and your band," came the terse reply.

Such courage! It impressed Geronimo, but he was ready to quit the fight.

"Tell Crook I will meet at the border to discuss surrendering," directed Geronimo.

In mid-March, Geronimo arrived at the meeting place of Cañyon de los Embudos. Crook arrived soon after, and Kaahteney was with him. His presence was meant to reassure the renegades. On March 25, Geronimo met with Crook. He explained that he had left San Carlos out of fear for his life.

"You told me that I might live on the reservation the same as white people lived. One year I raised a crop of corn, gathered and stored it, and the next year I put in a crop of oats, and when the crop was ready to harvest, you told your soldiers to put me in prison, and if I resisted to kill me."

Crook denied this. Geronimo went on to claim that he wanted peace, no more trouble and no more talk of his impending hanging. He wanted a good man placed in charge of the reservation.

"I know I have to die sometime, but even if the heavens were to fall on me, I want to do what is right. I think I am a good man, but in the papers all over the world they say I am a bad man; but it is a bad thing to say so about me. I never do wrong without a cause," he asserted. "There is one God looking down on us all. We are all children of the One God. God is listening to me. The sun, the darkness, the winds, are all listening to what we now say. To prove that I am telling the truth, remember I sent you word that I would come from a place far away to speak to you here and you see us now."

Although Crook grew angry as Geronimo spoke, he remained silent. Then he barked.

"You are a liar! You promised to live in peace on the reservation. You broke your promise and then killed innocent people! Your word cannot be trusted. You must make up your own mind whether you will stay on the warpath or surrender unconditionally. If you stay out, I'll keep after you and kill the last one, if it takes 50 years," replied Crook.

It soon became clear that the issue would not be resolved with a return to the reservation since local settlers feared for their lives. The warriors (and any family members who wanted to) would be sent East for two years where they could not cause problems in the American Southwest. After that they could return to live on the reservations. Geronimo agreed to the terms.

"Once I moved about like the wind. Now I surrender to you and that is all." Geronimo rose and shook hands with Crook. "My heart is yours and I hope yours will be mine." Later, after Crook had died, Geronimo revealed a more frank assessment of the man. "I think that General Crook's death was sent by the Almighty as a punishment for the many evil deeds he committed [against the Apache]."

Crook departed for Fort Bowie, leaving Maus to lead the Apache back to the reservation. Once he arrived, he wired Lieutenant General Philip H. Sheridan, commander of the army, of Geronimo's surrender. Sheridan was not pleased; government officials wanted the Apache broken. His reply, approved by President Cleveland, directed Crook "to enter into negotiations on the terms of their unconditional surrender, only sparing their lives." Anything less and Crook should "insure against further hostilities by completing [the Apache's] destruction...." Crook decided not to tell the Apache of the demand for their unconditional surrender because he was sure they would flee. Some of them did anyway. When Maus was ready to move out, he received word that Geronimo had made for the mountains. With him were 20 men, 14 women and 6 children. Crook didn't look forward to informing Sheridan of the news. When he did, Sheridan blamed him. Crook asked to be relieved of his duties and was replaced by General Nelson A. Miles, who arrived at Fort Bowie in mid-April to assume his position. The 77 Apache with Maus were placed under arrest and eventually sent to Fort Marion, Florida.

Miles had experience fighting Natives. His triumphs included the defeat of Crazy Horse in 1877. But fighting Apache in the mountains was different than fighting Sioux and Cheyenne on the plains. He quickly discovered that horses were of no value in the mountains and that soldiers couldn't easily meet the hardships that were readily conquered by the Apache. During April, he could only read the reports of Geronimo's raids in Sonora and Arizona. Mexicans bore the brunt of Geronimo's anger; they were killed on sight. But Americans and Mexicans alike were right to fear any report that Geronimo's warriors, with their white-painted faces, were nearby.

As Geronimo later recalled, "We were reckless of our lives because we felt that every man's hand was against us. If we returned to the reservation we would be put in prison and killed; if we stayed in Mexico they would continue to send soldiers to fight us; so we gave no quarter to anyone and asked no favors."

Tracking them was made more difficult because the renegade Apache had split into smaller groups. Even skilled Apache scouts (Miles had discharged most of them), could not easily follow the concealed markings of the Apache warriors, who walked on their heels to leave no footprints. Nevertheless, encounters occurred, although few deaths. In August 1886, Miles persuaded two Apache warriors to take a message to Geronimo. Lieutenant Charles Gatewood, whom Miles had placed in charge of the mission, accompanied them. Geronimo agreed to parley.

Gatewood informed him of Miles' demand: "Surrender and you will be sent to join the rest of your friends in Florida, there to await the decision of the president of your final disposition. Accept these terms or fight it out to the bitter end."

Geronimo agreed to surrender if he could return to the reservation. Gatewood could not give on this point. Geronimo asked about Miles, anxious to determine if he was trustworthy. Despite Gatewood's words of assurance, the Apache could not make up their minds.

Finally, Geronimo put the question to Gatewood. "We want your advice. Consider yourself one of us and not a white man....As an Apache, what would you advise us to do?"

"I would trust General Miles and take him at his word."

Geronimo spoke to his warriors after some moments of anguish, "I don't know what to do. I have been depending heavily on you three men. You have been great fighters in battle. If you are going to surrender, there is no use my going on without you. I will give up with you."

The Apache slept on it. The next day Geronimo and three warriors surrendered.

In early September, Geronimo arrived at Fort Bowie where Miles was waiting for him. Miles stated the terms of surrender. The Apache would have to give up their weapons and move to Florida. All that was done would be forgotten.

"I will take you under government protection; I will build you a house; I will fence your land; I will give you cattle, horses, mules and farming implements. You will be furnished with men to work the farm, for you yourself will not have to work. In the fall I will send you blankets and clothing so that you will not suffer from cold in the wintertime," promised Miles. "You will live with your tribe and with your family," he added.

"I will quit the warpath and live at peace hereafter," pledged Geronimo.

Once he agreed to Miles' proposals, there was a ceremony. Miles knew the importance of such events to the Natives. He placed a large stone on a blanket and pledged that the treaty would last until the stone crumbled to dust. On September 4,

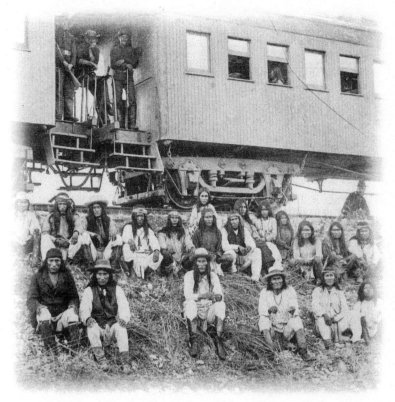

Geronimo, age 63, seated third from the right in front. After surrendering, he and his band were transported to Fort Marion, FL.

1886, Geronimo surrendered for the last time. His decision was greatly influenced by Miles, whom he said "talked very friendly to us and we believed in him as we would God."

Miles was just as taken by the Apache leader. "He [Geronimo] was one of the brightest, most resolute, determined looking men that I have ever encountered. He had the clearest, sharpest dark eyes that I think I have ever seen....Every movement indicated power, energy and determination."

In mid-September nearly 400 Apache rode a train to Fort Marion. A week passed before word came from President Cleveland that their leaders' lives would be spared. But the message also drew attention to the seriousness of Apache actions and the government's intention to ensure that there would be no more violence.

"By direction of the president, it is ordered that the hostile adult Apache Indians be sent under proper guard to Fort Pickens, Florida, there to be kept in close custody until further orders. These Indians have been guilty of the worst crimes known to the law, committed under circumstances of great atrocity, and the public safety requires that they should be removed far from the scene of their depredations and guarded with the strictest vigilance."

While at Fort Pickens, Geronimo and the others performed manual labor five days a week. They caused little trouble, although Geronimo was placed under guard a couple of times for being drunk. It was some months before their families were allowed to join them. The reunions were not complete, however, because the Apache children, including Geronimo's son, had been taken to the Carlisle Indian School in Pennsylvania. Geronimo was not against education, but he did not want children separated from their parents. After the War Department transferred the Apache to the Mount Vernon Barracks in Alabama in 1888, a local school was established.

Geronimo noted, "All the children go to their school. I make them. I want them to be white children."

Although all were pleased to be reunited with friends and family, the climate did not suit the Apache as demonstrated by the many cases of illness and death among them.

The Apache lived as prisoners in Mount Vernon until 1894. Geronimo continually pressed government officials to allow a move back to Arizona, but that was not to be because regional hatred against them remained intense. Finally, they were moved to Fort Sill, Oklahoma Territory. The Apache arrived on October 4, practically destitute, since their belongings had been destroyed in a fire along the way. Newspapers trumpeted the arrival of the feared Apache leader Geronimo but, at over 70 years, he did not command the respect among the soldiers he once had. They called him Gerry, which he did not like.

The process of assimilation continued at Fort Sill where each man was given a plot of land to farm. Geronimo enjoyed good success with watermelons. He believed it was important to set an example for his people. Although initially hesitant about the white man's religion (he felt he was too old for a new path), he even converted to Christianity (the Mission of the Reformed Church). He did not, however, abandon the traditional Apache ways, and there are numerous stories of his using his Power and ceremonies as a medicine man to minister to and heal the sick.

Despite his age, Geronimo's time at Fort Sill was busy. His status made him a celebrity, and he was invited to fairs and exhibitions. He made good money at these events, selling autographed pictures, bows and arrows and even buttons from his coat. The manager of the Louisiana Purchase Exhibition in St. Louis conceded that the old Apache was priced pretty high, "but, then, he is the only Geronimo."

In 1905, Geronimo was invited along with other noted tribal leaders to ride in President Theodore Roosevelt's inaugural parade. Woodworth Clum, the son of the agent who was so long at odds with Geronimo, arranged his appearance although he was none too pleased about it.

"Why did you select Geronimo to march in your parade, Mr. President? He is the greatest single-handed murderer in American history."

Geronimo, age 81 (center) while attending the 1904 St. Louis Fair. Geronimo was popular at exhibitions.

Roosevelt replied that he wanted to give the people a good show.

Geronimo was able to meet with the president, and he used the opportunity to make one last plea on behalf of his people:

> *Did I fear the Great White Chief* [when the American soldiers first arrived]*? No. He was my enemy and the enemy of my people. His people desired the country of my people. My heart was strong against him....I defied the Great White Chief, for in those days I was a fool. I ask you to think of me as I was then. I lived in the home of my people....They trusted me. It was right that I should give them my strength and my wisdom.*
>
> *When the soldiers of the Great White Chief drove me and my people from our home we went to the mountains.*

*When they followed us we slew all that we could. We said
we would not be captured. No. We starved but we killed.
I said that we would never yield, for I was a fool. So I was
punished and all my people were punished with me.*

*Great Father, other Indians have homes where they can
live and be happy. I and my people have no homes. The
place where we are kept is bad for us....We are sick there
and we die. White men are in the country that was my
home. I pray you to tell them to go away and let my people
go there and be happy.*

*Great Father, my hands are tied as with a rope. My
heart is no longer bad. I will tell my people to obey no chief
but the Great White Chief. I pray you to cut the ropes and
make me free. Let me die in my own country, an old man
who is punished enough and is free.*

Roosevelt could not grant the request. The reason had
not changed; he feared more bloodshed. The Apache would
remain at Fort Sill.

After the celebrations, Geronimo returned there, but not
for long. In February 1909, he rode to the nearby community
of Lawton to sell some bows and arrows he had made. While
there he got drunk. Riding back to his reservation home, he
fell from his horse into a puddle. He wasn't found until the
next day, and he was taken home. After three days, he was still
sick so he was transferred to hospital. He died from pneumo-
nia on February 17 far from the protective mountain spirits
of his home. He was interred in a Christian service, although
his wife insisted his belongings be buried with him.

CHAPTER FOUR

Crowfoot

Siksika Blackfoot, 1830–1890

IN THE EARLY SUMMER OF 1884, several Blackfoot bands gathered together at Blackfoot Crossing, just south of the Bow River, to celebrate their annual Sun Dance. The four-day ceremony, which the Blackfoot called Okan, was among the most important and complex of their celebrations. For countless generations, the Blackfoot had assembled when the Saskatoon berries bowed branches low so that the people could reaffirm their faith in the Sun spirit, the greatest of supernatural powers. Individuals danced to demonstrate their thanks to the Sun for favors granted. The ceremony also fulfilled other important functions. Filled with stories, songs and feasting, it tightened tribal bonds.

A Sun Dance also raised spirits, and this year there was a great need for that. Eyes were downcast and hearts were heavy as people remembered the once boundless herds of buffalo, all but gone. What had happened? Some looked to the treaty, made between the Blackfoot and the Canadian

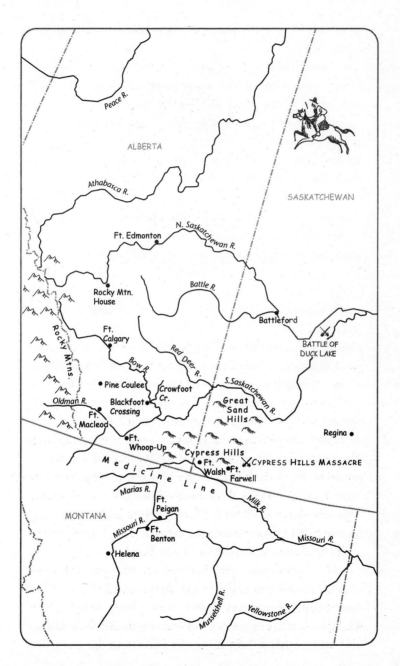

Peace R.

ALBERTA

SASKATCHEWAN

Athabasca R.

Ft. Edmonton

N. Saskatchewan R.

Battle R.

Rocky Mtn. House

Battleford

Rocky Mtns.

Ft. Calgary

Red Deer R.

BATTLE OF DUCK LAKE

Bow R.

Pine Coulee

Crowfoot Cr.

S. Saskatchewan R.

Oldman R.

Blackfoot Crossing

Great Sand Hills

Ft. Macleod

Regina

Ft. Whoop-Up

Cypress Hills

M e d i c i n e   L i n e

Ft. Walsh

Ft. Farwell

CYPRESS HILLS MASSACRE

Marias R.

Milk R.

Ft. Peigan

MONTANA

Missouri R.

Ft. Benton

Missouri R.

Helena

Musselshell R.

Yellowstone R.

government in 1877, as the origin of the present troubles, while others pointed to the arrival of the white man decades before. Although the Blackfoot might disagree about such things, none doubted that the situation in which they found themselves left much to be desired. Dependent on government handouts for survival, forbidden to travel from reserve to reserve without a government permit that was rarely forthcoming, and forced to obey laws that did not reflect their ways, the Blackfoot were demoralized. The Sun Dance at least allowed them to relive past glories, to talk again of the days when men hunted buffalo and warriors won honor with displays of courage against their enemies. Stories of the past fired the cooling passions of the Blackfoot to a heat that had not been felt for many moons.

At the height of the Sun Dance, a visitor arrived. He was a Métis named Bear's Head. Upon his arrival, he was led to the lodge of Crowfoot, one of the three most influential of the Blackfoot chiefs. Crowfoot was anxious to speak with Bear's Head, for news had reached the Blackfoot camp of the runner's mission. He came on behalf of the Métis leader Louis Riel, and rumor had it that he was to spread the news of Riel's imminent return to Canada and to foster support for his proposed rebellion against the Canadian government. Not so long ago in 1880, Crowfoot had rejected a similar proposal brought to him by Riel himself, while his band was camped along the banks of the Musselshell River in Montana. Crowfoot reflected on that meeting as he waited for the messenger.

"The Sioux and the Cree have pledged to join us in our fight against the white man," declared Riel. "With the support of the Blackfoot, it will be an easy matter to take control of the northwest. The Blackfoot will take Fort Macleod while the other tribes and Métis take Fort Walsh and Battleford. When we are in possession of the forts,

I will proclaim a provisional government, just as was done in Red River."

Crowfoot well remembered the success of the Métis in 1869–70. How could one forget the time when Natives led the resistance that forced the government to agree to terms dictated to it? But Crowfoot was a man of his word.

"I have made treaty with the white man," he replied. "I have promised not to raise my war club against them."

Crowfoot would never forget what Riel did next. He took a copy of the Cree treaty with the white man, threw it on the ground and trampled it.

"The Indians deserve better!" he barked.

Crowfoot could not disagree and remained silent.

"I am sending out runners to take word to Indian chiefs and Métis leaders of a great council that we will have in Montana. We will plan our attack. We will take back our land!"

Although what Riel proposed was appealing, Crowfoot was none too sure that a fight against the white man was in the best interest of his people. He was not inclined to join Riel, but perhaps he would listen to the words of the chiefs at the council. He never got that opportunity. The council never met. American officials got wind of Riel's plans, and they would not allow Natives to travel to the proposed meeting place. Crowfoot departed, leading his people on a desperate search for buffalo, with talk of rebellion little more than a fading and fanciful memory.

The buffalo hide that covered the entrance of his lodge was thrown open, and Bear's Head stepped inside. Crowfoot greeted him warmly, inviting him to sit to his right (the place for honored visitors). He asked Bear's Head of his recent troubles.

"I was imprisoned for vagrancy," confirmed Bear's Head.

Crowfoot, age 57, possibly taken during a visit to Prime Minister John A. Macdonald in Ottawa to speak for Native rights.

Crowfoot shook his head. "It does not seem right that a man should be arrested for doing nothing."

"The laws of the white man are strange and do not make sense," argued Bear's Head.

"And yet, they have helped us," replied Crowfoot, remembering well the efforts of the North-West Mounted Police to rid his people of the troublesome whisky traders and their poisonous firewater.

"Ha!" laughed Bear's Head. "White man's laws were always for the white man's benefit. They enforce them when it is to their advantage, and they break them when they see fit. Look at the rags your people wear. Listen to the rumble of their bellies. The white man's treaty promises have gone unfulfilled. They have lied, and we should take back our land!"

Crowfoot remained silent while those in his lodge made known their approval of Bear's Head's words. The messenger explained Riel's plan. It had changed little from the one of four years earlier. The Blackfoot would be responsible for capturing the south, their old home territory.

Bear's Head's message quickly spread throughout the camp, and it gained ready support from the younger warriors. Soon the local Indian agent was so concerned that he sent word to the Mounted Police in Fort Calgary, asking them to come and deal with the situation. Two officers soon arrived and arrested Bear's Head, only to see him escape on the return journey to Fort Calgary. Inspector Sam Steele and two constables showed up a few days later. Learning that Bear's Head was a guest in Crowfoot's lodge, Steele went straight there.

"Crowfoot!" he bellowed. "Come out so that I may speak to you." The interpreter who accompanied him was not needed to translate the determination in Steele's voice. When there was no reply, he added, "I know that the half-breed Bear's Head is in there. I will have him, dead or alive."

With that, Steele threw open the flap that covered the entrance of Crowfoot's lodge and entered it. Crowfoot and Bear's Head were seated inside.

"I have come to arrest this troublemaker," he declared as he looked to Bear's Head.

"He is my guest. He has done no wrong, and he will stay in my lodge," replied an equally determined Crowfoot.

"I think not." Steele placed his hand on his revolver, stepped around the lodge fire, grabbed Bear's Head by the shoulder, dragged him outside the lodge and ordered that he be placed in restraints.

"Why do you enter my camp and treat me with such disrespect?" asked the Blackfoot chief, who leapt to his feet and followed Steele outside.

"It is you, Crowfoot, who behaves badly," countered Steele. "You have always been treated fairly, and now you act as if you are treated unjustly. You have always received the greatest of kindness from the Mounted Police and the officers of the Indian Department. You are making a poor return for it."

Crowfoot was about to suggest that Steele look around to see what the white man's fair play had meant for his people when Steele continued.

"Come to Fort Calgary and see this man on trial. You will find that you are harboring a disturber of the peace."

Crowfoot knew that resistance would mean bloodshed. He let Bear's Head be taken away and followed him to Fort Calgary. Four days later, Bear's Head was acquitted of all charges although he agreed, at the magistrate's request, to leave the district. Crowfoot quickly left Fort Calgary, and with it he left much of the trust and respect he had for the Mounties. Bear's Head had been treated unfairly. It was becoming an all-too-common pattern. Daily Crowfoot witnessed the mistreatment of his people on the reserve, where officials commonly belittled them. If it wasn't short rations or extra charges for goods, it was the humiliation of racial slurs. There was a time when the Mounties had been the friends of the Blackfoot, but it was becoming clear that those times were gone. Frustrated, Crowfoot was starting to think that it was time to listen to the words of Riel and fight back. It would take little to convince his followers to accept such a course. Most had been ready to fight for some time and only awaited the word from their chief.

≈≈≈

In the summer of 1835 an old man was busy scouring the bush that surrounded his camp. Although he did not show it, Scabby Bull was worried. It had been early morning since he last saw his grandson Shot Close (Crowfoot's name as a child). Blood children were often given considerable freedom to do as they chose and to learn from those choices, but Shot Close was only five. One so young could find much danger in the wooded valley where his people camped. The sun would soon enter its lodge. Scabby Bull had searched the camp in vain; no one had seen Shot Close.

His already heavy heart heightened Scabby Bull's concern. Just that morning his daughter (Shot Close's mother), Attacked Toward Home, had left with her new husband Many Names. He was a Blackfoot, and tradition dictated that a wife live with the people of her husband. Neither father nor daughter doubted that Many Names would be a good husband. He had given Scabby Bull many horses for the right to marry his daughter. Still, the marriage came with a problem. Shot Close and Scabby Bull had grown close and did not want to be separated.

Blood children and their grandparents often developed intimate relationships, bonds that were pulled tight as much by artfully told stories of times past and future expectations as they were by responsibility and kinship. However, the relationship shared by Scabby Bull and Shot Close was a special one. Not so long ago Shot Close's father, Packs a Knife, was killed in a raid on the Crow, long-time enemies of the Blood. It had been a sorrowful time. Attacked Toward Home had slashed her arms and legs, cut her hair and painted her face dark, all in the traditional manner of mourning. Scabby Bull's lodge trembled with his daughter's constant wailing. Shot Close's younger brother, Iron Shield, was but an infant and hardly aware of either the loss or his mother's anguish. Shot Close was old enough to sense both, and it was only the calming influence of his grandfather that brought stability to his world. They remained close after the period of mourning had passed. In recognition of their intimate relationship, Attacked Toward Home and Many Names decided it was best if Shot Close remained with Scabby Bull while Iron Shield left with them.

It was not even a day since his daughter's departure and already Scabby Bull had failed in his responsibility. Terrible visions of the boy's fate tortured him as he made his way through the trees. Finally, he reached the height of the ridge that rose on one side of the valley. He walked to the edge of the forest, where the trees gave way to the great prairie. He was about to fall to his knees in despair when he saw something moving on the brown grass in the distance. He blinked his eyes and looked again, but it was not the boy. Instead he saw two people on horseback, likely Blackfoot, for they pulled a travois. As they came closer, Scabby Bull saw that they were Attacked Toward Home and Many Names. And riding with his mother was Shot Close!

Scabby Bull ran towards the group, and reaching them, pulled Shot Close from the horse. He was far too happy to be angry with the child.

"He followed you!" exclaimed Scabby Bull.

Attacked Toward Home smiled and nodded.

"We were far away before he caught up with us," explained Many Names. "The boy must have a powerful spirit."

"When we saw him, we decided to return, so that no one would be worried," said Attacked Toward Home.

"It is good you did, for there would have been great concern," replied Scabby Bull, careful to shield his wet eyes.

"Let us return to camp. There we can rest and resolve this problem," suggested Many Names.

The next day it was decided that Scabby Bull and Shot Close would join the family in the camp of Many Name's people. After days of travel north, the small party of five eventually arrived at the Red Deer River, where Many Name's Biters band was camped. Many Names gave his adopted son a new name, a Blackfoot one, Bear Ghost, and the family settled into their new life.

Although Bear Ghost was with a new band and tribe, there was little that was foreign to him. The Blackfoot were one of three bands, including the Blood and the Peigan, who spoke Blackfoot. While they called themselves Nitsitapi (the real people), they were commonly known as the Blackfoot because they dyed their moccasins black.*

The three bands did not share a rigid political connection, but they were close allies, often referred to as the Blackfoot Confederacy (which also included, at varying times, neighboring Sarcee and Gros Ventre). Although they had ancestral ties with the Algonquin tribes to the east, the Blackfoot considered their homeland to be in present-day Alberta, south of the Red Deer River, east of the Rocky Mountains and, in Montana, north of the Missouri River. Bear Ghost's people lived near the northern extent of that range. They had not been there for many generations before Bear Ghost was born in 1830 because it is likely that hostile Chipewyan had forced them southwest.

The Blackfoot prospered on the Plains. The early 1700s saw the introduction of both the rifle and the horse into

---

*For clarity, the Blackfoot band is referred to as the Siksika, the Blackfoot word for their band, while Blackfoot will indicate the grouping of all three bands. Also, an alternate spelling for Peigan is Piegan.

their culture, and by mid-century both had been fully
integrated, thereby enhancing the Blackfoot reputation as
skilled hunters and fearless warriors. While they stole horses
in raids, rifles came to the Blackfoot via the Cree, who traded
with white men to the east and north. It wasn't until 1754
that they saw their first white man, the explorer Anthony
Henday. Over the following decades, the Blackfoot had little
to do with whites. They were content to trade for their
goods, but they did not want the strangers in their hunting
territory. The British Hudson's Bay Company (HBC) had
established trading posts at Fort Edmonton and Rocky
Mountain House, and as far as the Blackfoot were concerned,
they were ideal trading partners. The HBC was content to
remain at its posts and let the Blackfoot come to them.
Relations with the Americans, however, were less comfortable
because they hunted and trapped in Blackfoot territory.
Occasionally there was violence. Not until 1831, when the
American Fur Company made peace with the Blackfoot and
established Fort Peigan on the upper Missouri River, were
American trappers safe. It was a sound economic decision for
the Blackfoot; they could play the HBC against its American
competitor for the best deal. Prosperity allowed the Blackfoot
population to grow to what was probably its largest number,
some 13,000. Of these, more than 4000 belonged to the
Siksika tribe of which Bear Ghost was a member.

As a child, Bear Ghost began to learn the skills necessary
to be a successful Blackfoot warrior. By the age of four he
had his first set of bow and arrows. A year later, he was riding
a cayuse. A warrior, however, needed more than a strong
arm, a sharp eye and good horsemanship. Blackfoot virtues
had to be internalized. Generosity, communal responsibility,
respect and wisdom—all traits that benefited the band—
were praised, but above all stood the precept of bravery.
Often the advice came in stories told around the flickering

light of an evening fire. Bear Ghost readily took to heart the lessons from such stories.

Scabby Bull sat near the fire across from the opening of the tipi. Around the fire sat Bear Ghost, Iron Shield and a few other children.

"Tonight I will tell stories of courage. Listen and you will learn that there are many ways to be brave," he encouraged his willing audience. He began with the story of Turtle going to war.

"A long time ago a camp with many lodges was set up near a lake. One day Turtle came to shore. He was anxious to get a scalp," explained Scabby Bull. "He crawled into one of the lodges. He found a woman there, and he killed her. As he tried to pull the heavy head from the lodge, the woman's husband arrived. He caught Turtle and brought it before the people. All agreed it should die.

"'Build a fire and we will burn him!' shouted one. Twigs and logs were enthusiastically piled for the pyre. All the time Turtle sought to break free so that he might rush to the fire.

"'He must belong in there,' observed one. 'It must be his place,' said another. 'We cannot burn him.'

"'Let's smash him between the rocks!' called another. Turtle crawled to a rock and hid under it. 'This will not do! He must have come from a rock.'

"'Hang him!' someone suggested. A sinew was quickly produced and made into a loop. Turtle grabbed the noose and placed it around his neck. 'This is no good! He is too willing.'"

"'Let us drown him in the deep water.'

"With that the Turtle cried, 'Please do not drown me!'

"'We have him!' Turtle was taken to a canoe and rowed out onto the lake. He was thrown overboard. Soon after he bobbed to the surface, singing, 'Turtle has a scalp!'

Although they had heard the story before, all the boys laughed at this. Scabby Bull sat silent for a moment, then spoke.

"Yes, it is funny, but it is also serious. Turtle was a good warrior. He was brave to enter the camp alone. He used his cunning to escape. A warrior must always think," advised Scabby Bear. "The good warrior has other traits," he continued. "Listen to the story of a Warrior's Duty.

"One day a warrior led his war party on a raid. After many days of failing to find the enemy, the warrior went out alone to scout. Soon he found two lodges. For a time he watched the lodges. He saw that a beautiful young woman lived alone in one of the lodges. That night, when the moon was high, he entered the lodge and slept with her. He visited her for four nights.

"The warrior's feelings for this woman began to get the best of him, and he thought of ways to save her," explained Scabby Bull. "He could lead her away and kill those in the other lodge, but they were her relatives and she would be sad. If he married her, then they would be his relations, but he was a leader of the war party and these were his enemies. Finally, he took these two lodges to his war camp.

"'I have married this woman,' he said.

"They went home and although they were from hostile tribes, they lived together.

"Be sure you know who your enemies are," suggested Scabby Bull, "and know that a warrior does not always have to raise his war club to vanquish them."

Throughout his childhood years, Bear Ghost enjoyed a life much as any Blackfoot child had over the previous 100 winters. Arrows fired at targets of stiff hide were soon directed at squirrels and small birds, activities that eventually led to a boy's first buffalo hunt, an important rite of passage to adulthood. The buffalo was central to Blackfoot culture, as it was to all Plains people. The animal informed their mythology and provided them with many of their material needs. It was the Blackfoot relationship with the great shaggy beast that shaped their nomadic ways. Little is known of Bear Ghost's first buffalo hunt, except that it was probably undertaken with Many Names at his side. Like other Blackfoot youth, he was taught how to cut up the dead animal, perhaps even how to make pemmican. While these were traditionally women's responsibilities, the skills came in handy when a warrior found himself alone.

In the early 1840s, Bear Ghost's world underwent significant change. A smallpox epidemic decimated the Blackfoot. The Siksika were reduced to 2100 and the Blackfoot nation numbered fewer than 6500. Eventually, the numbers rebounded, but more epidemics followed. Shortly after the outbreak, Bear Ghost made an important foray into the warrior's world. He participated in his first raid.

When they weren't hunting, celebrating or enjoying their leisure, men raided their Native enemies to the north and south. Such excursions were generally for revenge or to steal goods (especially horses) and didn't often involve the taking of an opponent's life. More important was a display of courage, such as striking an enemy or placing oneself in danger. When they became teenagers, Blackfoot youth were invited to take part in raids, although they did not seek such honors. They participated in the raids as apprentices, charged with watching, learning and performing menial camp tasks. Bear Ghost must have met expectations because he was allowed to take a new name. He chose Packs a Knife, his father's name.

Packs a Knife was still a teenager when his reputation as a warrior began its ascent. A Blackfoot party was formed to raid into Crow territory in Montana. Packs a Knife was one of the few youths invited, and he did so as a lesser member—

he had served his apprenticeship and had even occasionally acted as a warrior, but he still lacked the experience of many older braves. Just north of the Yellowstone River, scouts reported finding a large Crow camp. The Blackfoot approached carefully until they could see the camp. The leader of the raid waved his hand for all to slip back. Once they were sheltered from the enemy, he spoke.

"All have seen the large tipi in the middle of the camp?"

None could have missed it; it was painted with four red stripes.

"It is a Peigan lodge, taken by Crow raiders. Whoever gets to it and strikes it will be the future leader of his people in hunting and war," he declared.

All heard the words, but they affected none as they did Packs a Knife. When the leader gave the signal to attack, Packs a Knife made straight for the tipi. He ran low, but even crouched he was a tempting target for Crow warriors. A Crow shot fired from the brush tore through his arm, leaving a bloody flesh wound. The shock of the strike brought him to his knees, but only momentarily. He was quickly running again, still in front of the other Blackfoot, zigzagging his approach so as to challenge the rifle skills of the Crow, and reaching the tipi without being hit again. He felt faint as he struck the lodge and then fell to the ground, unconscious.

After the raid, Packs a Knife awoke surrounded by fellow Blackfoot. He was informed that his stepbrother, Three Bulls, had pulled him to safety. Summoning his strength, Packs a Knife declared that he had struck the tipi. Others verified his assertion. Everyone noted that he had shown great courage, and it was agreed that he had earned the right to take a hero's name. It did not take long for Packs a Knife to declare he would be known as Crowfoot.

It was not just any name. Only one other Blackfoot had used it, a relative of Many Names, who had through his skill and bravery become a chief. Once, on a raid against the Crow, he and his companions discovered an abandoned camp. As they searched through it, all were amazed when they found a large footprint in the mud. Each warrior in turn placed his foot in the indentation, and each found his foot too small. When the chief tried, he discovered his foot fit perfectly. He took the name Crow Indian's Big Foot, Crowfoot for short. Some time after, Crowfoot negotiated a peace treaty with the Shoshone. When he led a delegation into Shoshone territory to finalize the details, the party was ambushed and all were killed. That was 1828, two years before the birth of Shot Close. In the Blackfoot calendar, the year became known as the "When Crow Indian's Big Foot was killed." In the 20 years that had passed, none had been great enough to deserve the name. After the raid in Montana, those present knew that had changed.

"Yes," agreed the chief of the raiding party. "You have struck the tipi, and you will become a leader of your people."

Throughout his late teens and early 20s, Crowfoot developed an enviable record for bravery. He would eventually claim 19 battles and wear the marks of 6 wounds (most of which he earned before he was 30). Some of his wounds were serious, such as the ball Crowfoot took in the back during a wintertime raid against the Shoshone. On that occasion, only the quick action of Many Names (who spirited him away from the scene of the battle) and the healing powers of a shaman saved his life. The ball, however, was never removed, and it caused Crowfoot considerable pain later in life. Upon reflection he probably considered that there was good reason that the Blackfoot did not usually engage in raids when snow blanketed the ground.

Crowfoot counted many more successes than failures in battle, however. One raid against the Cree did much to ensure that few would question his bravery. When the party met up with the Cree, they retreated into a nearby stand of trees. Crowfoot was one of the first to run after them. Singling out a Cree warrior, he threw his rifle down so that he might be less encumbered in his pursuit. Ignoring the possibility of ambush, he pierced the woods and was soon close enough to the warrior to grab his braid. Crowfoot plunged a knife into his adversary's chest and took his life. Crowfoot then pulled the Cree's hair tight, slipped his knife across the man's forehead, and with a tug took his scalp. The Blackfoot warrior won great praise for his action.

It was not long before Crowfoot's reputation made him the leader of his own raiding parties, and he had no trouble attracting warriors to join with him. On one occasion he led some Siksika against the Cree. The opposing sides took shelter, making it difficult for either party to get a clear shot, so the encounter had all the makings of a lengthy affair with little gained. Crowfoot slipped out from behind his shelter and made his way to a small depression midway between the opposing forces. As balls and arrows whizzed past him, he took out his fire bag, from which he withdrew his pipe.

As he filled it with tobacco, he called to his brothers, "Come and smoke with me!"

It was not merely an invitation to smoke; it was a call to courage. The Siksika knew that if they declined, there would be accusations of cowardice. Slowly—and carefully—some crawled towards Crowfoot. Seeing this advance, the Cree retreated. The Siksika pursued and victory was theirs.

The battlefield was not the only place to display courage. Like most young Siksika, Crowfoot was a member of a tribal society. A half dozen such societies existed, all sharing similar functions: to preserve order in camp and on the hunt, to punish wrongdoers and to cultivate a warrior spirit. The societies were ranked according to prestige, which in turn was mostly a reflection of how long the society had been in existence. Crowfoot joined the All Brave Dogs, a society that ranked in the middle. He was not a prominent member of the group, perhaps because he had a certain unspoken disdain for these societies. Unlike many Siksika, he joined only one and had little interest in the other popular secret societies. Choosing the All Brave Dogs, however, revealed something more of Crowfoot's character. Its members had a particular reputation for bravery.

One year, while the Siksika had joined with the Blood to celebrate the Sun Dance, a war party of Pend d'Oreille attacked the camp and killed a warrior. As they retreated, they stopped long enough to kill a woman they unexpectedly encountered. Killing the woman was poor judgment because the delay proved sufficient for the warriors of the two tribes to catch up with them. Among the numbers of the pursuing Blackfoot were many All Brave Dogs. The Pend d'Oreille were routed.

As the victorious Blackfoot collected the weapons, Crowfoot grabbed a rifle at the same time as a young Blood warrior named Brave Dog. After a brief argument, Brave Dog let Crowfoot take the rifle, but Brave Dog's anger simmered. That afternoon, he arranged a victory party for the All Brave Dogs. Members, dressed in fine costumes, marched around the camp and sang their society song, announcing the forthcoming dance to the entire camp. Brave Dog, however, planned on something more than a celebration. He was going to use the occasion to ridicule Crowfoot. Perhaps Crowfoot suspected this, but as a member of the society, he was obliged to attend.

The celebration began with the All Brave Dogs marching two abreast through the camp. Two on horseback,

representing the society's founders, led the column in. They
sang as they marched, and drummers kept a rhythm. The
chorus of a popular song was often repeated:

> It is bad to live to be old; better to die young fighting
> bravely in battle.

All were well dressed, and some wore flowing war head-
dresses or carried colorfully decorated protective shields.
Eventually there was dancing, and when the food and
tobacco was finally brought out for the feast, Brave Dog
rose and looked to Crowfoot. In his hand he held a rifle.

"Come and take this rifle from me!" Brave Dog called
to Crowfoot.

By this time, all knew of the dispute. Some urged
Crowfoot to accept the challenge while he could hear others declare that he should never have taken the rifle.
Crowfoot sat rigid. If he met Brave Dog, one would have
to die, and the death of either would open a wound
between the bands. So Crowfoot remained seated and
accepted public ridicule, the worst punishment a Native
could endure. But it was an act of courage, one that also
demonstrated considerable wisdom. Soon after he sought
out Brave Dog, and certain in his belief that Brave Dog's
words had been spoken because he believed himself to be
right, Crowfoot praised him for his public rebuke.
Crowfoot's handling of the Brave Dog affair suggested that
neither his leadership abilities nor his reputation had been
tarnished by the episode.

Indeed, others in his tribe saw Crowfoot's potential.
One was no less than Three Suns, the chief of Crowfoot's
Biter band of Siksika. He had watched Crowfoot and was
well aware of his burgeoning leadership skills. It was generally not the Native way to bring attention to such matters,

for it might be seen as unduly meddling with one's life path, but evidently Three Suns saw something in the young Siksika warrior that demanded comment. Three Suns probably took the opportunity when Crowfoot was in his early 20s, and the conversation was surely a short one done in private, since such open flattery would have been most uncomfortable.

"Crowfoot, I have something for you," said Three Suns. He took from his side a small pouch and loosened the sinew that held it closed. Gingerly, he emptied its contents into his hand. It was an owl's head.

"This will be your protection," continued Three Suns. Perhaps the Siksika chief was aware that Crowfoot had never been granted a successful vision quest. All evidence suggests that to be the case (though, a vision quest was rarely given public comment). Undoubtedly, however, at some point in his young life Crowfoot had retreated to a desolate location on a hillside, where he fasted and offered prayers, hoping that some supernatural being would visit him and bestow its protection. All Blackfoot youth did so.

"Carry it always, and you shall become a great leader," advised Three Suns.

Crowfoot took the owl's head and tied it into his hair, where it was to remain for the rest of his life. Perhaps Three Suns had had a vision of his own because Crowfoot was to succeed him as band chief.

Crowfoot did, however, have one vision, the only one he is known to have had. As a young man, the Buffalo Spirit appeared to him and declared that he would become the father of his people. The spirit directed Crowfoot to kill a buffalo and to make a pair of leggings from its skin. He prepared them in the traditional manner. A single piece of leather sewn with a single seam served for each legging. The leggings reached from hip to ankle, were painted yellow and black and were decorated with quills and small pieces of fur. Crowfoot's leggings served as his holy charm.

The 15 or so years following the middle of the 19th century were good ones for the Blackfoot. Although pressures were exerted on the great buffalo herds to the south and east, they had little impact on the number of animals within the Blackfoot's traditional hunting territory. If anything, more buffalo came, since the herds migrated north and west. The impact of the white man, aside from his diseases, remained mostly positive. Most stayed clear of Blackfoot territory, and as yet, trade goods only complemented traditional practices. Perhaps the Siksika were surprised (and bewildered) to learn in the mid-1850s that they were "British" Natives and that their Peigan and some Blood relatives were "American." United States officials, interested in constructing a railroad through the northern territories to the Pacific coast, had negotiated treaties with some of the less powerful southern Blackfoot chiefs. The Siksika were considered too far north to be of any concern. The difference meant little to the Siksika at this point, but not so many years would pass before being a "British" Native meant a somewhat different experience from being an "American" Native.

Crowfoot also prospered during this period as suggested by his three wives (keeping more than one indicated a man's wealth). The years of his marriages are uncertain, but it appears that before he was 30, Cutting Woman, Cloth Woman and Packs on Her Back each lived with him. He would eventually have 10 wives, although usually only three or four at a time. Shortly before he became chief, he divided his family (he had numerous children, but only four lived to maturity) between his two large tipis, each made of 30 buffalo skins. Only the wealthy could afford such large dwellings, the standard size tipi being 12 buffalo skins.

Another indication of Crowfoot's prosperity was his large herd of horses, many of which had been taken during raids while others had been obtained by trade. By the 1870s, he owned more than 400. Crowfoot understood the value of trade, especially with the white man. He frequently visited Fort Edmonton and Rocky Mountain House, and was liked by the local traders. Skin color mattered little to Crowfoot. It was his belief that if a man could help his people, he was a friend; if he couldn't, he was an enemy.

Crowfoot's life took a dramatic turn in the mid-1860s, when Three Suns, chief of the Biter Band of Siksika, died. The band was divided on the matter of succession. While it was possible for one not related to the chief to assume his position, it was unusual. Many, therefore, looked at the younger Three Suns as a potential new leader. Crowfoot impressed others, and in 1865, it was decided that the band would split in two. Twenty-seven lodges followed Three Suns while 21 accepted Crowfoot as their chief, and became known as the Big Pipes band. The split was amicable and the two bands continued to camp close together. Although his followers were not yet numerous, Crowfoot had begun his swift ascent to the chieftainship of the Blackfoot. Throughout late 1865 and 1866, Crowfoot figured prominently in a series of events that earned him great praise and respect.

As winter tightened its grip in the closing month of 1865, a white man visited Crowfoot's Big Pipes band, a rare occurrence. This man was not to be deterred by fear of the Blackfoot because he obeyed a higher power. His name was Albert Lacombe, and he was a Catholic missionary with some 12 years experience in the West. Father Lacombe did not yet have the great reputation that he would eventually enjoy; nevertheless, the Plains Natives respected him for his generous nature and courage. On visiting Crowfoot's camp,

Crowfoot, age 56 (left), with his stepbrother Three Bulls and the respected missionary Father Albert Lacombe (standing).

Lacombe learned that the Big Pipes would soon be joining with Three Suns' Biter band for the winter. The Biters were already at the winter camp and Lacombe decided to go there and prepare for his missionary activities. During his first night there, the Cree attacked the camp. It was a large raiding party—some 800 Cree, 10 times the number of Siksika.

An exhausted Lacombe heard the call of Three Suns, "Assinow! Assinow! The Cree are attacking!"

Before he could step from his tipi, cracking rifles and war whoops shattered the night's quiet. Lacombe fell to his knees as balls tore through the buffalo skins of his lodge. He knew that he had to get out of there, and he believed that he might hold the key to stopping the attack. The Cree knew him, and he hoped that if he could talk to them, he could bring an end to the violence. Lacombe emerged from his tipi, and with the melee not far from where he stood, he called to the Cree in their own language. His pleas could not be heard over the din, and his black robe rendered him almost invisible on the dark night. His efforts were fruitless, and the Cree continued to advance on the camp. By morning they controlled half of it.

With the dawn, Lacombe decided to try again. He took a small white flag bearing a red cross and advanced towards the Cree lines. When Lacombe reached the peak of a small hill, he raised his flag above his head, but it had hardly caught the breeze when a bullet struck his shoulder and ricocheted, delivering a glancing blow to his head. Dazed, he fell to the ground and was quickly retrieved by the Blackfoot, who took him to one of the tipis not yet taken by the Cree. Fortunately, the bullet did little more than break the skin. He was resting when he heard the voice that would soon rescue the Biter's camp from sure defeat.

"Take courage! Hold fast!"

Lacombe did not recognize it, for he was not yet familiar with the man who called the words of encouragement. It was Crowfoot. Word of the attack had reached his camp, and he had rushed with his warriors to assist. Although those who followed him numbered fewer than the braves of the Biter band, they fought with such abandon that the tide of the battle turned, and the Cree retreated. They were pleased enough, because they had taken many scalps and over 300 horses, the Biter's entire herd. But they left before they could completely raze the village. All agreed that it was the determined example of Crowfoot, who threw caution to the wind as he charged through the camp, that had inspired and rallied the Siksika. Not only had his actions saved the Biter band from destruction, he had also saved the life of a powerful white man. The Blackfoot took notice of such a man.

The following summer an event occurred that had many discussing the likelihood that Crowfoot possessed some special connection with a spirit power. After the spring hunt, during which the Siksika bands had separated in search of buffalo, the bands gathered for the annual Sun Dance. As they prepared, word came of a grizzly bear attack. Some women were out picking berries when a large grizzly roared through the bushes. Any grizzly bear was considered to have strong powers, but one of this size was especially fearsome. The young boy who had been assigned to protect the women was mauled before he could notch an arrow, and he remained at the mercy of the grizzly.

Crowfoot was among those who rounded up the All Brave Dogs to respond to the emergency. It was not long before they reached the tangle of bushes and trees where the women had been berry picking. The grizzly was still threatening the injured boy, but the warriors' shouts and gunfire soon distracted it. They wanted to kill the bear before it was lost in the trees, but Crowfoot counseled patience.

"Ride to the other side of the stand of trees," he told some of the warriors. "The bear is likely hiding there. Flush it out, and call to me when you have done so."

Crowfoot was not their leader, but the All Brave Dogs responded to his direction. As they made their way around the trees, they found that many band members had gathered at a safe distance to witness this encounter with a grizzly. Warriors took turns charging into the brush in an effort to draw the animal out. Eventually they heard a rumble, and the grizzly charged out of its hiding place.

"Crowfoot! The bear is in the clearing!"

The sentence was not completed before Crowfoot, who had been waiting on the far side of the stand of trees, jabbed his heels into the midsection of his horse and sent it into the brush in pursuit of the animal. Branches tore at him as he pushed to get to the clearing. When he broke free, he raised his spear above his head. He urged his horse on until he was just behind the grizzly, and with a strong arm, he thrust his weapon into the animal's back. The grizzly roared, and Crowfoot's horse tossed its head up in fear. Seeing the terror in its eyes, Crowfoot quickly dismounted. Once on his feet, he continued to stab at the grizzly until it fell to the ground and lay dead. It was a great moment for Crowfoot. Many Blackfoot had seen his act of uncommon courage, and from that time on, everyone regarded him as a chief. He was probably formally recognized as such during that year's Sun Dance.

While Crowfoot was considered a chief, none yet saw him as one of much importance. Certainly stories were told of his courage and hushed discussions were held about what appeared to be his special relationship with the spirit world. But, at this time, he was merely one chief among many lesser Blackfoot chiefs, and his followers remained few—no more than 30 lodges. His position was soon to take a dramatic change. Crowfoot had demonstrated that he feared neither the enemy nor powerful spirits (though he surely respected both). In the fall of 1866, he was given an opportunity to show that he had the courage to stand against his own people—if he believed the cause to be just. In doing so, he was to distinguish himself from his counterparts.

Seen From Afar, the head chief of the Blood, decided that it would be to the benefit of his people if they avoided contact with American whites, who were increasingly hostile towards Natives. Rather than trade at the traditionally used posts on the Missouri River, they made a decision to go north, where they might trade with the Hudson's Bay Company. When the Blood arrived at the Red Deer River, they met up with some friendly Sarcee who informed them that large numbers of enemy Cree were camped nearby. To avoid a confrontation with the Cree, Seen From Afar decided that he would return south, but not until after his people had disposed of their trade goods. He sent a messenger to Fort Edmonton asking that a trading party be sent to his camp. The news was well received at the HBC post, so 15 Métis along with 30 Red River carts were soon dispatched.

Under the direction of John Cunningham, the trading party arrived at the Blood camp in October. By that time, the Blood were in the minority. The camp had grown in size and included some Sarcee, Peigan and many Siksika, most of whom were angry. While it might be acceptable to trade with the white man, it was not right that he venture into the heart of Siksika territory. Fueling their anger was the Cree heritage of the Métis because the Cree were Blackfoot enemies. Even as he led his party towards Seen From Afar's lodge, Cunningham sensed trouble. Seen From Afar did also, and he made a quick effort to defuse it by lighting his pipe and offering it to the trader as a sign of his friendship. While some of the Native chiefs joined them in the pipe smoking, Crowfoot was the only Blackfoot who did.

Smoke still lingered in the air, and the trading had only just commenced when they heard shouting. Big Swan, one of the three most important Siksika chiefs, was calling to his warriors. They gathered around him and pushed their way towards the traders. He stood close to Cunningham and Seen From Afar and verbally assaulted those who had come as guests.

"Since when do we allow white men and Cree half-breeds to come to our camp! They are no friends of ours. We do not trade with enemies. We deal with them in other ways," declared Big Swan, as his hand fell to the rifle at his side.

The speech continued along the same line for some time. Cunningham realized there would be no more trading and quietly directed his men to pack up the carts.

When he saw this happening, Big Swan barked, "Trader! Why do you prepare to leave? I, too, have goods to barter."

With that he threw some buffalo robes on the ground. Cunningham examined them and saw they were worn and full of holes. Black Swan did not want to trade. He wanted to bully Cunningham into giving up his goods for free. Cunningham would not be so easily cowered.

"No trade, Big Swan."

"Then we will take what we want."

With a quick move of his arm, Black Swan's warriors were at the carts, unloading them. It wasn't long before they were empty. Black Swan turned to the traders and brandished his rifle before them. Seen From Afar stepped between them. He would not allow harm to come to those he had invited. Black Swan did not appreciate the challenge to his authority.

"Kill them anyway," he directed his warriors.

Before they could move, Crowfoot stepped from the crowd and moved to Seen From Afar's side. He caught Big Swan's eyes in his own, a challenge in its own right.

"You people are dogs!" declared Crowfoot. "The whites should sweep you off the face of the earth."

Black Swan's shoulders drew back as if he had been struck. As he stood silent to consider this new challenge,

other chiefs joined Seen From Afar and Crowfoot in defiance of Black Swan. None, however, were Siksika. They led
Cunningham's party from the area and ensured they were
unharmed on their return trip.

Crowfoot's actions were unexpected. It was not usual to
so openly challenge an important chief; indeed, he might
have been put to death for it. Those who did not know
Crowfoot well might have seen the act as a rash display of
temper, a reasonable assessment since he was often explosive. Many of those present, however, saw the wisdom in his
stand. To massacre the traders would have had far-reaching
repercussions, not the least of which was that they might
cut off future trading possibilities. Crowfoot's courage was
also noted, even by Big Swan. Many might have disagreed
with what Crowfoot did, but all could see it was a principled act, taken because he had believed it to be right.
Although he expected no reward for what he had done,
one came from an unlikely source. Cunningham's superiors
at Fort Edmonton were so grateful that they gave Crowfoot
many presents, including a British flag and a scarlet uniform.
In the eyes of the local white population, Crowfoot had
become as important a chief as Big Swan and Three Suns.
Such recognition undoubtedly improved his status among
the Blackfoot as well.

The first indications of this greater status emerged
amidst tragic circumstances. In 1869, the Blackfoot were
again afflicted with smallpox. Although the number of
deaths did not approach the levels caused by previous epidemics, they were nonetheless significant. Among those
who died was Three Suns (the younger), the chief of
Crowfoot's old Biter band. The Biters made a quick decision to accept Crowfoot as their chief. No longer was
Crowfoot a minor chief; he was ranked with Big Swan.
Three years later Big Swan died of tuberculosis and

Crowfoot found himself one of two Siksika head chiefs. Some 1300 Siksika followed him, well over half their total population. By 1872, Crowfoot had become one of the most influential leaders among the Blackfoot.

Crowfoot's first months as a head chief among the Siksika were peaceful ones. It had been many years since he had fought his enemies; however, personal tragedy was to drive him back to those bloody paths. In the fall of 1873, his eldest son was shot dead during a raid against the Cree north of the Red Deer River. Crowfoot had three sons, but the loss of the eldest was a particular blow. Of the other two, one was mute and the other had failing eyesight. Crowfoot held out great hope for his eldest, who had shown promise as a young warrior. Perhaps he might even have followed in his father's footsteps. Instead, he met the fate of Crowfoot's father.

After the period of mourning, Crowfoot turned his mind to revenge. Satisfaction did not demand that the warrior who had actually killed his son be killed; the death of any Cree would suffice. Four warriors were dispatched to discover if any Cree were nearby. When they returned with news of a Cree camp, Crowfoot called for warriors to join him. His popularity meant that many offered to follow him, but Crowfoot chose 20 who were close friends and relatives. The raid was efficient. Crowfoot gave the signal to attack, and one Cree was quickly killed before the others escaped. His body was scalped and mutilated. With his revenge satisfied, there would be no more raids of reprisal. The pain of his loss continued as a dull ache, but circumstances would see that soon fade.

During the months following this incident, likely around 1873, the Blackfoot and the Cree made peace, one of numerous short-lived treaties. During this peace, Crowfoot had the opportunity to visit a Cree camp. While there, he

Cree chiefs Big Bear (1825–88) and Poundmaker (1842–86) in 1886. Big Bear and Poundmaker were men of peace whose values were tested by government parsimony and circumstances. Big Bear refused to make treaty until his starving people could no longer live off the land. Poundmaker, Crowfoot's adopted son, believed that treaty provided the best future for his people and he more willingly "touched the pen." The bands of both men, however, suffered from poverty and hunger on the reserves. When the North-West Rebellion erupted in 1885, followers of Big Bear killed settlers at Frog Lake and burned Fort Pitt. Poundmaker's followers pillaged Battleford and later countered an attack by the Canadian military at Cut Knife Hill. While most reports suggest that Big Bear and Poundmaker counseled peace and sought to rein in their more violent band members, both were sentenced to three years in prison after the rebellion was crushed. Neither served his full term.

met a young man. Although the brave was a few years older than his dead son, the resemblance between the two was startling. Crowfoot's wife suggested that their son had returned from the Great Sand Hills, the resting place of the spirits of the dead. Crowfoot talked to the young man, whose name was Poundmaker, and discovered that all his close relatives were dead. Crowfoot described the loss of his own son and invited Poundmaker to come and live in the Siksika camp. The relationship blossomed as Crowfoot and Poundmaker discovered that they shared visions for their people. Both men saw the best future as one of peace. Eventually Crowfoot offered to adopt Poundmaker. The young Cree agreed and became known as Wolf Thin Legs among the Blackfoot. Such a relationship was common among Plains Natives, and Wolf Thin Legs was eventually accepted as the son of Crowfoot. He continued to live with Crowfoot throughout the mid-1870s.

Crowfoot's world was to undergo dramatic change in the 1870s. Most Natives soon discovered that the best they could do was to adjust to it, which did not prove easy. The Blackfoot were oblivious to the cause of the change because it happened thousands of miles to the east. Under pressure from the British government, the Hudson's Bay Company had decided that its financial interest lay in selling its massive land holdings in North America (the drainage basin of Hudson's Bay, which extended west into present-day Alberta and south to the American border) that it had owned since 1670. They had a willing buyer. In 1867, the Dominion of Canada had been created, and politicians who envisioned a nation stretching from Atlantic to Pacific were anxious to take possession of the northwestern portion of the continent. In 1869, a deal was reached. But, while Canada held title to the territory, it did not have a presence there because it was without the funds to ensure one.

American entrepreneurs took note and decided there was financial opportunity in the wide open west.

In 1870, two merchants out of Montana, John J. Healy and Alf Hamilton, built a trading post at the fork of the Oldman and St. Mary's rivers, in present-day southern Alberta, then in the heart of Blood territory. They stocked Fort Whoop-Up, as it was soon called, with all sorts of trade goods but quickly found whisky and rifles to be the most popular items. By rights, liquor was off limits. Natives couldn't legally buy booze in the old Hudson's Bay Company territory. But HBC regulations were suddenly meaningless, and the Canadian government turned a blind eye to whisky peddling. When Montana merchants saw the money to be made in the booze business, other trading posts—called forts—quickly sprang up in what was rapidly becoming known as Whoop-Up country.

The sudden availability of liquor had a devastating impact on the Blackfoot. Liquor was foreign to their way of life, and they had a difficult time adjusting to it. The greatest of the problems faced was the violence that followed in the wake of drinking. Blackfoot turned on the traders and on each other. Others met with less violent but equally tragic ends. Some froze to death while drunk; others starved, all their trade goods wasted on whisky. Many more died at the hands of the firewater itself, since it was generally fortified with anything from iodine and turpentine to gunpowder. The effects of liquor ran rampant through communities. Those who didn't die were often left poor and demoralized. It even affected the balance of power with the Cree. They were too far north to trade at the southern forts and were thus relatively free from the liquor problems. As a result, they found it increasingly easy to take control of Blackfoot territory.

At first, Crowfoot took a practical view of the American traders. He wasn't against liquor; he drank it himself. He was not opposed to trade, having long since learned that it was beneficial to his people. If these new traders were honest and respected his people, they would be treated in kind. But it soon became apparent that some American traders cheated his people, using alcohol to strike crooked bargains. Crowfoot advised against trading at certain forts, but his words often fell on deaf ears. The lure of whisky was too powerful. Within a few years he recognized that liquor was an evil force among his people. Something had to be done, but self-restraint proved an impossible demand.

The Canadian government had also reached the conclusion that the issue had to be addressed. The violence was bad enough, but officials feared that the bloodshed might encourage American authorities to invade the territory under the pretense of protecting American interests. It wouldn't be a stretch, since it was well known that Blackfoot raided American settlers living in the United States for goods they could take into Canada and trade. Once the American army was in place, it would not easily be removed. The Red River Rebellion of 1869–70 in present-day southern Manitoba, occurring when no military or law enforcement was yet established in the region, had forced the Canadian government to negotiate terms with the Métis and other local settlers. There was a fear that the rebels' victory might spur others in the West to similar action. By the early 1870s, the Canadian government was considering the establishment of some sort of military force to send west to deal with the problem.

In early 1874, the problems of whisky, Natives and violence came to a head during one particularly ugly incident at the American-run trading post of Fort Farwell. It involved the Green River Renegades, a nasty group of wolfers out of Fort Benton, Montana. Wolfers were men who made their living poisoning wolves, men looked down on by all save, perhaps, the cattle barons who hired them.

Fueled by booze, they all but wiped out a band of peaceful Assiniboine who were camped near the Cypress Hills (in present-day southwestern Saskatchewan). The Cypress Hills Massacre, as it became known, made it clear to Canadian authorities that the time for consideration had passed. They had to get an agency of law and order on the prairies without further delay. In the spring of 1874, the North-West Mounted Police finally began their march west.

Crowfoot knew of the Mounties before he met them. The Canadian government wanted to prepare the Natives for their arrival, and to that end, they had dispatched Rev. John McDougall, a missionary respected among the Blackfoot. McDougall found the large Siksika camp on Crowfoot Creek, south of its traditional location (Cree incursions had forced the relocation), well stocked with whisky and animated with drunken rancor. He was directed to Crowfoot's lodge, strangely quiet amidst the laughter and shouting.

"Chief Crowfoot, I have come on behalf of the Grandmother [Queen Victoria], who wishes your people well," began McDougall. "She wants me to tell you that her police are coming from the East. They are coming to protect you."

"There are white men here, many who do not wish to protect us," remarked Crowfoot. "How will we know those who come from the Grandmother?"

"They will wear red coats. They will build forts in Blackfoot territory."

A decade ago, perhaps even five years ago, such an occurrence would have been unthinkable. Crowfoot remained silent, an indication of the great changes of those years.

"The Red Coats will stop the traders from selling liquor. They will stop the Indians from killing each other.

They will ensure that British justice exerts a lawful presence in these lands," declared McDougall. "All may expect to be treated fairly. Whether Indian or white, all will be subject to the laws of the Grandmother. The guilty will be punished. Killing, thievery, the liquor trade, all will come to an end."

When McDougall finished, Crowfoot rose and took the missionary's hand in his own. He placed both on his chest.

"My brother, your words make me glad. I listened to them not only with my ears, but with my heart also. The coming of the traders with their firewater and their quick-shooting guns has made us weak, and our people have been woefully slain and impoverished."

"If left to ourselves, we are gone," admitted Crowfoot. "The whisky is fast killing us off, and we are powerless before the evil. We are totally unable to resist the temptation to drink when brought in contact with the white man's water. We are unable to pitch anywhere that the trader is unable to follow us. Our horses, buffalo robes and other articles of trade go for whisky, and a large number of our people have killed one another and perished in many ways under the influence.

"You say this will be stopped. We are glad to have it stopped," conceded Crowfoot. "We want peace. What you tell us about this strong power that will govern with good law and treat the Indian the same as the white man makes us glad to hear. My brother, I believe you and am thankful."

The first act of the North-West Mounted Police upon their arrival demonstrated that Crowfoot's hope was not misplaced. In early October, the mud of the march still clinging to their boots, the Mounties shut down Fort Whoop-Up. Within days, they selected a site for their first post in the region, and before the worst of winter had set in, Fort Macleod (named for the Assistant Commissioner

James Macleod, who was in charge of the operation) was well under construction.

Crowfoot was pleased to see such quick and direct action, but he needed more to satisfy himself that these Red Coats were truly friends. His attitude towards the white man had been changed with the activities of the American traders. He no longer assumed that the white man's presence was of value. Only a few weeks had passed since the arrival of the Mounties before he put them to the test. He sent Three Bulls to Fort Macleod with evidence of two American traders selling whisky at Pine Coulee, about 50 miles north. Crowfoot wanted to see if the Mounties' actions would follow McDougall's words. Within days, Macleod himself led a party to Pine Coulee and found barrels of whisky that were proof enough of the accusations. Macleod had the spirits spilled out onto the ground. In addition, their trade goods, including 100 buffalo robes and 16 horses, were confiscated. The two men were arrested and one, who could not pay his fine, was placed in jail.

When word came in late November that the Red Coat chief was anxious to meet with the Blackfoot chiefs, Crowfoot was pleased. On December 1, Macleod and his officers met with the Blackfoot chiefs at a grand council. Macleod spoke first.

"I am James Macleod, the representative of the Grandmother in these parts," he said through his interpreter. "I have asked you here so that you might know our mission. I want there to be no misunderstanding about the law of the Grandmother, which we have come to enforce.

"The Grandmother has laws that must be obeyed by whites and Indians alike. There is to be no killing and no stealing. And that includes horses. Women and children are not to be harmed. If the laws are broken, the culprit," Macleod paused briefly for emphasis, "and let me say again that it makes no difference if he is Indian or white—will be punished. No one will be punished for something done that he did not know was wrong. Obey the laws of the Red Coats. They are there for your protection.

"Some of you might be afraid that we have come to take the land. That is not our objective," assured Macleod. "We simply want to ensure that all who live here can do so in peace."

Those were words that appealed to Crowfoot, ones that reflected his own outlook. He rose and shook hands with Macleod and the other officers in the room. Then he bared his arm, a sign of his own peaceful intent, and responded to Macleod's speech.

"I look to the Sun," he began as he lifted his hand skyward, "and thank it for telling the Grandmother to send these Red Coats. I thank the Red Coats for coming. Their words are what we want to hear," Crowfoot declared. "Their actions are what we want to see. The traders' liquor has been more devastating than enemy rifles. The Red Coats can save us from them. Then we may have peace. That is what my heart also desires."

The council concluded with both parties on good terms. Crowfoot believed that in Macleod he had found a man of his own heart, and it was the beginning of a friendship between the two. The Siksika chief immediately began to enforce the rules of the Red Coats. He forbade his young warriors to raid enemy tribes. Generally, his authority prevailed, especially since there was no longer alcohol to fuel Siksika aggression. Occasionally, however, his directions fell victim to the rashness of youth and they raided anyway. When he discovered this, Crowfoot had the stolen horses returned to their rightful owners, a course of action that could not have been imagined a few years before. To sooth the ruffled feathers of the braves, Crowfoot

replaced the horses he had taken with those from his own
herd. The Red Coats were not long on the prairies before
the violence of the Whoop-Up days was a fading memory.

Peace, however, brought a new problem to the Natives.
It made the prairies more attractive for settlement. Aware
that the Mounties effectively guaranteed their safety, Métis
and white settlers began moving onto the territory that had
once been traditionally Blackfoot. In the mid-1870s their
numbers weren't great, but Crowfoot and the other
Blackfoot leaders were concerned. Already the buffalo herds
were noticeably smaller in size, and the hunts were not as
bountiful as in previous years. If settlers chose to move into
Blackfoot hunting territory, they would prove a further
disruption. Without the buffalo it would be impossible to
maintain the Blackfoot way of life. In the summer of 1875,
Crowfoot took the problem to John McDougall.

"Your situation is not unlike that of the Indians who live
in the eastern parts of Canada. Treaties were signed that set
land aside for them and ensured that their rights would be
respected," explained McDougall. "It will be the case here.
In due time, treaties will be made and a settled condition
created in this country wherein justice will be given to all."

A few weeks later, a representative of the Canadian government came to confirm McDougall's comments. Near
Blackfoot Crossing, Crowfoot met the commander of the
Canadian militia, Major General E. Selby-Smyth, who was
on a tour of the West. Selby-Smith advised Crowfoot that
"his government's objective was to deal fairly with all tribes
in Her Majesty's domain and to extend uniform justice to
the Indians of the Plains."

Crowfoot found some comfort in such words. Certainly
the efforts of the Red Coats suggested that these newcomers meant what they said. But, as leader of his people,
Crowfoot had a responsibility to ensure that their interests

would be observed, and he wanted more than the rather vague assurances of McDougall and Selby-Smyth. He wanted a commitment from the Grandmother that would identify exactly what she would do to address their concerns. In the fall of 1875, Crowfoot called a council of the Blackfoot so that they might discuss protection of their interests. Fifteen chiefs gathered, including the five head chiefs. The document they drafted was translated and forwarded to Lieutenant-Governor Alexander Morris, the Queen's representative in western Canada. It emphasized the increasing immigration and subsequent loss of hunting territory. It also noted that the missionaries and Mounties were respected for their important services and that they continued to be welcome.

The chiefs' petition requested that a representative of the Grandmother come west to discuss Blackfoot concerns. Clearly, for some of the Blackfoot, this meant making treaty. Crowfoot's positive experiences with the Red Coats and missionaries suggested to him that the Grandmother could be trusted. However, others among the Blackfoot were not convinced that a treaty meant anything significant to the white man. Despite disagreement over what might come of the proposed meeting, there was consensus among the Blackfoot that the meeting itself was desirable. In 1876, when it became known that the Cree had made treaty, demand intensified. At that time, however, the Canadian government was suddenly preoccupied with a new Native problem. Word was that the Hunkpapa Sioux chief Sitting Bull was actively seeking to form an alliance with the Blackfoot, an alliance that would attack white settlers both above and below the Medicine Line (the international boundary).

The problems of Sitting Bull and his Sioux people with the United States had been mounting for some years. In

1868, the Sioux had made treaty with the United States, but American prospectors and settlers soon broke the Fort Laramie Treaty, as it was known, when they traveled onto reserve land. The Sioux harassed the newcomers, and the American government ordered that they return to their reserves or be considered enemies of the United States. Sitting Bull and his followers were among those who chose not to obey the directive. To bolster the Sioux's chances in a war with the American army, Sitting Bull appealed to neighboring tribes to join his people in the resistance. In late spring 1875, a Sioux runner arrived at Crowfoot's camp.

"Sitting Bull sends this tobacco as a peace offering," he explained. Had Crowfoot smoked it, he would be committed to war. He placed it on the ground.

"Though we are many days' travel from the land of the Sioux, the deeds of the great Sitting Bull are well known and highly spoken of here," replied Crowfoot.

"Sitting Bull invites you to cross the Medicine Line to join the Sioux in their fight against the Wasichu. You will get horses, mules and white women prisoners for your efforts. After the Wasichus and their Crow allies have been defeated, Sitting Bull pledges to come to the land of the Grandmother and join the Blackfoot in their war against the white man. The Red Coats are few and will be easily defeated," the messenger suggested.

"I cannot offer Blackfoot support until I know the views of my fellow Blackfoot chiefs," replied Crowfoot. He was not interested in joining Sitting Bull's fight, and he suspected the other Blackfoot chiefs would share his position. But he wanted there to be no doubt when he responded to the request.

The runner returned a few weeks later, and Crowfoot informed him that the tobacco would not be accepted. The Blackfoot would not fight the white men.

"Sitting Bull has many followers. When they have killed the Wasichus, they will cross the Medicine Line and kill the Red Coats and the Blackfoot for their refusal," promised the messenger.

The threat was troubling because the Sioux formed a large nation. As it happened, an inspector of the Mounties who was on patrol arrived in Crowfoot's camp soon after the Sioux messenger left. Crowfoot put the question directly to Cecil Denny.

"Will the Red Coats help us if the Sioux attack?"

"The Blackfoot are subjects of the Grandmother. As such, they can always expect the protection of the Mounties," confirmed Denny.

Crowfoot nodded. "And, if the Sioux attack the whites, as they have pledged to do, the Blackfoot will help. Two thousand warriors will join the battle."

Crowfoot continued with a somewhat surprising and very frank assessment of the future his people faced.

"We all see that the day is coming when the buffalo will all be killed, and we shall have nothing more to live on. Then you will come into our camp and see the poor Blackfoot starving. I know that the heart of the white soldier will be sorry for us, and they will go and tell the Grandmother, who will not let her children starve.

"We are getting shut in. The Cree are coming into our country from the north and the white men from the south and east. They are destroying our means of living. Although we plainly see these days coming, we will not join the Sioux against the whites but will depend upon you to help us," reasserted Crowfoot.

The Canadian government was grateful to hear of Crowfoot's loyalty. Queen Victoria directed that Crowfoot be thanked for his commitment. His decision was soon to become even more important. In the summer of 1876, Sitting

Bull and his followers defeated General George Custer and
the Seventh Cavalry at the Battle of Little Bighorn. By
March 1877, most of the victorious Sioux had fled into
Canada just east of the Cypress Hills, where the Mounties
promised them that they might live peacefully—though
temporarily—as long as they obeyed the laws. Sitting Bull
and his people, starving and tired of war, agreed. He also
thought that he might gain some influence with the Red
Coats if he could ensure the friendship of Crowfoot,
a known ally of the Mounties. To that end, Sitting Bull
again sent the Siksika chief an offering of tobacco.
Crowfoot accepted the tobacco, but informed the runner
that he would not smoke it until Sitting Bull made clear his
intentions. Some weeks later Sitting Bull visited Crowfoot's
camp. They smoked together, and when Crowfoot was
confident that Sitting Bull was no longer interested in
pursuing the violent course of action he had previously
suggested, a friendship was formed. The relationship was
recognized with a friendship dance, in which both the
Sioux and Siksika participated.

News of Sitting Bull's activities caused great concern in
the United States, where many concluded that he was
forming an alliance that would be used to attack those in
his old homeland. Perhaps Canadian officials were also
worried, despite Crowfoot's pledge of allegiance. In the
fading days of the summer of 1877, the Canadian government ordered the new lieutenant-governor, David Laird,
and Assistant Commissioner Macleod of the North-West
Mounted Police to organize a treaty meeting with the
Blackfoot (and some adjacent tribes). The negotiations got
off to a poor start because the Blood refused to participate.
Macleod had originally proposed that the treaty council
meet at Fort Macleod, but Crowfoot objected because he
did not want such an undertaking to occur in a white

man's fort. Macleod consented and suggested Blackfoot Crossing as the location.

The problem was that Blackfoot Crossing was wholly in Siksika territory. Macleod did not see the problem, for he considered Crowfoot to be the leader of all Blackfoot. He wasn't. Although he was the most vocal about peace and often spoke on behalf of his people to the white men, Red Crow, a Blood chief, actually held greater influence in tribal decisions. Crowfoot recognized his importance, and when Laird outlined the government's treaty offer at the council, he declared he would not make a decision until the Blood arrived and he could consult with Red Crow. A couple of weeks passed before they arrived, and until that time, the treaty was in doubt. Red Crow, however, supported it.

On September 21, after many nights of discussion with his people, Crowfoot addressed the treaty commission:

While I speak, be kind and patient. I have to speak for my people, who are numerous, and who rely upon me to follow that course which in the future will tend to their good. The plains are large and wide. We are the children of the plains; it is our home and the buffalo has been our food always. I hope you look upon the Siksika, Blood and Sarcee as your children now and that you will be indulgent and charitable to them. They all expect me to speak now for them, and I trust the good spirits will put into their breasts to be a good people—into the minds of men, women and children and their future generations.

The advice given me and my people has proved to be very good. If the police had not come to the country, where would we all be now? Bad men and whisky were killing us all so fast that very few of us, indeed, would have been left today. The Police have protected us as the feathers of the

A painting by A.B. Stapleton of the 1877 Treaty 7 Council. Crowfoot speaks to Lieutenant-Governor David Laird.

bird protect it from the frosts of winter. I wish them all good, and I trust that all our hearts will increase in goodness from this time forward. I am satisfied. I will sign the treaty.

All the head chiefs, even those who had reservations, signed what became known as Treaty 7. Crowfoot believed that the Blackfoot would remain strongest if they occupied a shared reserve, and at his insistence, they were granted one along the Bow River. Land was distributed on a predetermined ratio: one square mile for each family of five. Also included were annual payments that amounted to a few thousand dollars a year and an offer of cattle (or farming implements) so that the Blackfoot might make a transition to ranching once the buffalo were gone. In return, the Blackfoot ceded 50,000 square miles (the Blackfoot retained the right to hunt in the area as long as they did

not molest the settlers) and pledged to obey Canadian law.
The Blackfoot chiefs were given medals and Union Jack
flags, and the negotiations closed with the Mountie band's
rendition of *God Save the Queen*.

The great shared reserve that Crowfoot envisioned was
not to be. Shortly after the treaty council, Red Crow
informed Macleod that the Blood wanted to have their
own reserve farther south. Realizing that a geographic
division of the Blackfoot would undermine their unity
and lessen their strength, Macleod quickly agreed. Crowfoot
also saw this and he visited Macleod to express his anger.
Perhaps, suggested Macleod, his decision was a violation of
the treaty, perhaps not, but he would not force the Blood
onto a reserve that they did not want. To Crowfoot, it
appeared as if the Red Coats were unduly interfering in
Blackfoot matters, and he did not like it.

Such political problems were quickly overshadowed by
more pressing concerns. The late 1870s saw the virtual disappearance of the buffalo from the Canadian prairies. The
reasons were numerous, but the most significant one was
the American policy to slaughter the buffalo in an effort
to bring the Plains Natives in the United States under
control. One result of this was that shrinking herds no
longer migrated north in significant numbers. Without the
food source, many Siksika were on the verge of starvation.
Government rations were forthcoming, but they were
inadequate. Crowfoot heard rumors of buffalo in Montana,
and in the fall of 1880, he decided to take his people there.

The Blackfoot found only misery below the Medicine
Line. Local residents protested their presence. Some saw
Crowfoot as just another murderous Indian, waiting for an
opportunity to go on the warpath. Ranchers claimed the
Blackfoot were raiding their cattle herds and urged
Montanans to stand up and fight for their property and

rights. It is likely that cattle were killed because Crowfoot's people were starving, and he had to ensure that they were fed. Without the orderly presence of the Mounties, the Siksika were again subject to the liquor trade. The booze peddlers soon owned what few trade goods the Natives possessed, including most of their horses. The final assault on Native well-being came in the form of a mumps epidemic. Weakened by hunger and poverty, many Siksika fell victim to the disease, including Iron Shield, Crowfoot's only full brother.

By the spring of 1881, there was still no sign of the buffalo, so Crowfoot took his people farther south. They made it to the Musselshell River, unfamiliar territory well beyond the traditional range of the Siksika. Still, they found no buffalo. Because resources were so scarce, Crowfoot was forced to divide up his tribe. Some wandered back to Canada, desperate for rations. Crowfoot decided to lead those thousand or so who remained with him towards the Yellowstone River, but they met only with trouble there. A Siksika hunting party returned to camp with a herd of 70 horses, taken from the Crow. Such a raid once brought honors, but no longer. These horses had been taken from a Crow reservation that was under the protection of the American government. Crowfoot knew that the army would soon be in pursuit.

In the hope of preventing retaliation, Crowfoot and some of his most trusted followers took the herd back to an army post. There he learned that several cavalry companies had been already dispatched to deal with the situation. Their orders were uncompromising: "move those Indians or bury them." Crowfoot did not want the blood of his people on his hands, so when he returned to camp, he directed his followers to prepare to return to Canada. Most were forced to walk; they were ragged, emaciated figures who carried their few remaining belongings on their backs. They traveled for more than a month before they crossed into Canada and reached Fort Walsh in the Cypress Hills. The Mounties gave them rations but ordered them to move on; the Sioux were in the region, and trouble had to be avoided. They finally reached Fort Macleod in August. During the entire journey, not one buffalo had been seen. Fears were confirmed as reality. The Blackfoot could no longer depend on the animal that the Sun had provided as the foundation for their way of life. For many Blackfoot it mattered little. Since 1879, some 1000 had died.

Those who survived found themselves fully dependent on the rations provided by the Indian Department, a government agency responsible for Natives. It was not a pleasant situation for the Blackfoot. Indian Department employees had little respect for their charges, who often found themselves scorned and belittled. Rations tended to be of an inferior quality and were rarely enough to adequately meet their needs (limited quantities saved the government money). The Blackfoot had a difficult time adjusting to beef, which they found too sweet, but when the meat ration was changed to pork (a meat unfamiliar to the Blackfoot), most rejected it outright. The Siksika also found that they were charged for goods—notably the head and offal of the cattle—that they believed the treaty guaranteed to be free. Conditions were so desperate that the women fought over discarded flour sacks from which they might make clothing.

In September 1881, Crowfoot and the other chiefs were presented with an unexpected opportunity to take their concerns to the Canadian government when the Indian Commissioner Edgar Dewdney and the Marquis of Lorne (the governor general of Canada) visited the reserve on a tour of the West. The governor general's party brought with it a good omen; their guide was Poundmaker. Crowfoot had not seen his adopted son in many years and was pleased to see him a tall, strong warrior, unharmed by the hunger and poverty that had ravaged his own people. The two were able to spend some time together, and Crowfoot learned that Poundmaker was a chief, his band living near Battleford (Saskatchewan). Lord Lorne extended a formal invitation to the Blackfoot chiefs to meet with him. They accepted, and the Blackfoot arrived at the camp in traditional formation. The chiefs and warriors led the party, riding the few bony horses they still had, amidst gunfire and shouting, as if they were preparing for battle. The women and children followed. None could fail to notice, however, that the Blackfoot were not the people they had been a handful of years before.

Led by Crowfoot, the chiefs walked to the governor general's tent, each carrying a Union Jack, symbolic of their loyalty. To reinforce the peaceful relationship, they smoked the sacred pipe. Then each of the chiefs spoke. Crowfoot addressed the gathering last, his words little different from those spoken by the others. Rising, he shook hands with Lord Lorne. Then, ensuring that his Victoria medal was visible on his ragged clothing, he leaned heavily on his staff and made his plea.

The buffalo are gone. Perhaps it is true what we have heard and that the Sun made a hole into which they disappeared. It must have been a big hole, for there were once so many, the plains were brown with their number. My people have nothing. We are starving. The wail of those who mourn for our dead is always heard. We need food if they are to be silenced.

But food is not enough. We were once a proud people, a people who looked to no others for our keep. We wish to be that way again. But how can we be self-sufficient in this strange world without buffalo? Show us the way.

"The old days are gone," sighed the governor general, who had heard similar pleas in other Native camps. He had yet to feel any compassion. "The Blackfoot can no longer wander the plains in search of food. Turn your efforts instead to breaking the land. Your future lies in farming."

"I shall take your advice," replied Crowfoot. "I have been first in fighting; I shall now be first in working." As a chief, he had a responsibility to lead the way.

Neither the governor general nor the Indian commissioner made any effort to deal with the poor and often dishonest treatment of the Blackfoot by government agents. The problem simmered, and Crowfoot's efforts to keep a lid on it challenged his skills. Many young Siksika were anxious to attack those who treated them with such disdain. Crowfoot counseled peace. He continued to use diplomatic channels to deal with the situation, but the local farm instructor (the most prominent government official on the reserve) and the Indian agent (who delivered the annuities, but who also lived in Fort Macleod) were unreceptive and began calling him a troublemaker. The pot finally boiled over in early January 1882.

Bull Elk, a minor Blackfoot chief, purchased a steer head for $1. While he waited for his wife to help him carry the head home, the piece was sold to a different Native. When Bull Elk finally tried to take it, he was told he couldn't. In anger and frustration, Bull Elk fired a couple of rounds at the ration house, whereupon the Mounties arrested him. As three Mounties tried to escort the prisoner back to the guardhouse, they found their way blocked by Blackfoot. Inspector Francis Dickens, the Mountie in charge, was knocked to the ground. The situation was rapidly turning ugly. The only hope was that the Blackfoot would pull back, but that did not seem likely. At that moment, Crowfoot arrived. He had heard of the dispute and was as angry as the other Blackfoot.

"The warriors have told me why you hold Bull Elk. I want to hear it from your lips," demanded Crowfoot.

Dickens explained the situation.

"He is innocent!" Crowfoot barked in reply. "You have no cause to arrest him!"

Dickens submitted to Crowfoot's demand that Bull Elk be set free. Crowfoot agreed to release him when it was time for a trial, but only after the chief had first been consulted. The situation defused, Dickens then sent to Fort Calgary for reinforcements. Inspector Crozier soon arrived. He wasted little time in making the arrest. Crowfoot, incensed that the Red Coat had entered his village and taken Bull Elk without even the promised consultation, set off in pursuit of Crozier with a couple of hundred warriors.

On reaching them, he demanded, "Do you intend to fight?"

"Certainly not," replied Crozier, "unless you commence it."

Crowfoot evaluated the situation. It would be easy to kill the Red Coats and free Bull Elk, but that would not be the end of the matter. Rations would stop and many more Red Coats would come. Crowfoot agreed to let the party continue on if he could accompany them and witness the trial. Crozier consented.

Crowfoot's old friend James Macleod, who had since retired from the Mounties and served as a district magistrate, subsequently sentenced Bull Elk to two weeks in the guardhouse. The punishment was for firing his rifle in a threatening manner, as Macleod agreed that there had been no cause to arrest him in the first place. The whole affair soured Crowfoot's relations with the Mounties. They had treated Bull Elk unfairly, differently than they would have treated a white man in similar circumstances, and he never trusted the Mounties again.

The episode did, however, bring change to the workings of government officials on the reserve. Edgar Dewdney had been promoted to the position of lieutenant-governor of the North-West Territories while maintaining his position as Indian commissioner. To relieve the tensions, he replaced an unpopular farm instructor with a retired Mountie who was liked by the Blackfoot. Cecil Denny, another retired Mountie, was appointed the new Indian agent. Denny's work had often brought him into contact with the Blackfoot, and he had a good understanding of their problems and a willingness to address them. He replaced the offensive practices of the old regime with more just ones. The Blackfoot responded. In his report at the end of 1883, Denny noted that the Blackfoot had turned in 1100 sacks of potatoes for storage and future use. Crowfoot, he added, set the example by growing his own crops of turnips and potatoes.

Still, signs showed that the goodwill nurtured in the months following Denny's appointment would not be allowed to mature. In the spring of 1883, surveyors from the Canadian Pacific Railway arrived and began marking the route for the new line. Although it did not cross Blackfoot territory, it came uncomfortably close. Rumors had it that the markers indicated where new white settlers would build their houses. When Crowfoot expressed his displeasure, Dewdney himself came and held council to ease Blackfoot fears. He convinced Crowfoot that the railroad would be beneficial for his people because it would ensure that rations could be quickly accessed in times of need. Crowfoot eventually agreed to remove his opposition to the line, but some among his own people thought he had been bribed to do it (an accusation for which there is no evidence).

Adding to the problems were new orders (in 1884) from the government in Ottawa. Rations were to be cut, and the

Blackfoot were not allowed to leave their reservation. Denny resigned in protest, but his action did not delay policy implementation. The reduction in rations cut costs, but they were also designed to strengthen the order that forbade Blackfoot travel. Perhaps, it was reasoned, hungry Natives would be more obedient. By 1884, there was good reason to keep the Blackfoot submissive and isolated on their reserves. Louis Riel was again actively promoting rebellion, and no one had forgotten the success he had enjoyed 15 years earlier.

Bear's Head, a Métis, arrived at Blackfoot Crossing with Riel's message. He was returning to Canada to lead the Natives in a fight to regain their lands. Crowfoot had little time to consider it because the Mounted Police soon arrived to arrest Bear's Head. Crowfoot objected to the harsh treatment of his guest, but when the Mounties agreed that he could accompany the party to Fort Calgary for the trial, Crowfoot submitted to the arrest. Bear's Head was acquitted of the charge of disturbing the peace, but he was asked to leave the district. Crowfoot considered this to be unjust. Innocent men did not have conditions placed on them. It seemed just another example of the white man's increasingly dishonorable treatment of Natives. It was wrong. Crowfoot had had enough. It was time to seriously consider Riel's proposal.

Word of the mounting unrest on the Blackfoot reserves had reached Lieutenant-Governor Dewdney, who was well aware of the potential cost of suppressing a rebellion. The Dominion government could not afford to pay for it, nor could they afford to lose potential settlers who would undoubtedly be turned off by the bloodshed. In a move that demonstrated something of his shrewdness, he invited Crowfoot and the other leading chiefs to visit Winnipeg. At the time, the population of the city was 22,000.

Crowfoot was faced with the sobering reality of the white presence.

"They are as plentiful as flies in the summertime," he observed. "It is useless to oppose them."

Dewdney further defused the situation by persuading Denny to reassume his position as Indian agent. His first act was to double the rations, thereby removing another major Blackfoot grievance.

As the first months of 1885 slipped by and rumblings of the Native resistance became louder and suggested it was inevitable, Crowfoot was finally forced to choose sides. It was a difficult decision, one not helped by the fact that Poundmaker, his adopted son, was deeply enmeshed in the troubles. Crowfoot desperately wanted to help him, and mounting pressures to do just that came from the more militant among his own people and the Cree, who threatened to attack the Blackfoot if they did not join in their cause. But Crowfoot remained worried that fighting was not in the best interests of his people. He remembered the large numbers of whites he had seen in the eastern cities. He could look to the north and see the new railroad that could quickly bring many soldiers.

As he thought about what to do, word came that violence had erupted near Duck Lake, Saskatchewan. A decision had to be made. Crowfoot sent word to the other Blackfoot chiefs, asking them of their decisions. Two of the most influential, Red Crow and Eagle Tail, were opposed to fighting. Crowfoot had not long received their words when Dewdney visited his camp, seeking a council. Crowfoot, who trusted Dewdney, agreed and the meeting took place in mid-April.

"I have come to pledge my government's support to the Blackfoot," declared Dewdney, his eyes scanning numerous minor chiefs in attendance. "I have heard the Cree threats, but I promise that the Dominion government will protect its faithful subjects. You must shut your ears to any rumors that the Cree will attack you.

"Soldiers, who even as we speak are arriving in this country, will not hurt the Blackfoot," assured Dewdney. "They come to punish the bad Indians for killing the whites. The Blackfoot have nothing to fear as long as they remain faithful to their treaty."

Crowfoot rose and shook hands with Dewdney and his associates.

"I pledge my loyalty to the Grandmother. I promise that my people will not cause the government any harm.

"If the government wants to help the Blackfoot," he added, "my people are ready to do all they can. Although I am but one chief, I will do my utmost to ensure that no Blackfoot raises a rifle against the white man."

Dewdney left, confident with Crowfoot's word. His confidence was not misplaced. When hostilities intensified in May 1885 and many of the younger Blackfoot advocated joining their Native brothers, Crowfoot would not accede to their demands. Some grumbled that more interested in keeping the goodwill of the whites than he was in supporting the Native cause. But Crowfoot had concluded that his people would be best served if they remained neutral. The North-West Rebellion did not enjoy the success of the one 15 years earlier; the fighting was over by June. Those Blackfoot who doubted Crowfoot's leadership had come to share his view. The white population also praised Crowfoot and hailed him for his loyalty.

Despite his increased popularity, all was not well in the months following the rebellion. Crowfoot, whose health had been deteriorating for some time, was confined to bed. Another of his children died, and others would soon fall to tuberculosis. Just as devastating was the news that Poundmaker was imprisoned for his activities during the rebellion.

Crowfoot thought the imprisonment unjustified, and he was pleased that Dewdney was working to have Poundmaker's three-year term shortened. His efforts were partly exerted in recognition of Crowfoot's loyalty during the rebellion. Dewdney was also motivated by Poundmaker's own poor health. He was afraid the chief might die in jail and thus foment unrest. He was set free in March 1886, and he managed to visit Crowfoot before he died in July.

Crowfoot received an unexpected visitor in late 1886. While on a tour of the West on the inaugural run of the Canadian Pacific Railway, Prime Minister John A. Macdonald stopped at the reserve. The visit was short, but the prime minister invited Crowfoot to visit him in Ottawa. Although he was weak, Crowfoot accepted and made his way there later that year. While he traveled with other chiefs (including Red Crow) who had been loyal to the Canadian government during the rebellion, Crowfoot received the kindest accolades. As the chiefs toured eastern Canada, he was lauded at every stop. When he finally reached Macdonald's house in mid-October, he took time to give one of his few speeches.

> *We have come a long way to see you at your house and our own are far, far off. We remember you both* [the prime minister and his wife] *when you came to our land this summer. We had a good feeling there, and the lady gave our people money and presents. We hope the Great Chief will think of our people. Since the white man came, the buffalo have gone away, and now we need to be helped by the white chiefs. We want big farms, but what shall we do with what we cannot eat? I see this morning that you do not forget your own people—they sell what they do not want. That is what my people want to do.*

Macdonald assured him that all would turn out well in the end as long as the Blackfoot remained peaceful and patient. The prime minister then pressed Crowfoot to continue touring eastern Canada, but he was too ill. He returned to his reserve, pleased that he had had an opportunity to speak for his people and to let the Great Chief know that they wanted only the fair treatment given to the white man. Crowfoot also returned with the certainty that he had chosen the right path for his people. They would never have been able to defeat the great numbers of white men he had seen in the east.

Crowfoot lived a few more years, but he never fully recovered. He continued to promote the Blackfoot Confederacy, occasionally traveling to other reserves. He advised the Blackfoot to adapt to their new lives. Weak as he was, he hoed his field until he was forced to his deathbed. Before he died he thanked the government for aiding his people and to Lieutenant-Governor Dewdney in particular. His last words were ones of courage and beauty.

"A little while and Crowfoot will be gone from among you; whither we cannot tell. From nowhere we come, into nowhere we go. What is life? It is as the flash of a firefly in the night. It is as a breath of a buffalo in the winter-time. It is as the little shadow that runs across the grass and loses itself in the sunset. I have spoken."

Crowfoot died on April 25, 1890. His body was dressed in full ceremonial clothing, and all his personal possessions were placed with him in his coffin. A Roman Catholic priest read the burial beside a local Catholic cemetery near the Bow River. While the Indian agent wanted the coffin buried, the Blackfoot objected. As a compromise, the top of the coffin was left exposed and a small log house was built over it for protection.

CHAPTER FIVE

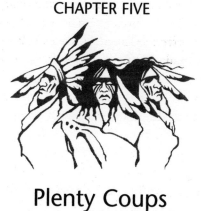

Plenty Coups

Mountain Crow, 1849–1932

IN THE HEAVY RAIN of a yet another chilly, gray late summer's day in 1876, a sprawling column of more than 1000 weary American cavalry headed for the Black Hills under the command of General George Crook. Crook was a Native fighter who had earned his stars battling the Apache and other Southwestern tribes. Those in the middle and at the end of the column trudged through the sucking path muddied by those at the fore. They'd been on the move for over a month, searching for Sioux north of the Black Hills. They hadn't even found cold fire pits, and their supplies were rapidly dwindling. Hungry, cold and tired, the men mostly rode or walked in silence, having long since discovered that cursing the situation made no difference.

Crook couldn't do much about the weather, but he was determined to address the supply issue. He sent Captain Anson Mills and an advance party to the Black Hills to return with some food. Within a day Mills stumbled on

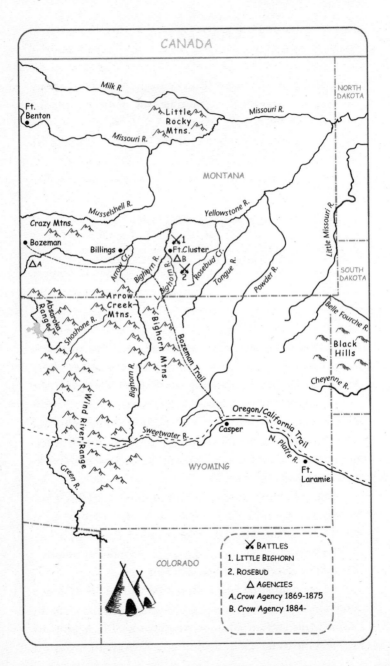

CANADA

NORTH DAKOTA

Milk R.

Ft. Benton

Little Rocky Mtns.

Missouri R.

Missouri R.

MONTANA

Musselshell R.

Yellowstone R.

Crazy Mtns.

Bozeman

Billings

×1 Ft. Cluster
△B
×2

Arrow Cr.

Bighorn R.

Bighorn R.

Rosebud Cr.

Tongue R.

Powder R.

Little Missouri R.

SOUTH DAKOTA

△A

Arrow Creek Mtns.

Absaroka Range

Shoshone R.

Bighorn Mtns.

Bighorn R.

Bozeman Trail

Belle Fourche R.

Black Hills

Cheyenne R.

Wind River Range

Sweetwater R.

Casper

Oregon/California Trail

Green R.

WYOMING

N. Platte R.

Ft. Laramie

COLORADO

× BATTLES
1. LITTLE BIGHORN
2. ROSEBUD
△ AGENCIES
A. Crow Agency 1869-1875
B. Crow Agency 1884-

a small camp of Miniconjou Sioux. He gave the order to attack. Within hours, Crook arrived with the main body of his command. By then, many more Sioux had come because runners had carried word of the Wasichus to adjacent camps. Among their number was Sitting Bull, and rumored to be nearby were Crazy Horse and Spotted Eagle. The battle continued until dusk when both sides fell back under the shelter of night. Crook was in his tent preparing his strategy for the next day when a junior officer interrupted him.

"Sir, this Indian scout wants to speak to you. Won't say what it's about, but claims it's important. Name's Plenty Coups."

Crook recognized the man who stood next to the officer. He was one of the more important Crow scouts. His tribe was friendly with the United States. They had been for two or three generations, ever since the first treaty made in the 1820s. Along with the Pawnee and the Shoshone, the Crow often scouted for the cavalry. The relationship served both parties well: the army benefited from the Natives' intimate knowledge of the land, and the Natives were able to continue to wage war against their traditional—and America's new—enemy, the Sioux. Crook dragged his hand through his hair and sighed. Tired as he was, the general knew that he must meet him.

"Plenty Coups, it is good to see you. What news do you bring?"

"Three Stars, army must retreat."

"Retreat?"

"Only defeat will be found here."

"That's hardly likely. We outnumber them. We're better armed."

"On this day, it will not be enough to defeat the Sioux."

"Well, what will?"

Plenty Coups fell silent. He reflected on the day's battle. As always, he had fought hard against the Sioux. To him they were more than longtime tribal foes. When Plenty Coups was not yet a man, they had killed his older brother during an unsuccessful Crow raid. In later years, he had avenged that death. He followed his success with other raids, where a young Crow warrior could prove his bravery. A memory of one such battle had resurfaced earlier during the day's battle, amidst the smoke from the firing rifles and burning Miniconjou village.

Plenty Coups remembered the time he led 20 Crow towards the winter camp of the Sioux on the Bighorn River. He carried the pipe and he kept spirits high with songs of bravery and war. When they finally found signs of the enemy, Plenty Coups fell silent, slipped into a wolf hide and crept to the top of a nearby hill. He howled, confident that against the pale moon any observer would surely take him for the gray animal. He finally spotted the Sioux party and scampered down the hill to inform his fellow braves. Plenty Coups outlined the plan of attack. They would take horses and scalps and count coup (strike the enemy with coup sticks). It would be a great victory. And it was. Plenty Coups had led the Crow into the Sioux camp, where his great war whoop caught the enemy by surprise. Whistling arrows soon gave way to thudding war clubs and slashing knives. On that day Plenty Coups' bravery had gone unmatched. Alone, he had advanced on four Sioux who had taken shelter in a nearby cave. Using rocks and trees as shields, Plenty Coups dodged the raining arrows and skipped to the cave until he was close enough to count coup on one of the Sioux. It was the bravest act a Crow could perform. He returned to his village to great honor and celebration.

But on this day, north of the Black Hills with Three Stars' army, there had been no counting coup, no honor

Plenty Coups, age 31. He had a reputation as both a warrior and a thoughtful leader.

achieved with acts of bravery. Perhaps, he thought, it was the way of tomorrow. Even at the age of 27, Plenty Coups sensed that the traditional ways of a warrior were disappearing. Courage was now found in an ability and willingness to adapt to a changing world. His dreams had told him to keep peace with the white man, dreams that revealed to him that his people would be best served through alliances with the powerful newcomers. It made sense. Who could argue that a grateful heart is not more generous? If he could so serve his Crow brothers and sisters, there was honor in that.

But it wasn't notions of service that took Plenty Coups to Crook's tent. He wasn't sure what it was.

"What will?" Crook again barked, growing impatient.

"On this day…perhaps nothing," Plenty Coups conceded. With that he left.

Once Crook was again alone in his tent, his eyes fell back to the papers that lay on the table in front of him. But he did not see what was there. Try as he might, he could not forget the words of Plenty Coups. Crook had not enjoyed great fortune against the Sioux. At the Battle of the Rosebud a few months previous, he had sent the attacking Sioux into retreat. Indeed, his men had suffered fewer losses than the Sioux. Yet, regardless of his description of the confrontation to his superiors, it was far from the victory he had anticipated. And he heard troubling rumors of a similar warning given to Custer by his scouts before he had ordered the Seventh Calvary to attack the Sioux at the Little Bighorn River. Custer had ignored their attempts to dissuade him and had died.

The next day, Crook turned his troops towards the Black Hills. He told others that he believed his men were too tired and hungry to wage effective battle. The Sioux continued to harass column's flanks as they departed, but the troops suffered no losses, and the harassment soon stopped. There are those who say that Crook's decision on that day saved his troops from the fate of the Seventh Calvary. It was a decision based on the advice of Plenty Coups.

~~~~~

Faces the Buffalo North (Plenty Coup's name as a child) ran with his older brother along the banks of Mission Creek, his dog nipping at his heels. Faces the Buffalo North could not keep up—he was only five and his brother was twice that age—but it didn't matter. They laughed as they ran, falling occasionally to the ground and wrestling in the tall grass. They had left the Crow camp early in the morning, before the sun was up, while the dew was heavy on the ground. When they told their mother that they planned to go hunting, she had enthusiastically prepared them a lunch of pemmican and dried elk meat. Faces the Buffalo North was excited, for it was his first journey away from camp.

"Look!" cried Faces the Buffalo North. "A beaver! Mother would be proud to roast its fatted tail tonight."

The brothers fell to their bellies and snaked towards the animal. Their desire, however, did not yet match their skill. The animal sensed the approach of the strange creatures and slipped lazily into the water beyond reach. With a laugh, they continued on, disturbing a resting flock of blackbirds and sending them scattering into the air. Faces the Buffalo North watched as his brother took his bow and let loose an arrow into the small black cloud. A pierced blackbird fell at the young boy's feet. Faces the Buffalo North smiled as he picked it up. His brother had been good with a bow and arrow for as long as he could remember. He had often seen him best older boys in the buffalo chip game, the object of which was to shoot an arrow closest to the center of the rolling chip. His brother would be a great warrior, and Faces the Buffalo North admired him. The older sibling also cared deeply for his brother, especially since their father was dead. While two uncles addressed the younger boy's education, he also took special care in watching over Faces the Buffalo North. Few relationships among the Crow were stronger than that of siblings.

The sun was dipping below the horizon when they finally made their way back to camp. The village was busy, more so than normal. The light of the fires, usually obscured by storytellers and their eager audiences, was cast deep into the camp, illuminating the people who were hurrying about. Some were sorting goods and packing gear. Others were dismantling hide tipis. They were preparing to move. Faces the Buffalo North ran to his mother's tipi and handed her the blackbird. Otter Woman smiled and sat down. She patted the robe next to her, bidding Faces the Buffalo North to sit next to her.

"Some day you will be a mighty hunter and will bring to our tipi much buffalo meat," she said. "It has been foretold. Let me tell you the story. Your grandfather had a dream. He saw you as a chief among our people. He saw you count many coups in your long life. For this reason, he said that your name will one day be Aleek-chea-ahoosh [Many Achievements or Plenty Coups]. It is a name to be proud of, but it is also one to be earned. Rest now, for tomorrow we move."

"Why mother?"

"It has to do with a treaty we have made with the white men."

Faces the Buffalo North crawled under his buffalo skin blanket. He was tired, and his eyes closed when his head hit the ground. As he dozed off, he could hear his mother singing the song that she often used to lull him to sleep.

Every day go out to fight the enemy,
Every day be very strong and brave.
Be fleet of foot,
And sure with bow and arrow.
Always make the enemy run.

The Crow were moving because tribal leaders had signed the Fort Laramie Treaty of 1851 with representatives of the United States government. Along with some Sioux, Cheyenne and Arapaho, the Crow agreed to cede an enormous amount of territory in the present-day states of Montana, Wyoming and North Dakota. In return, they were to receive an annuity of $50,000 (originally for 50 years, but later reduced by the American Senate to 10 years without either the knowledge or consent of the Natives) and reservations. The Crow reserve was 38.5 million acres in Montana and Wyoming, roughly bound by the Sweetwater River to the south, the Powder River to the east, the Musselshell River to the north and the Wind River Range to the west. It took some years for the treaty's terms to affect the band of Faces the Buffalo North and it was the mid-1850s before they moved.

The Crow—Absaroka (Bird People) as they called themselves—were a Siouan-speaking people who had split off from the Sioux in the late 18th century. Since that time, the Sioux and the Cheyenne had pushed them to the northwest into the traditional territory of the Blackfoot (who quickly became their enemies) and away from their ancestral home around the Black Hills.

Although they did not hesitate to raise the war club when necessary, the Crow accepted this relocation with resignation, perhaps because they considered their western migration preordained. Old Man Coyote, the creator/trickster of Crow legend, was said to have purposefully placed the Crow there. "They can fight the rest of the tribes," said Old Man Coyote. "They can have fun that way." While the Crow might have had fun, certainly their position relative to the hostile neighboring tribes, which greatly outnumbered them, ensured that they became determined warriors. Their bravery brought prosperity. They were said to have

more horses—a common indication of wealth among
Plains Natives—than any other tribe east of the Rocky
Mountains.

By the time Faces the Buffalo North was born in 1849,
the Crow were divided into two groups, River and
Mountain, based on little more than geographic preference.
His people were the Mountain Crow, and they lived mostly
in the high terrain between the Musselshell and the
Yellowstone rivers. Faces the Buffalo North was born
there, on the southern fringe of that range in the Crazy
Mountains (near present-day Billings, Montana). The Crow
were further divided into clans. During Faces the Buffalo
North's early years, 13 clans roamed the Plains, each named
after some characteristic or event associated with its members. He was a Burnt Mouth by birth, but after the death of
his father, he was raised by the Newly Made Lodges. He
was born into a people still reeling from a series of disasters
suffered in the first half of the 19th century. The split with
the Sioux had not been amicable, and in 1822 the Sioux
and their Cheyenne allies attacked the Crow main camp.
The men were away and it's said that thousands of Crow
women, children and old men died. Some 400 more were
taken captive. In the 1830s, Crow numbers were further
ravaged by a smallpox epidemic. By the 1850s, their numbers
were reduced to no more than 3600.

Faces the Buffalo North was also born into a people
who already possessed a tradition of good relations with
the United States government. While the first recorded
encounters with the white man did not occur until 1802,
by 1825 the Crow had made a peace treaty with the
Atkinson expedition out of St. Louis. The government
pledged to protect the Crow, a pledge they were surely
happy to receive given their decimating 1822 encounter
with the Sioux and the Cheyenne.

As a young boy, Faces the Buffalo North would have
had many opportunities to play games that honed the skills
necessary to be a Crow warrior. An especially popular
game was magpie, which saw boys cover themselves in
mud, sneak into camp to steal meat and return to the forest
to eat their plunder. Undoubtedly the attack was often
imagined to be a raid on a Sioux camp. Older boys followed on the buffalo hunt, which provided the Crow with
their main source of food (and a great deal of their other
equipment). They couldn't participate in the hunt itself, but
once the men were finished, boys were permitted to roam
the area in search of orphaned calves. If a boy was successful in bringing one down, he might give its skin to
a favored young girl. She might otherwise receive the hair
of a wolf or coyote in tribute as a makeshift scalp. Most
hunting was done on horseback, so from infancy, the boys
knew the feel of a trotting horse. But it wasn't skills alone
that prepared boys for manhood. Also important were the
stories that explained Crow culture and set down moral
precepts. The transmission of such knowledge was not
pedantic, and boys listened undoubtedly with glee to the
colorful exploits of Old Man Coyote or to the adventures
described in the many Crow hero tales.

One of the most important rituals in the extended transition into adulthood was a boy's vision quest. A vision
quest was an undertaking in search of a personal revelation,
a blessing that might be used for the good of the community. Faces the Buffalo North was about nine years old
when he made his first attempt. He may have seemed
young, but he was motivated by the recent news of his
brother's death. He was killed along the Powder River during a raid on the Sioux. Perhaps Faces the Buffalo North
hoped that a spiritual Helper might visit him and give him
the power necessary for successful revenge. It was early

spring and the cool dampness fought with the first of the year's warm breezes when he set out. Travel was difficult for he was still weak from the loss of blood caused by the self-inflicted wounds made as he mourned his brother. Faces the Buffalo North went to a stream near the Crow camp, shattered the thinning layer of ice and slipped into the cold water. He bathed and drank deeply, both acts believed by the Crow to cleanse and bring good health. Refreshed, he made his way to the Buffalo's Heart Mountain, and after four days of fasting, a voice came to him and said that he had come to the wrong mountain. He returned to his camp, determined to try again.

Faces the Buffalo North was in camp for only a handful of days when he renewed his efforts to seek his first vision. As before, he purified himself, but on this occasion he took time to build a sweat lodge for cleansing his body once he reached the Little Rocky Mountains. Following tradition, he left the sweat lodge wearing moccasins only and carrying his buffalo robe. Nothing else was needed because neither food nor water was allowed to pass his lips. His body was covered with ashes and sage because he did not want to smell like a man. The first night, he huddled under the shelter of a pine tree. By the second day he climbed nearly to the top of the southern peak of the Two Buttes. He was thirsty and tired, his moccasins torn by the sharp rocks and bloodied by his cut feet. He could no longer see his village.

He prepared for the long nights ahead by making a bed of sage and cedar. Then he called for his vision. For long hours he walked along a sloped crest of the mountain, calling for assistance. None came. The falling sun found him exhausted, lying on his back and facing east so that he might greet it directly upon its return. Tired as he was, the night was a difficult one. The sounds of the forest seemed strange and human voices joined the cries of the nocturnal animals and the whistling wind. Faces the Buffalo North closed his eyes tightly, but even that failed to shut out the evil spirits lurking in the woods. He fought off drowsiness and was awake to see the rising sun. Again he pleaded for a vision, but as he lay in the darkness that night, he had yet to receive one.

Faces the Buffalo North fell asleep and awoke under a twinkling, milky sky. He could see by the position of the Seven Stars (the Big Dipper) that morning was near. As he thought about yet another day of fasting, his aching body begged for surrender. But he hardened himself for the task, and as he did, he heard a voice.

"Faces the Buffalo North."

The young brave's heart leaped like a trout after a fly. But he remained still as he answered.

"Yes."

"They want you, Faces the Buffalo North. I have been sent to fetch you."

"I am ready."

Faces the Buffalo North got to his feet. In the darkness, he felt a Person (as he described it) slip by his side, a Person of unknown identity, bathed in a strange light. He followed the Person over the summit of the mountain and then down its slope across the plain. Faces the Buffalo North could feel no rocks beneath his feet and he could not hear the footfall of the one who led him. The night was pierced only by the howl of coyotes, and when they came upon a circle of those animals, the Person stopped. Nearby was a lodge.

"Come, Faces the Buffalo North," said the Person as he lifted the robe that covered the lodge's opening.

He stepped in. He saw no fire, but the same strange light that cloaked the Person lit the interior. The lodge was filled with Persons unknown to Faces the Buffalo North. The Persons were old and he could tell by their countenances that they were warriors. The array of coup sticks and strong, beautiful eagle feathers embedded in the ground told him that they had been counting coup.

"Why have you brought this young man into our lodge!" demanded one. "He is not one of our kind and has no place here. We do not want him."

Faces the Buffalo North glanced towards the speaker on the south side of the lodge and he turned cold. He wasn't sure who had spoken, but he trembled at who he saw gathered there: the Winds, the Bad Storms, the Thunders, the Moon and the Stars, all powerful beings, much stronger and braver than man.

"Come, sit with us, Faces the Buffalo North," came a reassuring voice from the north side of the lodge. The Person who had first appeared to him guided him towards the speaker and then vanished. He knew none of those among whom he sat.

"Take these," directed the one who was the head of those near him. He handed Faces the Buffalo North several eagle feathers. As he took them, Faces the Buffalo North realized suddenly that the giver was a Dwarf Person and that all who sat around him were also Dwarfs. He thought of the stories he had heard about these beings. They were said to have great strength and were believed to be benevolent. Good thing, for he would need their protection in this place! Legend had it that they lived in the Medicine Rock, not far from the lodge.

"Stick one of your feathers in the ground before you count coup," directed the Dwarf chief.

Faces the Buffalo North hesitated. He had not yet counted coup and did not wish to mislead those gathered in the lodge. But he moved quickly when the Dwarf chief shouted for him to proceed. He thrust the quill of a feather into the ground.

"That is the rider of the white horse," said the Dwarf chief. "I first stuck him with my coup stick, and while he was unharmed and fighting, I took his bow."

"Nothing can be greater than that," bellowed the Thunders.

Faces the Buffalo North was directed to stick another feather in the ground and did.

"That is the rider of the black horse," declared the Dwarf chief. "I first struck him with my bow. While he fought with me armed with a knife, I took his bow and his shield."

"Enough!" cried those on the south side of the lodge. "It is the best that one can do."

"Count no more coup," suggested the Bad Storms. "We are glad you have admitted this young man to our lodge and we think you should give him something, some strong Medicine to help him."

"He will be a chief," observed the Dwarf chief, "and I can give him nothing. He has the power to become great if he chooses to use it. He must use the powers given him by Ah-badt-dadt-deah (the Great Spirit). How it is used makes differences among men."

Then the Dwarf chief turned to Faces the Buffalo North.

"The Dwarf people have adopted you and we will be your Helpers in this life. We have nothing to give you but advice."

"In you, as in all men, are natural powers. You have a will. Learn to use it. Make it work for you. Sharpen your senses as you sharpen your knife. Remember the wolf smells better than you do because he has learned to depend on his nose. It tells him every secret the winds carry because he uses it all the time, makes it work for him," observed the Dwarf chief. "We can give you nothing.

You already possess everything necessary to become great. Use your powers. Make them work for you and you will become a great chief."

There was nothing more. Faces the Buffalo North woke up on his mountainside bed, certain of two things—his destiny lay in his own hands, and the Dwarf people would be his protector. Faces the Buffalo North left his boyhood on the hill. He likely also shed the name by which he had long been known (it had been given to him by his godfather and it recognized an important event in that man's life). He became known as Swift Arrow.

All Crow were not granted visions, so Swift Arrow knew that his experience on the Two Buttes meant that he had strong Medicine. Yet, despite his revelation, he longed for more and he found himself restless once back in camp. He soon set out in search of another vision. On his first attempt, he could not dream. Undeterred, he returned with three others, although they separated after sweat bathing and before they reached the mountains. After two days of hunger and thirst, Swift Arrow realized that it was necessary to make a greater sacrifice if he was to dream. He decided to cut off the third joint of the little finger of his left hand. It was the act of a warrior and not unusual among the Crow. Strangely, when he severed it, no blood flowed. Swift Arrow struck the finger against a log to open the wound. Successful, he began to walk and call for his Helpers, perhaps using the traditional Crow invocation.

"Uncle, you see me. I am pitiable. Give me something good. Let me live to old age, may I own a horse, may I capture a gun, may I strike a coup. Make me a chief. Let me get good fortune without trouble."

Before sundown the Dwarf chief and some of his people arrived. They carried him back to his bed and they shared a pipe. Eventually Swift Arrow fell asleep, only to hear a voice. A Person was directing him to approach a bull buffalo visible on the plains below. He did, but when he reached the animal, it changed into a man wearing a buffalo robe. The man sunk into the ground and beckoned Swift Arrow to follow. Although fearful, he followed and was led towards the Arrow Creek Mountains (the Pryors). As they walked, Swift Arrow found himself amidst great herds of buffalo. He was afraid they might gore or stomp him, but his guide reassured him, counseling courage. They passed a lodge where Swift Arrow could hear babies crying within. He was told not to go inside because if he did and touched the children, he would not enjoy success in his life. Swift Arrow hurried along. When the man stopped, he began to shake a ceremonial rattle and to sing. Seeming to respond to his call, great numbers of buffalo emerged from a hole in the ground. They were beyond counting, but soon they all disappeared on the plains.

The man sang again, and from the hole emerged a new creature. It was similar to a buffalo but possessed a long tail and was spotted. Many such creatures emerged and filled the plains around him. He could tell that there must be a message here, but Swift Arrow did not yet have the wisdom to understand it. His guide then showed him an old man; it was Swift Arrow. The guide and the old man vanished suddenly, and Swift Arrow found himself alone in a forest. He watched as the Four Winds prepared to unleash their forces against the trees. As they did, their onslaught was ushered in by the booming Thunders. The storm was so ferocious that it left only one tree standing.

"What does it mean?" Swift Arrow whispered in his dream. He was granted an answer.

"In that tree is the lodge of the chickadee. He is least in strength but strongest of mind among his kind. He is willing to work for wisdom. The Chickadee Person is a good listener. Nothing escapes his ears, which he has sharpened by constant use. Whenever others are talking together of their successes or failures, there you will find the Chickadee Person listening to their words. But in all his listening he tends to his own business. He never intrudes, never speaks in strange company and yet never misses a chance to learn from others. He gains success and avoids failure by learning how others have succeeded or failed yet without great trouble to himself. There is scarcely a lodge he does not visit, hardly a Person he does not know, and yet everybody likes him if he minds his own business, or pretends to.

"The lodges of countless bird people were in that forest when the Four Winds charged it. Only one lodge is left unharmed, the lodge of the Chickadee Person. Develop your body, but do not neglect your mind, Swift Arrow. It is the mind that leads a man to power, not strength of body."

When Swift Arrow awoke, he found his friends waiting for him. They took a sweat bath and then ate. All the while, Swift Arrow was puzzled by his dream. It reinforced what he had learned on his vision quest, the importance of using his mind. He also knew that the chickadee was his Medicine, and he would make a medicine bundle reflecting that, but he was unclear as to the rest. He would consult the elders of his tribe.

When he returned to camp, his uncle White Horse took him to the tipi of Yellow Bear, where the elders were assembled. Swift Arrow told them the entire dream. When he finished, Yellow Bear lit his pipe and passed it around the lodge, to his left, as the sun goes. The pipe made the circle four times before he spoke.

"White Horse, your nephew has dreamed a great dream." Then Yellow Bear explained its meaning.

"In Swift Arrow's lifetime, the buffalo will disappear and be replaced by the cattle of the white man. These newcomers will take and hold the country. The Four Winds represented the white man. The trees were the tribes of the Plains. After the battle, only the one tree, the Crow, which never made war against the white man, will remain standing. The tribes who choose to fight the white man will suffer defeat, but the peaceful Crow would avoid that future and the tribe could keep their lands. Swift Arrow will live to be an old man, although he would be childless and witness these changes. Finally, he will live differently than his Crow ancestors in a home where the Person took him on Arrow Creek."

Some years passed before Swift Arrow passed through a second important rite of manhood: he counted his first coup. He sensed that the time was near when he saw a great circling eagle, considered a symbol of war, swoop low near where he stood. He rushed to his close friend Big Shoulders.

"The eagle has come to me. Tomorrow I go in search of the Sioux camp," he confided. "My brother's death will be avenged."

"Swift Arrow, your sorrow is my sorrow. You will not go alone," Big Shoulders replied.

They traveled for two days before they reached the Musselshell River, where they knew the Sioux hunted for buffalo. The excited conversations that had sped their journey were no longer heard. The enemy might be around the next bend in the river or behind an outcropping, so silence was necessary. The warrior's habits, formed by years of observation, reflection and practice, guided their actions. They rode slowly, all senses in tune to their surroundings. They had no fear, although they shared an unspoken worry that their hearts boomed so loudly that they might be revealed. When they caught sight of the Sioux camp, the pair picketed their cayuses. Swift Arrow took the small stuffed chickadee from his medicine bundle and held it high as he prayed for its assistance. This *baaxpee*, or power, would surely be needed. Then he tied the stuffed bird beneath the left braid of his thick, black hair. Before they set off on foot, they checked their bows and arrows, and with a tight grip on the handles of their war clubs (long, straight, carved sticks with an oval rock attached at the top by a thong), they slipped into the bush. When they saw that the forest growth was thinning, they fell to their knees and crawled to its edge.

Swift Arrow and Big Shoulders watched the Sioux hunters as they rode through the buffalo herd. The friends were safe enough because the braves were far too preoccupied to be watching for enemies. But how could they attack? The number of Sioux was far too great for them to ride down from the bluff. The pair wanted to count coup, but they also wanted to return and tell others about their bravery. So they waited while the sun rose high into the sky and began to descend to its lodge. It was not easy, lying there in the heat of the day, without drink, without movement, but they had learned that patience was as important to the successful warrior as a strong bow arm. As the pair waited, they considered their strategy. To be successful, one of the Sioux had to leave the main body and venture towards their hiding place. As the time passed, they played the attack over and over again in their minds, so that they would be prepared to act when the time arrived. Finally it did.

A wounded buffalo separated from the herd and limped towards them. Surely the Great Spirit directed its course! A Sioux brave on horseback followed it. When he was close enough, the young men leaped from their lair. Other braves in the distance spotted them, but their call of warning came too late for their friend. When the Sioux finally saw them, he had time to unleash a single arrow. It flew wide of its mark. As he tried to set the notch of a second arrow, Swift Arrow threw himself upon the harried rider. Big Shoulders grabbed the horse's head and stilled the startled animal. With a well-practiced swing of his arm, Swift Arrow unsheathed his knife and sliced it across the Sioux's scalp. The brave screamed and with a jerk pulled back. But Swift Arrow did not let go of the scalp, and it tore free with a sucking noise. His face bloodied, the Sioux ran back to his people, faced with a future of humiliation. Swift Arrow did not care about the brave's life, for the scalp itself was the great coup.

Swift Arrow and Big Shoulders did not wait to see if the Sioux chased them; they turned and ran for the woods. Swift Arrow's arms pumped as he ran, and the scalp, clenched tightly in his fist, sprayed droplets of blood. As they retreated deeper into the woods, the shouts of the pursuing Sioux became fainter, until they were no longer heard. Likely the Sioux thought that the forest was full of Crow waiting to ambush them. Nevertheless, Swift Arrow and Big Shoulders did not linger, and their ragged breathing returned to normal only after they had ridden some miles on their cayuses. The pair returned to great celebrations and feasting. The *aassahke*, members of the Newly Made Lodges clan, sang praise songs and offered prayers in recognition of this important first coup. But in later years Swift Arrow would recall not so much the joy of his tribe but the whispering voice that carried from the trees and spoke so gently to him.

"Do not grieve for me any longer. You have avenged my death. Think no longer of snows that have fallen but of those yet to come. Make many coups. Grow strong and courageous and you will be a worthy chief of our people."

From left: Pretty Eagle, Bull Nose, Spotted Horse, Enemy Hunter, Plenty Coups, Big Shoulder and Short Tail.

Swift Arrow would never forget his brother, but the pain of the memory was never quite as sharp.

By this time, those in Swift Arrow's band had come to hold a high opinion of him. It wasn't just his first daring coup, although that demonstrated something of his bravery. For some time others had seen special qualities in him. Elders talked of his visions as they smoked their pipes: he would be a great leader. Warriors discussed his abilities as they readied their weapons: he would picket many horses. Women whispered that he would make a good husband for their daughters: they would never want for meat over a fire. Swift Arrow seemed to have taken to heart the Crow dictum to excel at all things. So Chief Pretty Eagle was less surprised than pleased when, during a gathering of braves, Swift Arrow jumped to his feet in support of the chief's proposition to raid the Sioux in retaliation for their successful plundering of Crow horses.

"Our chief has spoken. We must show the Sioux that Crow warriors do not have the hearts of women. The trail of the enemy runs to the Valley of the Greasy Grass (Little Bighorn River). I know as I have seen it. I will follow that trail and take our horses back," declared Swift Arrow. "I will be brave, and the Sioux will not forget that a Crow is always to be feared."

Although Swift Arrow was only about 20 years old and still, for the most part, unproven, Pretty Eagle thought so highly of him that he appointed him the holder of the pipe for the 20-strong Crow war party. He would plan the raid and lead it. The chief's confidence was not misplaced. The entire Sioux party of 20 warriors was killed, and no Crow suffered injury. They took 100 horses. Swift Arrow counted two coups; he scalped a Sioux while the brave was still alive and he struck a dead one with his war club. As his dream had foretold, the first was riding a white horse, the second a black one. Pleased with their success, the Crow made their way back to the main camp.

Although they were eager to return, Swift Arrow directed the braves to make a detour along the way, to a grassy stretch where he knew that buffalo roamed. An important ritual needed to be addressed. They killed a buffalo and mixed its blood with water and charcoal to form a dark paint. The warriors covered their clothes with the mixture, and those who had counted coup drew special markers to identify their acts. The braves rubbed pure charcoal over their faces. When they returned to camp, their blackened faces would inform all that enemies had been killed. With the important work done, they continued on their way.

A runner was sent from the returning party, so the Crow camp was prepared when the victorious braves arrived. Long days of apprehension gave way to a flood of exuberance. Usually feasts to honor and to give thanks for the triumphs of returning warriors occurred a few days after their return, but this occasion was special. These were young braves, many of whom had just experienced their first Sioux raid or coup. Villagers prepared for the celebration that would begin at nightfall. Food simmered on fire pits, the prime boss ribs of the buffalo reserved for warriors. The scalp pole was erected. It would be the centerpiece for the stories and dance of the night. Young women hurriedly selected their finest doeskin outfits and most colorful beads. Boys talked excitedly of the courageous deeds they would hear described, wishing secretly they were the ones telling them. When the braves neared the camp, the men, women and children rushed along the trail to greet them. It was truly a time to be happy.

No one was more content than Swift Arrow. Seeing the waiting crowd, he was touched more deeply than he could have imagined possible. The pride he had felt following the great Crow victory was infused with a powerful love of his people, of their land and their ways. Just as Swift Arrow thought that his heart could beat with no greater emotion, his eyes caught sight of Knows Her Mother, the young Crow woman with whom he had fallen in love. With a fleeting glance from her he understood the difference between a slow stream and a raging river. As he wondered about these new feelings, Chief Pretty Eagle walked towards him and began to speak. Was he honoring their triumph? Swift Arrow did not know, for he was thinking only of Knows Her Mother. Eventually he looked down at Pretty Eagle, who seemed to have finished talking, and smiled in gratitude. Then, amidst the cheering and laughing, he dismounted and walked to Knows Her Mother.

They had courted for some time. In the safety of the shadowed forest around the camp, Swift Arrow had played his flute and he had sung for her. They had picked berries together. He knew of some friends who more boldly lifted the tipi pegs of their young women's lodges in an effort to reach in and touch them. Swift Arrow would not do that. Brave as he was, he feared touching her mother (the possibility of touching her father was beyond contemplation!). If he was caught, his hands would be tied together at opposite ends of a long stick; he knew his face would burn with hot blood then. As he approached, Knows Her Mother's eyes fell to the ground. He put his hand under her chin and lifted it so that she might see what was in his heart. In her eyes, he saw his every dream and hope reflected back. There would be no proposal of marriage to the young woman. It would come later, to her mother. He might be young, still less than the usual marrying age of 25, but he had counted coup and that was considered sufficient to allow a Crow brave to marry.

Swift Arrow felt an arm embrace his shoulder. It was Bell Rock, a warrior of Swift Arrow's age. He pulled him away from Knows Her Mother, eager to hear the story of his exploits. Knows Her Mother watched as the two walked back to camp, Swift Arrow's rapidly moving arms and hands suggesting that he was already well into his story. Not so far gone, however, that he did not give one last parting glance over his shoulder. Knows Her Mother hurried to get in front of the warriors, so that she could join in the dance that led them into the camp.

The setting sun found the Crow gathered around fires, sharing stories and preparing for the feast. Swift Arrow let it slip that he was going to approach Knows Her Mother's mother to ask permission to marry her daughter. His friends knew it was a serious step in a man's life, but that did not mean there would be no jesting or teasing. In that Big Shoulders took the lead.

"So my friend Swift Arrow is to be married! Many camps will have disappointed women tomorrow. I hope he is not rushing into this," reflected Big Shoulders. "As good as buffalo is, one likes a little elk or bear!"

Swift Arrow lifted his head and joined in the laughter. They fell silent when they heard some of the elder men begin the praise songs. Later the singers would receive gifts in return for their efforts. When the singing was completed, one of the braves who had been on the raid against the Sioux leaped up and struck the scalp pole with his coup stick. Soon only the beating of drums and the low, melodious chant of the women could be heard. The warrior danced around the pole and described the events of the raid. The courage of the Crow braves was highlighted, as were the dancer's own actions. Other warriors joined the brave, last of all Swift Arrow. All personal distinctions disappeared quickly as those gathered lost themselves in the slow rhythms. The music makers, the onlookers, the dancers were all Mountain Crow, bonded in the celebration of a great victory. As with so many Native ceremonies, its purpose was to unite the people. In this it was effective.

Later that night, while his exhausted people slept, Swift Arrow slipped out onto the plains. He was far too excited to rest and he had an important task to address. He gathered some 20 of his cayuses, representing a sizeable amount of wealth, and took them to the tipi of Knows Her Mother. There he picketed them, a gift for her mother. If the animals were gone in the morning, Swift Arrow would know that his offer of marriage had been accepted. He slept hardly at all that night and was up before the whole of the sun had appeared. The cayuses were gone! The pair was soon married. Although Swift Arrow was to have 10 more wives, it is doubtful that the love he felt for any of them was more than that he felt for Knows Her Mother, whose virtue, skill and beauty placed her close to the ideal of Crow womanhood.

It was probably around this time that Swift Arrow changed his name to Plenty Coups, and it was justified. Throughout his 20s, Plenty Coups continued to develop as a leader of his people. Particularly evident were his triumphs as a warrior. Such bravery and success in battle were sure to draw attention, and soon the leaders of the Foxes came calling. The Foxes' function was to lead the Crow in war against their enemies. They decided when raids would be undertaken, planned them and prevented braves from going off to fight by themselves, a practice that might have demonstrated bravery but left the camp weakened. The Foxes held great authority within the tribe. Plenty Coups had idolized the club's members since childhood, so he jumped at the chance to join the band of elite warriors. He enjoyed success as a Fox, which came as a surprise to none since his dreams had revealed greatness.

By 25, he was a chief of his people. He hadn't held the honor long when, in 1876, representatives of General Crook came to his village on the Rosebud Creek. Gold had been discovered in the Black Hills of South Dakota, and the Sioux and Cheyenne had gone on the warpath to stop the miners from invading the sacred region. The army was searching for scouts who were willing to fight against the hostile Plains tribes. The Mountain Crow had some experience because they had served occasionally in such capacity since the late 1850s. Plenty Coups' answer came easily. Like the chickadee, he had been observant. He had noticed that Iron Belly, a leader among the first group of Crow to join forces with the cavalry, was the wealthiest man in his tribe. All knew that his wealth was founded upon his friendly relations with the white man. And hadn't the man in his dream told him that the Crow would also benefit from such a friendship? Plenty Coups would follow the teachings of his dream and he said as much to his people.

> *Let us help this man. His men here say that he has many soldiers in his camp and with them we shall whip our old enemies. Besides, we shall make the white man our friend. When the war is over, the soldier chiefs will not forget that the Absaroka came to their aid. This is a fight for future peace and I will carry the pipe for all who will go with me to the village of Three Stars.*

Plenty Coups' position was not readily accepted. Although white settlers were few, their presence had become more noticeable in Wyoming throughout the early 1860s. The Union Pacific Railroad arrived in 1867, a sure sign that even more settlers would be coming. At this time, fewer than 2000 Mountain Crow lived there, and the newcomers argued that the vast land they controlled was excessive. The Fort Laramie Treaty of 1868 drastically reduced Crow holdings by more than 30 million acres. Nevertheless, Plenty Coups was persuasive and 135 braves joined him. He sensed that he'd made the right decision when he first laid eyes on Three Stars' camp at Goose Creek in Wyoming. Countless tents stood in straight lines. Men dressed in blue were drilling and they were as orderly as the tents. The wagons and horses were as the blades of grass. It was an imposing sight, one that any warrior might admire, and it demanded an appropriate Crow response.

The arriving braves put their war bonnets on their heads, cried the war whoop and bolted down the hill into the valley, firing their guns as they rode. While the army knew that the Crow were coming, the soldiers must have held their breath as they watched the hard-driving warriors with their faces painted and wondered whether they'd be ambushed. But the soldiers took Crook's lead and remained steadfast. As the Crow approached the columns, Three Stars saluted them. All of the white men heaved a sigh of relief. Shoshone scouts supplemented the camp, and as Plenty coups looked upon the great crowd of allies, he was confident that he had made the right decision. Their enemies would be defeated. Then came the Battle of the Rosebud and sober second thought.

General Crook's assignment was to bring in Crazy Horse and his band of hostile Oglala Sioux. To do the job, he was given command of 1200 men. Crazy Horse found Crook resting with his men at a bend in the Rosebud Creek and attacked the surprised cavalry. Only the determined resistance of the Crow and Shoshone braves prevented an indisputable victory for the Sioux. As it was, the soldiers used the valuable time given them by their aggressive Native allies to prepare for battle. Once in formation, Captain Anson Mills led a charge that forced the Sioux to retreat. It drew a quick response from the strategically minded Crazy Horse. He surprised the soldiers by driving hard into their center. Knives and war clubs flashed and crashed as the opposing forces tumbled together in hand-to-hand combat. The soldiers were no match for the Sioux's long-practiced skills in close warfare, and they were saved only when Mills was able to circle around the Sioux and attack from the rear. With that the Sioux retreated and abandoned the battle. No one counted Sioux losses, but 31 soldiers and one Crow warrior died.

Plenty Coups had known before the attack that Crazy Horse was near, since his Wolves (scouts) had so informed him. He shared the intelligence with Three Stars, who bade him not to worry, because he had help coming from Generals Terry and Custer, both in command of nearby divisions. It was good news, but Plenty Coups wasn't enthusiastic about Three Stars' chances of getting a message to his white brothers with the great numbers of Sioux roaming about. However, even without reinforcements, he was confident that Three Stars' men and his Native allies could take the Sioux. It didn't turn out that way. Although Crook claimed victory, Plenty Coups figured that Crazy Horse had whipped them. The Crow didn't do poorly. They had fought the enemy courageously and they had helped the white men in their battle. They took 10 scalps, as well as a good number of horses, saddles and blankets.

Had Plenty Coups' Medicine been weak, his scalp would have dangled from a Sioux waist. His horse was shot from under him and, as he heard the approaching Sioux argue about who would take first coup on him, he scampered towards the shelter of an outcropping. He was bloodied by the fragments of rock that splintered from the bullets exploding around him. He knew that even strong Medicine wouldn't protect him long in that spot, isolated as he was, so he made a quick run for a nearby horse. Mounting it, he rode hard towards the soldiers, his red flag snapping in the wind (an indication to the soldiers that he was friendly). Then, as he sensed the danger was finally behind him, his horse went down with a bullet through the heart. Fortunately, many riderless horses roamed the battlefield, and Plenty Coups quickly found another and made it back to safety.

As the Crow scouts proved valuable to Crook, the general kept them on the army payroll. Plenty Coups scouted throughout the winter and it's likely that he saved the general's men from a near certain massacre in the fading days of summer. It's not known exactly when Plenty Coups decided to go back to his people, but by 1878 most of the Sioux had settled on reservations and the era of Great Plains warfare was in its twilight. The services of the Crow were probably not needed by the cavalry after that time. It was just as well, since his people needed him then more than ever.

In the decades that followed, Plenty Coups saw the dreams of his youth materialize. He witnessed the Great Plains fill with homesteaders and others making their way farther west. He watched, without surprise, as tribes that had waged war against the white men were treated with parsimony by the victors. Plenty Coups was determined that the United States government not forget the assistance that his people had rendered it. The attitude allowed him to emerge as a key intermediary between the Mountain Crow and the government officials.

As white settlement in Montana increased throughout the late 1870s, government officials were pressured to further reduce the size of Crow holdings. Settlers didn't only want Crow land. They were also concerned with intertribal warfare. As the decade drew to a close, the Crow rode north more frequently into traditional Blackfoot and Yanktonai territory to access the dwindling buffalo herds. While large-scale violence was rare, many skirmishes occurred. Fort Custer was built at the mouth of the Little Bighorn River to deal with the matter and conflict was soon minimized. Nevertheless, settlers remained worried. In 1880 the government responded to their concerns and proposed a council with the Crow. Officials took the position that it was best for the Crow to cede territory that they could no longer control effectively, particularly around the Yellowstone River.

A commissioner submitted the idea to some 50 Crow chiefs and headmen. Iron Bull had been chosen as their principal speaker. He declared his friendship for the Americans but declined to sell any more Crow land. Speaker after speaker followed his lead until Plenty Coups, who was determined to take a more prominent leadership role among his people, took the floor.

"I have a heart and I thought I had a mind. The white men think for me," he acknowledged. "I do what the white men want me to do."

Plenty Coup's proposal, which offered a new path for his people, accepted the changed reality of the American West, at least as Plenty Coups understood it. The buffalo were disappearing, their raids against old enemies decreased, and each day the white men were building their houses closer to Crow territory. Plenty Coups considered that the one thing that remained constant was the necessity of maintaining a friendship with the white man. While Plenty Coups was well respected, not everyone shared his interpretation of the shifting landscape, and the council decided not to follow his lead. The proposed land sale would not be accepted. The United States commissioner responded by announcing that the Crow would send a delegation to Washington to speak directly with the president.

Plenty Coups was among the six chosen. Officials in Washington pressured the Crow delegation to cede more land than they wanted to, but they held fast to a limited land sale. It seems that they were not unanimous; Plenty Coups, for one, was eager to appease. Ultimately, the delegation agreed to the government's terms, largely because they feared they would be held captive in this foreign land unless they did so. They pledged to try to sell the agreement to their people upon their return west. However, Iron Bull held fast to his original position, and only 1.6 million acres were sold

Plenty Coups, age 59. He was chosen principal chief of the Mountain Crow, the last man to hold that position.

(for $750,000). It was the smallest amount that the government would accept. Friends or not, it seemed that the Crow were treated little differently than other Plains Natives, who were also forced into accepting massive land sales. It was a defeat for Plenty Coups, who was criticized by some for his position, which they saw as overly and obsequiously ambitious. Like the observant chickadee, however, he had learned an important lesson: submission did not bring him standing among the Crow. In future, the moderation of his dealings with American authorities would be tempered by toughness.

His first opportunity to display his resolve came when the Northern Pacific Railroad signaled its intent to lay track west of Bismarck into Crow territory. As the railroad workers hammered their first surveying stakes at Arrow Creek, Spotted Horse and a band of Crow warriors met them, demanding they leave. Government officials responded to the entreaties of Northern Pacific executives and held council with the Crow to resolve the issue. That the Crow were divided was clear when they could not agree on a principal speaker. Although some Crow did not want the railroad to go through their land, including Iron Bull and Spotted Horse, they did not speak out. Only those in support of making an agreement spoke. Sensing that a position advocating consensus would serve both his community and his own ambitions, Plenty Coups took the floor.

"I will touch the pen and sign for all the Crows," he declared, "if you will pay us $30,000."

They settled on $25,000, which most Crow deemed adequate. It was a victory for Plenty Coups. He had cooperated with white officials yet had defended Crow interests. Many of his people came to believe it was a balance that would serve them well. Plenty Coups' criticism of his white allies also strengthened his position among those Crow who did not trust the government. Skeptics found comfort in Plenty Coups' assertion that the white man was confusing. As he put it, they "too often promised to do one thing and then, when they acted at all, did another. They spoke very loudly when they said their laws were made for everybody, but we soon learned that although they expected us to keep them, they thought nothing of breaking them themselves. They told us not to drink whisky, yet they made it themselves and traded it to us.... Their Wise Ones said we might have their religion, but when we tried to understand it we found that too many kinds of religion existed among white men for us to understand, and that scarcely any two white men agreed which was the right one to learn. This bothered us a good deal until we saw that the white man did not take his religion any more seriously than he did his laws.... We have never been able to understand the white man, who fools nobody but himself."

These strange characteristics were not enough to undermine Plenty Coups' efforts to cultivate and maintain friendship with the white man. Plenty Coups adapted his lifestyle to more closely reflect the new world he saw. In the early 1880s, he took his 150 followers to the upper reaches of Arrow Creek, one of a half dozen Crow communities on the reservation. Just 30 miles south of Billings, it was a good location. It did not seem to be so at first, as ranchers illegally grazed their livestock on Crow lands. Aware that considerable revenue was being lost, Plenty Coups and other leaders negotiated with local ranchers to lease Crow land. Shrewdly, they leased it to two men, who were made responsible for keeping trespassers off the territory as part of the agreement.

Leading by example, Plenty Coups began farming, which he saw as one of the few ways he could meet his chiefly obligation of providing for his people and reducing their dependency on agency handouts. It was an uncomfortable undertaking because the Crow had abandoned agricultural activities after the arrival of the horse in the early 1700s, except for the harvesting of tobacco (which was the tribe's "means of living," important in their ritual and ceremonial life). Initially Plenty Coups worked on the agency farm but soon he started his own. He also took to ranching, although he often lamented that beef was never as tasty as the buffalo he was raised on. As the local chief (and government favorite), he lived in a sparsely furnished two-story frame home built by the Indian Office. Open to visitors and those in need of accommodation, the house quickly became the center of the community's activities. Plenty Coups met there with Natives and government officials alike to discuss the business of his people. He also operated a store that was more like a contemporary food bank where band members could come for supplies and tools. While profits were never Plenty Coups' main objective, within a decade he was one of the most prosperous Crow. By that time, he was also one of the tribe's most respected members.

By his early 40s Plenty Coups had learned much since settling into reservation life. Most importantly, he had decided that he would not allow his friendship for the white man turn him into a toadying tool to further their interests. Indian agents discovered something of this attitude in 1890, when commissioners were yet again sent from Washington charged with reducing the Crow reservation. The summer had been a patchwork of drought and hail and few farmers in Montana had much of a harvest. The Crow were affected equally and they asked their Indian agent (government officials had the final say on economic matters pertaining to Natives on reservations) to apply money paid for grazing leases to extra beef rations, until farming provided adequate supplies. The request was forwarded to Washington, which responded with an offer to buy two million acres of Crow land. The Crow were divided. Those who lived far from the proposed land were content to sell it. But the sale would have meant that the boundary of the reservation would be only a few miles from Plenty Coups' home and, more importantly, that his band would lose the lucrative grazing income from the Montana ranchers.

Plenty Coups' position among his people allowed him to speak first at the council convened to discuss the land sale.

"If you white men put in all your money to buy that land you would not pay all it is worth....I don't want to have bad feelings against Indians or whites, but I want my country to remain," he declared. "If there is anything you love and I want to buy, you won't sell it. The Great Father buys and buys from me and this time I won't do it."

All were aware of Plenty Coups' amiable relationship with the white man, so his statement came as something of a surprise to those assembled. But experience with the white man had soured Plenty Coups' belly. He made known his conclusion in blunt statements.

"A few more passing suns will see us here no more, and our dust and bones will mingle with these same prairies. I see as in a vision the dying spark of our council fires, the ashes cold and white. I see no longer the curling smoke rising from our lodge poles. I no longer hear the songs of the women as they prepare the meal.

"The antelope have gone; the buffalo wallows are empty. Only the wail of the coyote is heard. The white man's medicine is stronger than ours," he conceded. "His iron horse rushes over the buffalo trail. He talks to us through his whispering spirit [the telephone].

"We are like birds with a broken wing."

Plenty Coups was not one to simply give up. But even his powerful statement could not persuade everyone to accept his position on the land sale. So the Crow chief changed his tactics. Sensing that the sale was inevitable, he set about improving the commissioners' offer. Ultimately, the Crow were given more cash, 2500 head of cattle, an irrigation system to aid farming efforts, yearly annuities, day schools, a blacksmith's shop and a gristmill. The Crow considered it a good deal given the circumstances.

It was difficult for Plenty Coups, as it was for most Crow, to see traditional lands slip into the hands of the white man. Natives held a special relationship with the land because it provided physical and spiritual sustenance. While the Natives could not prevent the white men from satisfying their appetite for more territory, Plenty Coups was at least determined to ensure that the ways of the Crow were not lost. He was particularly active in promoting the Tobacco Society. While the rituals that surround the society remain mysterious, it is understood to have involved ceremonies designed to pass on critical components of Crow culture between generations. For that reason, government and religious officials had long tried to suppress it. Their failure to do so is evidence of Crow resilience.

Plenty Coups also supported the Beaver Dance, "the only dance our fathers left to us and...about all the enjoyment the older Indians have." Christian Crow pressured officials to prohibit the ceremony, which they called religious animal worship. Plenty Coups, who was a baptized (though not a practicing) Catholic, obviously did not share the sentiment. On this matter, those who objected suffered the Indian agent's cold shoulder. Most Indian agents opposed traditional Native ceremonies, but the agent in charge of Plenty Coups' reservation felt that the dance was harmless and purely recreational, although he probably realized it was not within his ability to prohibit the activity even if he wanted to. Plenty Coups also helped establish a new club known as the Crazy Dog society. In many respects, it was similar to the Crow societies of old. Crazy Dogs wore special outfits, sang songs, danced, feasted and engaged in the time-honored tradition of wife stealing. One activity that Plenty Coups seems not to have promoted was the Sun Dance. Uniting tribes people and bolstering their confidence, the dance had been central to Crow life

Plenty Coups, age 72 (center), in Washington in 1921. With him are White Face Bear and Frost.

for generations and for that reason the government had prohibited it. As a young man, Plenty Coups had participated in the Sun Dance; he had even offered his flesh as the principal dancer. However, his thoughts on the dance after it was prohibited were not recorded.

In 1904 the prominent Crow chief Pretty Eagle died, so at age 55 Plenty Coups emerged as the principal chief of the Mountain Crow. In subsequent years he promoted friendship between the white men and his own people. During World War I, he counseled Crow braves to enlist in the armed forces. When the Unknown Soldier was interred at Arlington National Cemetery in 1921, Plenty Coups was the Native representative at the ceremony. He was also asked to give the final blessing. He did so dressed in ceremonial splendor and speaking in Crow.

> *I am glad to represent all the Indians of the United States in placing on the grave of this noble warrior this coup stick and war bonnet, every eagle feather of which represents a deed of valor by my race. I hope that the Great Spirit will grant that these noble warriors have not given up their lives in vain and that there will be peace to all men hereafter.*

Plenty Coups' presence and short speech revealed much. During his life he had seen many Native warriors die for their beliefs. Yet, in holding fast to his and being flexible where necessary, in remaining true to his dreams, he and his people had persevered. While his presence at the ceremony represented an attempt by the American government to cast a positive light on its relations with American Natives, it is no less true that Plenty Coups' ability to link the event with the courage and traditions of his own people and to do so in a prayer to the Great Spirit suggested the course his life had taken had not been in vain. When he died in 1932, the Crow people decided that there would be no more Crow chiefs. They too recognized his wisdom.

CHAPTER SIX

Wovoka

～～

Northern Paiute, 1858–1932

WOVOKA SAT IN HIS WICKIUP, his eyes fixed on the small fire inside. Even deep in thought he could hear the rush of the nearby Walker River and feel the sudden coolness that came with the sun's descent beyond the western hills of the Mason Valley. His thoughts did not wander. They had remained focused for many days on a most distressing question. How was it that the Northern Paiute had fared so poorly since the white man had come to their valley? Life had not been easy in the old times, which were not so long ago, but his people had listened to and obeyed the spirits and they had managed well enough. The generation since the arrival of the white newcomers had seen much in their lives change for the worse. Many Natives had been forced onto reservations, while others had taken work as poorly paid laborers. There was poverty, disease and numbing disillusion. Wovoka knew that other Natives had it little better. He had been north and seen the plight of those who lived

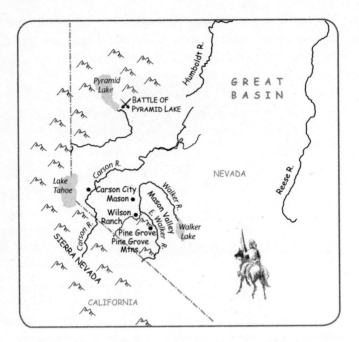

on the Great Plateau. He had heard of the events on the Great Plains to the east. The sights and stories did not differ. Wherever the white man went, Natives suffered.

It troubled Wovoka greatly. He was a respected man among his people, a dreamer whose visions helped the needy and benefited all. Perhaps he might have admitted that, on occasion in the past, he had used trickery and deception to increase his influence within the community. But he would have pointed out that it was not a bad thing. The secrets of the prophets and medicine men among his people included many tricks. He knew of no ruse, however, that could help his people during this time of great adversity. Instead, he had devoted long nights and days to prayer. Increasingly, he sought to communicate with the white man's spirit beings. He did not pray as a Christian, for he did not truly understand the religion. But he did believe in the power of the spirit world and he suspected that the white man's success must in some way be attributable their God. Countless prayers had given him no answers until this night in the late 1880s.

As Wovoka gazed at the fire, he slipped into a trance. His wife, Tumma, soon found him slumped over and deathly cold. She managed to lay him out on his blanket. When news of his condition spread, the wickiup filled with visitors. Many had hushed disagreements. *Was he dead?* Most could not accept that Wovoka had died. This was, after all, the son of Tavibo, a dreamer and medicine man with considerable powers of his own.

No, some suggested, *he was alive, visiting heaven.* For two days, the optimistic tried to bring him back. They doused him in water, force fed him, blew into his lungs and applied coals to his feet. There was no response. They had abandoned both their remedies and their efforts when Wovoka's eyes opened. In the shadowy light of the wickiup, he looked to his wife and spoke in a whispering voice.

"I have traveled along the Milky Way. I have visited the other world."

Tumma was less concerned about where he had been than she was about his health.

"Eat," she said, bringing him a bowl of stew.

"I will not eat until the sun rises," he replied.

The visitors could no longer hold their tongues.

"Wovoka, tell us of your journey," said one.

"What did you see?" asked another. "What can you tell us?"

"Brothers and sisters, please, no questions," replied Wovoka, as he raised a trembling hand for silence. "I have talked to the spirits of our dead people. They have taught me much."

He fell silent for a moment.

Wovoka, age 57, wore white man's clothing, but strapped an eagle feather to his right elbow, a symbol of his Native ancestry.

"Organize a dance." He gave instructions about the appropriate location and necessary preparations. "There I will tell you what I have learned."

With that, he asked Tumma to clear the wickiup. When all were gone, he sat up and began to chant. Throughout the night and into the next day, Wovoka continued, stopping only when word came that the dance preparations were complete.

As he rode on a wagon to the dance ground, with long, thick blankets tight around his shoulders, he observed the gathered crowd. He recognized most people in the crowd as local, but word of his trance and forthcoming revelation had spread quickly, and other Northern Paiute came from beyond the valley. When he reached the spot readied for him, the wagon stopped and he stood. He threw off the blankets and began to share what he had seen and the lessons he had been taught.

"I have been to heaven!" he cried. "There I saw many Indians. They were from the plains where the sun rises and from beyond the mountains where the sun sets and from places unknown. They walked arm in arm. All were beautiful," he smiled. "They were wiped clean of the desires and urges that cause people trouble. The physical ailments that bring pain were no longer even memories. And our brothers and sisters stood proud. They were servants to no one, equal to all."

"I longed to remain there," confessed Wovoka. "Why would one leave a place of such peace and happiness? But they knew my thoughts and spoke to me.

"'Go back to your people. Tell them of the things that you have seen and the things that you hear. Jesus is upon the earth. He moves as in a cloud. The dead are all alive again. When friends die, do not cry. Do no harm to anyone. Do not fight. Do right always. Do not tell lies, Work for the white man, and do not cause trouble for them.'

"They gave us much to consider, much to do. And they told me to bring the dance back to my people. They called it a dance of goodness. 'It will make your people free and it will make them happy.' That is what they said."

With that, Wovoka stepped down from the wagon. From the crowd he selected men and women. He painted signs of red ochre on their faces. He arranged them into a circle and bade them to hold hands, their fingers interlocked. Then he sang to them the song he had heard in his vision. There came to be many songs associated with the ceremony, but what this first one was is unknown. Once those chosen had mastered it, Wovoka started them dancing. Their movements were slow and precise. In rhythm with the singing, the left foot was lifted so that it was barely off the ground. When it was placed back down, the right foot slipped into the spot the left foot had occupied. Eventually, moving from right to left, the dancers completed a revolution. The circle was enlarged as more joined. Wovoka introduced more songs.

For five continuous nights they sang and danced. On the sixth day, Wovoka called for a dance in the afternoon. When the celebrants arrived, he directed all to plunge into the Walker River.

"Your sins will be washed away and you will be pure before God and the other spirits," he told them.

The ceremony was ended with a feast.

Wovoka's teachings found a ready audience and soon Northern Paiute villages along the western Nevada border were alive with the ceremony that he had delivered. His standing with them took on giant proportions. Here was a dreamer with a great prophecy. Could it be believed? Some pointed to his past visions and argued that there could be no doubt. Those who were less certain had only to wait.

A young boy who had seen only 12 winters stood at the mouth of the Walker River, where it joined with Walker Lake. He was in search of a deer; he wanted to make his first kill. It was an important undertaking, one that would allow him to leave the world of childhood and become a man.

Over the past few days, he had walked north to the southern bend of the Walker River, but he had spotted nothing larger than a rabbit. He was tired of hunting such small animals that fed only the children. He longed to kill a large animal, something that could feed the adults. On this day, he traveled south past the fork of the Walker River and along the East Walker River. He strained his eyes, hoping to see something move against the silvery gray of the desert sagebrush that seemed to color even the lush growth along the river. In the distance, he could see the hills that rose from the west side of the river. Although no animals were visible, he remained hopeful and set about walking resolutely along its shoreline.

The boy would become known as Wovoka although that wasn't yet his name. When they were young, the boys of his tribe were given nicknames, but Wovoka's has been long forgotten. As his eyes scanned the land ahead, he reflected on his father's observation that it was difficult to become a man. Not since the days of the tales of old had there been many deer and antelope in the desert lowlands. Since the arrival of the white man, even the few that had been seen occasionally seemed to have vanished. But Wovoka was determined, and he would not return to his village until he was greeted as a man.

As he approached the mountains, the sun began to slip into the great water to the west of them. It was a good time to hunt because the animals liked to drink in the twilight, and Wovoka watched with greater care. There! Not more than an arrow's flight away, a deer stood at the shore's edge. There was no shelter between Wovoka and the animal, so he dropped to his belly and snaked just a little closer. Slowly, he raised himself, his arrow already notched. When he stood, the animal looked at him. Too late! The arrow was already unleashed. It struck true and the deer fell to its side.

Wovoka ran to the animal and slit its throat to ensure its death. Never had he felt so happy! But, as darkness fell, he realized that he had a new problem. It was too late to return to the village for his father, as was custom after a first kill. Much to his dismay, he would have to wait. His thoughts drifted back to the cautionary tales of his childhood. He remembered Tiya, his mother, warning him about the wild cats, big owls or snakes that might sneak in from the darkness to take him away. But that fate awaited only those who misbehaved. Surely they would not attack one who had achieved such a feat as his. He was an adult, and the animals that made a boy's blood run cold should no longer have such a chilling effect. Or so he told himself. He finally decided that it made good sense to light a fire, and soon the dancing flames warmed him.

He endured an uneasy night, and with the rising sun, was on his way back to his village. Without hesitation, he made his way to his family's wickiup, a lodge made of brush and weeds and covered with willow branches. Wovoka called to his father, Tavibo, who had also slept little during the previous night. Tavibo had the power of visions, but nothing had been granted to him of these days and he waited anxiously as any father might.

"Father! Mother! I have killed my first deer!" declared Wovoka, who's frame seemed suddenly to fill the wickiup's entrance.

Tiya smiled and Tavibo nodded and grabbed his quiver, in which he kept his hunting knife.

"Show me the way," he directed his son.

Tavibo was a respected medicine man among his people. He also possessed *bbooha* (power) that was manifested in visions. Although there was no way to ensure that Wovoka would share his power, it was expected. He had taught his son the ways of a medicine man. He chanted the songs until Wovoka joined him and eventually could sing alone. He took him through the valley, along the river and into the desert, carefully pointing out the plants that might be used to heal. Tavibo shared the spells for exorcising spirits and showed him the hand tricks that appeared mystical to the uninitiated. And Tavibo prepared Wovoka for the visions he might someday have. In hopeful anticipation, Wovoka took note of his father's careful advice.

"Remember what you dream and follow it closely. Do not anger the spirits, for they will abandon you. Without the power they bestow, people will no longer turn to you in their need."

When they arrived at the kill site, Tavibo skinned the deer and carried the meat home, as tradition dictated. At the village, he put the meat on the ground and cut some long sticks of willow. He fashioned them into a hoop, tying them with willow bark. He then collected some sagebrush that he tied around Wovoka's wrists, ankles, knees and waist.

"These will give you endurance," said Tavibo. "Do not remove them until the sun has gone to its wickiup five times. While you wear the sagebrush, you may eat only the outside flesh of the deer. The rest will be eaten by the others in the village. Now, stand on the skin."

The deer's hide was on the ground beside the meat. Once Wovoka stood atop it, Tavibo lowered the willow hoop over his son's head.

"Give to him deer," called Tavibo.

Wovoka then stepped out of the hoop. Tavibo raised it again and lowered over his son, saying "rabbit." He repeated this many times, until all the animals had been named. With that, the ceremony was completed, and Wovoka was a man.

All Northern Paiute boys experienced this ritual. The tribal name was roughly translated as "true Ute" (indicating

the peoples' strong link with the Ute tribe to the east),
although the Paiute called themselves Numu. The Northern
Paiute were one of a half dozen tribes who lived in the
Great Basin of the present-day western United States.
The bowl-like Great Basin has as a rough lip of the Rocky
Mountains (to the east), the Sierra Nevada (to the west), the
Columbia Plateau (to the north) and the Colorado Plateau
(to the south). Clouds rarely passed over the mountains to
bring rain to the territory, resulting in desert terrain, punctu-
ated with occasional lakes and valleys with streams flowing
down from higher elevations.

The Northern Paiute had called the region home for
centuries before Wovoka's birth around 1858. Over the
generations, they had learned to live off the limited
resources found in the area. Necessity made them
a nomadic people, well tuned to seasonal rhythms and
offerings. Summer found them on the hills and plateaus
harvesting berries or pine nuts from the piñon trees. In the
winter, they were in the desert lowlands hunting small
game, especially rabbit. Year round they foraged for grubs
and insects and collected plant roots. As they looked to the
ground for so much of their sustenance, the Northern
Paiute and the other Great Basin Natives were known to
the local white population as "Digger Indians."

The demands of life in the Great Basin were challenging,
but Wovoka knew that they were not without purpose. He
had often heard the story of the Northern Paiute's nomadic
lifestyle. It was one among many told by Narro-gwe-nap, the
keeper of the legends, during the tribal council meeting. But
that assembly was held infrequently, so Wovoka often asked
his grandfather or father to tell the stories of his people.

"Before the Northern Paiute lived here, they called the
high mountains that overlook the great western waters
home," explained Tavibo. "They lived there with Tobats and

Northern Paiute pine nut harvest, 1912. Pine nuts were collected from the sacred piñon trees and were a food staple.

Shinob, powerful spirits. One day Shinob told the people that they had to move.

"'Travel across the desert to the mountains of the rising sun,' he directed. 'Take these seeds so that you might always have food in your new home.'

"The journey was a difficult one. Neither the weak, who did not have the strength, nor the foolish, who drank their water too quickly, lived to see the Northern Paiute home. But when the others reached the red mountain country that would be their new home, they were pleased. The many caves would provide shelter and the streams that slipped through the valley bottoms would provide water to moisten their gardens. The people were careful with their harvest, storing it for winter. Many animals roamed the land, and the hunt gave their meals variety. Life was happy, and the Northern Paiute remembered to give thanks to Tobats and Shinob," noted Tavibo.

"As the years passed, the summer rain and the winter snow came less often. The watering places dried up and the crops withered. There was no food to store. Discouraged hunters returned with little meat; all the big animals had gone. Even the birds and rabbits and squirrels seemed to have disappeared."

"The wise men decided that the Northern Paiute should appeal to Tobats and Shinob. If they would not send food, all would surely die. So the people went to the top of the mountain, and for three days cried to Tobats and Shinob. Finally, Shinob came to them."

"'What is all this crying? What is all this bad noise about?' he roared.

"The people explained that they were hungry. They told Shinob that their seeds no longer grew and that the animals had left in search of food.

"'All the animals?' asked Shinob. 'What of the little ones?'

"'They too have gone," came the reply. They were getting frustrated explaining the situation to Shinob. The great spirit was also growing impatient.

"'The big animals have gone in search of food. The birds have gone in search of food. The little animals too. The animals and birds were smart. You should have as much sense as they do,' scolded Shinob. 'It is a large country, and there is always food to be found. Follow the animals and the birds, and they will lead you to it. Go. Look for their tracks.'

"The Northern Paiute left their caves and followed the game to where it led. They have ever since been a nomadic people," concluded Tavibo.

"And a strong people," added Wovoka, who, like all Northern Paiute, had learned early in life something of what hardiness meant.

Wovoka was born during an unusual period of considerable change for his people. For generations his people had lived as the spirits had directed, and they had come to accept it as reasonable people accept what is necessary. Small groups of families, who were related by marriage—with no bands and chiefs—ranged within well-known territories that varied from about 100 to 200 square miles. Usually, these groups were known by some type of unusual food available in the territory. Wovoka grew up among the Toboose tukadu, or Taboosi-eaters, who harvested the grass bulb nuts along the banks of the Walker River. They were his father's people. His mother was not a Toboose tukadu although she was a Northern Paiute.

In the early decades of the 19th century, the white man appeared. Until mid-century, only a handful of trappers inhabited the region. They were friendly with the Northern Paiute. These people had little effect on the traditional practices of the Northern Paiute, but it would not be so with the next wave of white newcomers. Drawn by the discovery of gold at Sutter's Mill in California in 1848, overlanders came by the hundreds, and soon, the thousands. Throughout the 1850s and 1860s, increasing numbers of these white men decided to settle in the homelands of the Northern Paiute. The fertile bottom lands and the well-timbered lower elevations of the mountains proved inviting territory, especially to ranchers. Prospectors also came in search of gold. In the late 1850s, Hoc Mason moved into the northern end of the valley that Wovoka's people called home (in present-day western

Nevada). No one asked the Northern Paiute's permission to inhabit the valley, nor was it given. The area was thereafter known as the Mason Valley. For a people who measured change in generational terms, the rapid construction of cabins and fences was undoubtedly confusing.

The impact on the Northern Paiute was immediate. Bands formed, an organized response on the part of the Northern Paiute to deal with the intruders. Wovoka may have been born into the Tovusi band although it seems his father belonged (for a time at least) to Chief Numaga's band at Pyramid Lake. Whatever their band name, Wovoka's people remained more commonly known as Toboose tukadu. Some of these bands went on the warpath to defend their interests. The Northern Paiute had no great history as warriors, however, so the battles were scattered and mostly ineffective at halting white incursions.

Only two major battles occurred during Wovoka's youth, both to the north. The Pyramid Lake War of 1860 had a direct effect on Wovoka. The war was set off when white traders kidnapped and raped two Northern Paiute girls. Chief Numaga and his warriors killed five traders in their successful rescue attempt. Local miners raised a volunteer force to seek revenge. The ad hoc force was soon replaced by 800 army regulars and volunteers that defeated the Northern Paiute at Pinnacle Mountain. Tavibo was taken prisoner during the Pyramid Lake War, and it's likely that his full Northern Paiute name, Numu-tibo'o (Northern Paiute White Man), came from the experience. The Snake War (1866–67) was a more substantial defeat for the Natives because 800 warriors from the neighboring Walpapi and Yahooskin Northern Paiute bands were forced to surrender. Following these defeats, most Paiute gave up on armed resistance. Instead, they tried to adjust to the presence of the newcomers, or to abandon the valleys and move into the western mountains or onto reservations. Adaptation or flight made the best sense because it was all too evident that bows and arrows were no match for bullets and rifles.

As they watched lifestyles and land slip away from them, some frustrated Northern Paiute turned to their spiritual leaders, men who had supernatural powers given to them by spirit helpers. While some men were given sorcery (bad power), most were given good power to be used for the benefit of the community. Good power might be manifested in a special ability to hunt, to heal or to have special visions. Some even claimed to be bulletproof. Those so blessed with good power were especially important during times of crisis because they might provide solutions to problems that proved too challenging to be solved by traditional practices. Their powers were much in demand during this troubling time.

As an important medicine man with the power of prophecy, Tavibo was sought out for guidance. His power brought him a vision. It was not the normal practice for one to reveal a vision, for fear that it might upset the spirit that bestowed the power and cause it to flee. Tavibo, however, revealed what he saw. Perhaps he wanted to bring hope to his people, or maybe he wanted the glory and respect given to one with a great vision. He never gave the reason for telling his people that an earthquake would swallow up the white men, thereby leaving the land to the Natives. Even the Northern Paiute had difficulty accepting this. An earthquake that would kill whites and leave Natives unharmed? It seemed unlikely! Tavibo also wanted clarification and sought another vision. He saw a earthquake that swallowed everyone. Then he saw the resurrection of the Natives.

Tavibo's vision attracted many supporters, but when the earthquake failed to materialize, most drifted away. Others came to question his abilities as a medicine man after the deaths of some of those he had treated. The customary rule of thumb was that if three people under the care of a medicine man died, he would be put to death. But Tavibo was a powerful man. He may not have been a chief, but he was certainly influential in the southern end of the valley that the Toboose tukadu called home. Some claimed he could make it rain and others said that he was bulletproof. Realizing, however, that his failures were raising threatening questions about his power, he revealed another vision. The earthquake would indeed come, but only *his* followers would be saved. The vision swelled the ranks of believers. But wish as they might, what Tavibo saw in his vision never occurred, and into the 1870s, his followers were few. The visionary and his prophecies would have, however, an unforeseen impact. Wovoka would soon share his father's visions.

When Wovoka entered his teenage years in the early 1870s, he had a decision to make. Throughout the late 1860s, many Toboose tukadu had moved north to the Pyramid Lake reservation. Others were determined to remain in their homeland. Wovoka chose to count himself among their number. Perhaps he did not want to live far from the shadow of Holy Mountain (Mount Grant) to the south. Northern Paiute mythology held that Holy Mountain was the place of the tribe's creation, and it remained home to some of their most powerful spirits. Perhaps he thought of days to come and figured that it made poor sense to move to a reservation where he would be only one prophet or medicine man among many. Wovoka did not yet know whether he had any power, but he was hopeful. Ironically, while the white men forced many from the valley, it was their presence that allowed Wovoka to remain. While the bottomlands provided good territory for ranching, ranches required large tracts of land, which left little room for the development of large urban settlements. Furthermore, there was so much land available for farming in the Northwest (Wyoming, Montana, Idaho) that it was difficult for ranchers to attract men to work their spreads. This need resulted in a unique situation. Natives lived side by side with white men, a sight unseen in most of the West.

Wovoka took employment with David Wilson, for whom others in his family (but not his father) had worked occasionally. It appears that he was separated from his parents and two younger brothers at this time. Wilson's family had settled on the Missouri Flat at the southern end of the Mason Valley in the early 1860s. Wilson thought that the boy was a little lazy, but in Wovoka's defense, it was difficult to be motivated to work as an unskilled laborer clearing sagebrush, planting crops, pitching hay and cleaning stables. At least Wilson could be thankful that the boy shared his mother's quiet demeanor and not his father's wildness. Wovoka soon shed the outward appearance of a Native. He cut his hair short (eventually it would be cut straight across at the back of the ears, a style he would maintain) and replaced his rabbit-skin leggings with denim pants. A singular marker of his Native ancestry remained: he continued to wear an eagle feather above his left ear. In later years, he would strap it above his right elbow. Perhaps most significantly, he was given the name of Jack Wilson, presumably because he worked on the Wilson ranch.

Wovoka's ability to move into the white man's world was eased by the relationship that he formed with Bill Wilson, the eldest of his employer's family, who was about Wovoka's age. The pair had known each other since they were children, and they had developed a close friendship that was blind to skin color. Wovoka had already shown some aptitude for learning English, and he progressed more quickly as he spent more and more time with Bill, who also picked up a smattering of Paiute. Wovoka's education did not stop with language. As Bill's close friend, he enjoyed unique access to the Wilson household. He was allowed to eat at their table. He listened to

mealtime prayers of Mr. Wilson and, on Sundays, the Bible
readings of Mrs. Wilson. Many of the stories were strange and
sounded nothing like what Tavibo had told him. His attention
was most keen when Mrs. Wilson read about Jesus. Here was
one with great power, who could heal the sick and feed the
hungry. Most interesting, however, was the resurrection and
accompanying claim that followers would be saved. Wovoka
could hear in Jesus' story the echoes of his father's vision. He
spent many long nights in his wickiup thinking about both.

Although immersed in white culture throughout these
years, Wovoka did not completely abandon his Native ways.
Ranching allowed him great freedom in the fall and winter
when the animals were out to pasture and work was sparse. As
with most of the laboring Toboose tukadu, Wovoka returned
to the traditional practices of his people during those months.
He filled his days with hunting, fishing and collecting piñon
nuts. He may have felt guilty during these outings because
they suggested to him that his activities among the white men
sometimes demanded that he forget what was important to
his people. Collecting piñon nuts surely reminded him that
the Northern Paiute held the tree in high regard (perhaps
even as sacred). Already he had spent many long, hard days
cutting piñon trees, primarily for use in the Wilson's gold
mine at nearby Pine Grove, but also for smelting, fence posts
and winter fireplaces. He likely got his name from his profi-
ciency in the work; Wovoka meant "Wood Cutter."*

Many were upset that the white men were destroying
the groves. A Northern Paiute who participated in the

---

*It is not clear whether he was called by Wovoka or Jack Wilson in his
adult years. In the white community, he was known as Jack Wilson, and
there are references to Northern Paiute also calling him by that name. In
the broader Native community (and likely even among some of his own
people), he seems to have been called Wovoka.

desecration would surely have been frowned upon. It was
not the Native way to confront another, but Wovoka would
have undoubtedly sensed their displeasure. Perhaps his dis-
comfort was one of the reasons why Bill (who was unlikely
to worry about such matters) often accompanied him when
he returned to the Toboose tukadu. The white boy was
accepted because of Wovoka's standing as Tavibo's son.

Eventually, living in two worlds proved confusing for
Wovoka. He looked to the world of the Toboose tukadu and
saw it in ruins. Those who had not been forced by the white
man from the Mason Valley lived mostly a precarious existence on the fringes of the land not yet settled by whites. He
easily found evidence of his people's poverty and ill treatment. No Northern Paiute in the Mason Valley owned land.
Natives were paid $1.50 a day during harvest while their
white counterparts received $2 plus board. When with his
people, Wovoka listened as elders gathered around fires and
complained of the changes. Some told stories of past victories (although there were few victories to remember). Some
speculated that there might be more ahead if the people rose
up against these newcomers. Most listeners shook their
heads. To many it seemed as if the spirits had abandoned
them. There could be no hope of victory without their
assistance. Wovoka surely wondered if the power bestowed
by the spirits could even help his people. He knew the white
man well. He also had powerful spirits who made him strong
and allowed him to prosper.

When he compared the two worlds, Wovoka concluded
he wanted to share in the prosperity enjoyed by the white
man. But how could he? Because he was a Toboose tukadu,
his future seemed determined. He could work for the
white man, but he sensed that success in the white man's
world would always remain out of a Native's reach. He
shared his sorrows with Bill Wilson.

"Well, you are practically a white man," chuckled Bill. "You dress like us and speak English. You're as welcome in my house as anyone else I know. Everyone calls you Jack Wilson."

"I think that it is not what's on the outside that matters," replied Wovoka. "My blood is Paiute. And all can see that the Paiute are servants of the white man."

"We can change that!" said Bill excitedly. "Let's become blood brothers."

"Blood brothers?"

Bill explained to Wovoka the custom that would bring the two close.

"We'll get my brothers Joe and George and head up to the rock cove. They can be witnesses. And when we're done, there'll be no one saying that you're anything less than my brother, a white man at that."

It wasn't long before they were at rock cove. Bill unsheathed his knife and played it against his thumb to test its sharpness. Satisfied, he looked to Wovoka.

"Jack, we're here with Joe and George to perform this solemn ceremony. Take this knife and cut my wrist. Not too deep, mind you," he added quickly.

Wovoka took the knife and deftly slipped it across Bill's wrist, leaving a thin red trail.

"I'll do the same to you."

When Wovoka's wrist was cut, Bill grasped his arm and placed the cut against his own.

"My blood runs into yours. That makes you about as white as a man can be."

Bill let Wovoka's arm fall. Wovoka looked at it. After a moment he turned and walked to the rock face. He rubbed his fingers against an outcropping of ochre and walked back to Bill. He put a red mark on his blood brother's head.

"What'd you do that for?" asked Bill.

"My blood also runs through you. I guess that makes you Paiute as much as it makes me white."

Bill hadn't quite considered that and his tanned face appeared suddenly washed out.

"What the heck!" he exclaimed finally as the smiling group scampered down the hillside.

Exciting as it was, the youthful ceremony soon lost its promise. Blood brother or not, others still saw Wovoka as Jack, a Digger Indian ranch hand down at the Wilson spread. Gradually Wovoka accepted that he was not white and that no mystical ceremony or intimate relationship could make him one. With this realization, he found himself less frequently in the company of the Wilson brothers. He spent his time among the Toboose tukadu, where he was faced regularly with their desperate situation. He heard stories of the plight of other Natives, the Sioux wars and the long flight of the Nez Perce. He learned that none fared well against the white newcomer, who did not seem to want peace or friendship, but land and domination. The desires of the white man had brought the Natives nothing but tragedy—illness, degradation and poverty. Wovoka didn't need stories to know the truth in this. He had to look no farther than his own Mason Valley.

One spring in the early 1880s, Wovoka failed to show up at the Wilson's for the seasonal work. He had joined with a group of Northern Paiute from the Pyramid Lake reservation. They were migrant workers who followed the hops harvests through California, Oregon and Washington. The work brought Wovoka into contact with other Native groups, and he discovered firsthand the truth in the stories he had been told about the white man. His own shoulders sagged as he saw the resignation in the faces of so many of his brothers and sisters. They seemed to have accepted their lot as servants to the white man. To ease the pain of this new world, many had turned to the mind-numbing effects of the white man's firewater. Those who could not afford to buy booze, stole or drove their wives and sisters into prostitution to raise money. Wovoka could not see how firewater made the situation any better, although he could hardly condemn anyone for seeking the temporary escape it provided.

Wovoka discovered, however, that not all Natives had surrendered. When he traveled north into Washington state he came to a Yakama reservation along the Yakima River. Several Northern Paiute lived there. They told him of the recent Bannock War. In 1878, the Bannock tribe had joined with the Northern Paiute from Nevada and Oregon in the most significant resistance witnessed in the region for some years. They skirmished with volunteer forces and stirred up unrest in local reservations. General Oliver Howard led his forces out of Fort Boise and ended the short-lived resistance after about four months. The defeated Northern Paiute were sent north to the reserve.

While at the reserve, Wovoka also discovered other ways of resisting the white intrusion. He came into contact with some Yakama who were practitioners of *Tschadam*, the Indian Shaker Religion. *Tschadam* was founded in 1881 by Squ-sacht-un (John Slocum), a Squaxon of the Salish people, a tribe from the Northwest Coast. Native religions blossomed during this period and like many of them, *Tschadam* had its roots in earlier religious movements, in this case the most important of which was the Dreamer Religion founded by the Wanapam Smohalla. In his dreams, Smohalla visited the Spirit World, where he was directed to return and teach his people. He told them he had learned that the traditional Native way of life would be reestablished. It would be free of white influences, and indeed, free of whites, as they would be killed by resurrected Natives.

While *Tschadam* was similar to the Dreamer Religion, it more fully integrated Christian notions of God, heaven and hell, likely brought to the region by missionaries.

The precepts of *Tschadam* came to Squ-sacht-un during an illness. His relatives thought him dead and were building his coffin when he rose and told them he had been to heaven and had talked with the Christian God, who had given him instructions for his people.

"Abandon the white vices, love one another and pray often," he told them.

Tschadam was known as the Shaker Religion because participants shook and twitched while in the meditative state necessary for removing sins. The popularity of *Tschadam* was soon evident in the many churches that its followers built in the Pacific Northwest. White leaders were concerned, as they were about any influential movement in the Native community, so they had Squ-sacht-un and other leaders jailed. Wovoka learned of *Tschadam* while its founders languished behind bars.

Wovoka experienced *Tschadam* firsthand when his Yakama friends invited him to a ceremony. As far as he could determine, the ceremony had been called to help a sick man. It was dark when Wovoka arrived, and he slipped quietly into the background when those who helped to perform the ceremony, the *Shapupulema*, entered the lodge, waving their hands and blowing so as to chase away any evil spirits. Each wore cedar laurels adorned with two candles. Individual *Shapupulema* also carried a candle and a different colored, lightly woven cloth. During the ceremony, the cloths were held in front of the candles, casting the interior of the lodge in an ever-changing rainbow of colors. The *Shapupulema* chanted and rocked as a *Tschadam* priest blew on the sick man. Wovoka watched as the ill man began to shake, whereupon the *Shapupulema* performed with greater urgency.

Wovoka soon found himself responding to the sounds and colors. His eyelids became heavy, his chin slumped to his chest and all went black.

When he awoke, only the sick man, still prostrate under a blanket, and his wife remained. She gave Wovoka some food. After he ate, Wovoka left the lodge and stepped into the sunlight. He'd been in a trance throughout the night. He struggled to remember what had happened, but his last memory was of the sick man shouting and shaking fiercely. Seek though he might, he could recall nothing after that. But the man was still sick. Had the ceremony done nothing for him? He asked the woman.

"He will sleep for two, maybe three more days. He will visit heaven. He will awaken and be fine," she replied.

What is this power? wondered Wovoka.

Even when he returned to his own people in the Mason Valley, the question remained. As he thought about it, he made another important decision. He would no longer travel from his homeland. He would remain with the Toboose tukadu and help them as he could. His presence was welcome. Many of his people thought that he could offer them great assistance. As the son of an important medicine man, it was believed that Wovoka might share his power. Although community members did not go so far as to tell him that he should follow in his father's footsteps—such blatant interference was not the Native way—subtle pressures were exerted on him to do just that. People came to his wickiup seeking help with problems and illness. In these days, however, Wovoka had little interest in healing; the power of a medicine man was tenuous. If many died—as was often the case when they contracted the white man's diseases—prestige and material benefit disappeared quickly, and the healer could be put to death.

For a time, Wovoka was content to perform the magic his father had taught him and to offer limited visions of the future. The tricks and the prophecies brought him some notoriety, and soon his small wickiup was well stocked with the offerings of thankful callers. But Wovoka longed for something more. He was not content to be known merely as the son of Tavibo. He wanted his powers to be recognized in their own right. His father, though, was a great dreamer who had seen glorious visions. Wovoka had to demonstrate to the people that he, too, had a spirit helper that could reveal great things. He made a plan that would suggest he had such power.

It was a hot July day when he called for a séance at his wickiup. Once those invited were settled, he chanted and began his hand tricks. Certain he had their attention, he slipped into a trance and began to tremble and then to shake, much in the fashion of the sick Yakama man he had seen. He spoke the words of a Paiute sorcerer, and with his glazed eyes fixed on the small, crackling fire, announced his vision.

"Tomorrow it comes. I see it. At the white man's bridge. At noontime it comes. The air is hot. The sky is hot. The sun, he is hot. But you shall see. At the white man's bridge. In summertime. In hot summertime. And you shall see what I see. It is ice," declared Wovoka. "It is ice. Floating down river in hot summertime. You shall see."

His pronouncement was met with silence, broken soon by laughter. Ice? In July? Surely this man did not have the power of Tavibo. It was foolishness. Nevertheless, the next day saw many curious Toboose tukadu crowded the bridge and the shoreline. Wovoka arrived and pushed his way to the edge of the bridge at its center. For a short time he stood and waited under the oppressive sun. All were quiet. The silence was shattered when someone shouted, "It's noon!"

More time passed. The Natives began to murmur and laugh. Nervously, Wovoka mopped the sweat off his face with an old handkerchief. It wasn't the heat alone that made him sweat. He had staked much on this vision. Should it not come to pass, he would become an object of derision among his people. But Wovoka remained confident. He threw back his shoulders and looked skyward to the sun. He began to chant, and his song hushed the onlookers. Still, it didn't help to realize his vision.

Who could have believed such nonsense in the first place? Wovoka felt the hands of the skeptical grip hold of his clothing.

"There's no ice in the river," shouted one.

"Good!" called another. "Wovoka won't get cold when he's thrown into it!"

He felt himself being pushed closer to the edge of the bridge when a third voice rang clear above the murmurs of agreement.

"Look! The ice! It floats down the river!"

And, indeed, there it was. A great bluish chunk bobbed along with the current. Smaller pieces followed in its wake. The crowd erupted into cries of praise and song. As the ice neared the bridge, braves jumped into the river to scoop up pieces, for this was great power. Wovoka had seen ice in summertime, and the ice came. He did not need to look to the people to know they were in awe. Soon word of his vision would spread, and Wovoka would have the reputation he desired.

The fulfillment of his desire, however, was never in doubt. Upstream, Bill Wilson and his brothers had dumped a wagonload of ice they had packed in sawdust and held in storage after the spring thaw. It was a common practice, and there wasn't a rancher in the Mason Valley who wouldn't have guessed the source of the miraculous downstream ice floe, but the Northern Paiute were apparently unaware of it. Not only was the vision a fraud, but so was the ceremony leading up to it. The trance was fake and the shaking done consciously, both for effect. Wovoka was a good actor, though, and none suspected it. All the Toboose tukadu saw was a young man in his early 20s, a dreamer with great power. That the spirit helpers would come to him during the time of his people's greatest need fired the dying embers of their hope. Perhaps there was good reason not to accept defeat.

The manifestation of his vision considerably enhanced Wovoka's standing among his people. No grass grew on the path to his wickiup; the trail was well worn by the feet of the many Natives who came in search of advice or doctoring. Wovoka gave them counsel and prophecies. If his visions did not materialize or his advice proved questionable, he could always point to the mystical ways of the spirit helpers, which everyone knew could change on a whim, or he could blame those seeking advice for failing to properly follow his instructions. The skills of a medicine man were more easily measured, and so he remained content to leave most of the risky business of healing to others. Wovoka's reluctance on the matter did not diminish his reputation in the eyes of the Toboose tukadu. His lodge was well stocked with food and furs, the offerings of petitioners and others who were pleased to have such a powerful dreamer in their midst.

Wovoka's prosperity allowed him to take a wife, which he did in the mid-1880s. Finding one could not have been difficult, for his power made him much sought after. Her name was Tumma, and she was either a Northern Paiute Agi tukadu (Trout-eater) or a Bannock. If the traditional practices of Northern Paiute courtship were still in place, Wovoka would first have become friends with her brothers. Upon learning from them that Tumma had no criticisms of him, Wovoka visited her at night in her wickiup with a gift of meat. Courting continued until she slept with him. The marriage was consummated when Tumma allowed him to stay for breakfast. Once they were married, Wovoka changed her name to Mary Wilson. Before the end of the decade (the 1880s), they would have a daughter Zohoona and a son Billy, named after Wovoka's blood brother.

Wovoka continued to impress his people during these years with his accurate visions. For the most part, however, his visions involved elaborate tricks. A memorable one occurred under a great cottonwood tree on a bank of the Walker River. The grass was well trampled by the many Toboose tukadu who sought to be near Wovoka. They talked in low tones as they waited. Wovoka joined in their discussions, oblivious to the promised spectacle. He had not said what it would be, so speculation ran high. A piercing cry hushed the crowd. The secret was revealed! A large block of ice, weighing some 30 pounds, had fallen from the heavens and landed on the blanket spread out at Wovoka's feet. All remained silent as they contemplated this singular event. Only the suspicious among the onlookers, a few white men who did not hold to notions of Wovoka's powers, concluded that the block of ice had been hidden in the branches of the cottonwood and had fallen from there once it had melted sufficiently. It was clear enough to them why Wovoka had not revealed his vision. Had he done so, the Northern Paiute would have had their eyes trained skyward and seen the deception.

The event was followed by a religious ceremony, likely of Wovoka's design. The ice block was placed into a washtub.

"We will wait for it to melt," said Wovoka. Once it had, he dipped a cup into the water.

"Come, my brothers and sisters," he directed as he held the dripping cup above the tub. "Drink the ice water that has come from above."

The Toboose tukadu drank it in great gulps. Once the water was gone, Wovoka spoke again.

"Take your clothes off. Go to the river and walk into it."

Wovoka was solemn as the Toboose tukadu slipped into the river. It was not an act that required second thought on their part, for the river was often used for spiritual cleansing, just as rivers across the land were used by other Natives for similar purposes. It's likely, however, that Wovoka had another reason. Throughout days and nights of contemplation and prayer, Wovoka seems to have concluded that his people should seek out the power of the white man's God. If the Northern Paiute were blessed by God's power, their lot might improve. Commanding the Toboose tukadu to go into the river served probably as a sort of baptism in Wovoka's eyes, at least as he understood the Christian ceremony. It was an invitation to God.

It wasn't long after this when, one day in 1886 or 1887, Wovoka fell into a trance while in his wickiup. Tumma found him, and despite the efforts of her and others to revive him, he would not rise. There was no trickery here. Many feared that he might be dead. Such fears were misplaced. After two days, Wovoka awoke. Despite many questions, he revealed little of what had happened during his trance, noting only that he had visited the spirits of his people's dead and that they had taught him much. He told his wife to have the elders organize a ceremonial dance, and he outlined the preparations they were to make. Following a night of fasting, Wovoka was ready to share his vision with his people.

He had been to heaven and there had seen beautiful things. Many there were Natives. They lived in peace and were free of the bonds of servitude. Despite his desire to remain in the tranquil place, he was directed to return to the Northern Paiute and to bring them important teachings. He was given a moral code that talked of peace, honesty and hard work. And he was taught a dance and songs to accompany it. Performed properly, it would give a glimpse of heaven and hasten the day that would again see Natives free and happy.

His vision explained, Wovoka made preparations for those gathered to perform the new dance. Once a select few had mastered the movements and the song, the circle increased in size until more than 100 were dancing. The dance continued for five consecutive nights. On the sixth day, Wovoka took the Northern Paiute to the Walker River and directed them to dip into it. He told them that it would wash away their sins, a further indication of the influence of Christianity. With a feast, the ceremony was complete.

Wovoka's vision in the late 1880s planted the seeds for what would soon flourish as the Ghost Dance. The ground proved fertile because his people's desperation made many want to believe in what he had seen. The ceremony was also very similar to the traditional Northern Paiute Round Dance, held in anticipation of successful fish runs and piñon nut harvests. Wovoka's teachings spread quickly beyond the Walker Valley. Many Northern Paiute throughout western Nevada began dancing and living according to his precepts. There seemed little difficulty in accepting the visions of the son of a known dreamer, of a young man whose visions had already demonstrated something of his own power. Nevertheless, skeptics remained. For many of those, however, doubt disappeared following the mystical events of 1889, events that placed the reputation of Wovoka beyond assail.

Late in 1888 Wovoka took his family to the Pine Grove Mountains, where he was going to chop trees for the Wilsons. There was nothing unusual about the job since he often took on such temporary work. At almost six feet tall, he was a big man, and he threw his thick shoulders and long arms into the work. He had chopped almost a cord of wood when he heard a great noise that seemed to come from above. He put down his axe, looked up for the source of the noise and collapsed. He was taken back to a lodge, where he lay in a state of unconsciousness for weeks. Evidence suggests that he had fallen victim to scarlet fever, which had run its course through the Walker Valley in the spring of the year.

He awoke on New Year's Day, 1889. Carefully he made his way to the entrance of his wickiup. He glanced out. Nightfall seemed to be approaching. Oddly, however, the Northern Paiute were greeting it with shouting and gunfire. Wovoka looked around in search of an explanation for this curious behavior. Finally, his eyes turned skyward. The sun was slipping behind the moon!

The eclipse was a disastrous occurrence for the Northern Paiute. The sun was their greatest deity and it appeared as if a sky monster was devouring it. The land would be plunged into eternal darkness and life itself might come to an end. Their loud noise was designed to scare the monster away. When he realized what was happening, Wovoka slipped onto the open space before his wickiup, sat down and began to chant. Slowly the sun began to reappear. Those who saw the dreamer were certain that his intercession had driven the monster away. Wovoka had saved them and the world! With the sun again firmly in its place, Wovoka stumbled back into his wickiup, where he again collapsed. When he awoke a few days later, he had another vision to share with his people.

When his strength was recovered, he had Tumma assemble the village elders. He described his great revelation.

"God came and took me to heaven again. There I saw all our dead people. They were turned young again. Their bellies were full. They danced and were happy."

"God told me many things," continued Wovoka. "He gave me power over the natural elements. He taught me five songs that I can use to make the weather. Then He said, 'You will now share the American presidency with Benjamin Henry Harrison. Harrison will be president of the East; you, Jack Wilson, will be president of the West!' He has made me invulnerable. Even if soldiers should try to kill me, they will fall down, as if they had no bones, and die.

"God gave me rules that we should live by." They were the same as those he had shared before. No lying, stealing or violence. The Northern Paiute should get along with each other and other Native tribes. And they should work for the white man.

"God said that the Northern Paiute and other Natives should dance for five nights in succession.

"If we do what God has said, a great reward awaits us. We will be young and strong again in heaven. Life will be as it once was!"

Later that same month, the Toboose tukadu and other Northern Paiute celebrated the Ghost Dance according to Wovoka's directions. As the rules given to him became widely known, more of the people strove to live by them. Followers took to calling Wovoka a prophet. Some sought to induce his trance state. Those unsuccessful sometimes turned to wild herbs and some died from poisoning. Others remained unconvinced. They needed more than Wovoka's descriptions and teachings before they would believe. The prophet looked to the skies and delivered that as well.

Wovoka's power over the natural elements was most dramatically demonstrated as fall gave way to winter in 1889. For more than a year, the Mason Valley had suffered under drought conditions. Desperate ranchers dug countless wells to water their stock. The Toboose tukadu watched helplessly as their few crops browned and threatened to shrivel for a second year. They were all too aware that another year of the same would bring disaster. They went to the prophet. In November of the following year, the local newspaper, the *Walker Lake Bulletin*, described what happened.

> *The Indians wanted rain, and they assembled in conclave, and [Wovoka] appeared, and they asked for water.... The result was that the most severe storm of that stormy winter followed. After about a month of incessant rain and snow the Indians had enough, and again they sought [Wovoka] and asked him to let up. And lo and behold, the clouds rolled by, and soon the papers began blowing about the fine climate.*

It wasn't just that Wovoka had brought the rains. He had prophesied that they would come within three days and they did. Controlling the weather was impressive enough, but it was only one of Wovoka's powers. He was also bulletproof. The Northern Paiute were probably not likely surprised to learn of his power over bullets. It was a traditional power that Tavibo had long claimed to have possessed. Even before his visions, Wovoka demonstrated that he had a way with bullets. His special abilities often allowed him to heal those injured with gunshot wounds. After the New Year's Day vision, however, it was clear that something more than skill was at work.

Wovoka staged a demonstration, probably in the fall of 1889 during the Toboose tukadu annual rabbit hunt, that left none in doubt of his power over bullets. Many gathered to witness the display. Wovoka appeared, cloaked in a heavy robe. In one hand he held a muzzle-loading shotgun. He bent over and took a pinch of dust from the ground.

"Powder," he explained as he dropped it into the barrel of the rifle. He then reached over a second time and took up a handful of sand.

"Shot," he declared, again letting it slip down the rifle's barrel.

He packed in paper as wadding. Wovoka gave the rifle to his brother and walked to a nearby spot. He took off the robe, spread it on the ground and stepped onto it. He looked to his brother, who trained the rifle on him.

"Fire!" called Wovoka.

The rifle's crack split the still air. Wovoka staggered and shook himself vigorously.

"Come! All!" he cried. "See what Wovoka does to bullets!"

The Natives hurried to him. They took note of his shirt, riddled with small holes. At his feet on the blanket, they saw the shot. Before their eyes was the evidence. The Prophet was indeed bulletproof!

By this time most Northern Paiute believed in the Prophet and few needed additional proof of his power. However, since Wovoka's vision in 1889, the Mason Valley saw a slow stream of Natives from other tribes come to see Wovoka for themselves. They had heard of the western visionary and of his dreams, and while all of the visitors believed in visions and special powers, most required something more than stories and rumors. They wanted to speak with this dreamer and see the ceremony revealed to him. Then they might know whether the stories were true. The first to arrive were the Ute, and by summer, Shoshone and Northern Arapaho came. The largest delegations of 1889 came in November—Northern Cheyenne, Arapaho, Shoshone, Bannock and Sioux. It is likely that Wovoka showed them his bulletproof power. The demonstration convinced the visitors that Wovoka did indeed have special powers and that his dreams should be believed.

It is difficult to follow the trail of the Ghost Dance as it fanned out from the Mason Valley, but it is necessary to try in order to understand Wovoka's influence. Unfortunately, the messages delivered by visiting Natives to their tribes did not always reflect what are considered to be Wovoka's original visions. There are several reasons that might explain the discrepancies. Most who visited Wovoka did not speak his language and so differences may have occurred during translation. Wovoka's message may also have been altered slightly by the members of the tribe that received it. It's also possible that Wovoka had other visions that elaborated on or modified what he had seen in the late 1880s. The written record doesn't suggest this, but it is known that Wovoka gave instructions to followers not to reveal his vision to white men, so it is unlikely they would have written anything down (even if they could write, a skill most did not possess).

There are, however, two letters explaining the Ghost Dance that were known to be written by visitors to Wovoka, both of whom met with the Prophet in August 1891. One was written by Casper Edson, an Arapaho, while the other was dictated by Black Short Nose, a Cheyenne, to his daughter. They are in broken English and not always clear. However, in the 1890s, the United States government hired ethnologist James Mooney to undertake a study of the Ghost Dance. Generally his study is well respected. He was shown the letters and he rewrote them placing them in the context of what he had learned. They were known as the *Messiah Letter* (the two original letters were called this), and it appears here as Mooney rewrote it.

> *When you get home you must make a dance to continue five days. Dance four successive nights, and the last night keep up the dance until the morning of the fifth day, when all must bathe in the river and then disperse to their homes. You must all do in the same way.*
>
> *I, Jack Wilson, love you all and my heart is full of gladness for the gifts you have brought me. When you get home*

I shall give you a good cloud [rain?] *which will make you feel good. I give you a good spirit and give you all good paint. I want you to come again in three months, some from each tribe* [the Indian Territory].

There will be a good deal of snow this year and rain. In the fall there will be such a rain as I have never given you before.

Grandfather [a universal title of reverence among Indians and here meaning "the messiah"] *says, when your friends die you must not cry. You must not hurt anybody or do harm to anyone. You must not fight. Do right always. It will give you satisfaction in life. This young man has a good father and mother.* [This reference may be to Casper Edson, the young Arapaho who wrote down this message of Wovoka for the delegation.]

Do not tell the white people about this. Jesus is now upon the earth. He appears like a cloud. The dead are all alive again. I do not know when they will be here; maybe this fall or in the spring. When the time comes there will be no more sickness and everyone will be young again.

Do not refuse to work for the whites and do not make any trouble with them until you leave them. When the earth shakes [at the coming of the new world] *do not be afraid. It will not hurt you.*

I want you to dance six weeks. Make a feast at the dance and have food that everybody may eat. Then bathe in the water. That is all. You will receive good words again from me some time. Do not tell lies.

The letter indicates significant changes in Wovoka's teachings. He is referred to as the messiah although exactly what this meant remains unclear. Wovoka denied that he was the Son of God, just as he denied being a prophet (which is, however, how most Natives saw him). The end of the world and the resurrection of Natives upon a new one seems not to have been mentioned before. Some interpreted this part of the prophecy to mean a rapidly approaching time when Natives would again live as they once had, free from the white man, on plains and plateaus where buffalo and deer were plentiful. Wovoka spoke little of this matter.

Wovoka's powerful message held much appeal for Natives. The previous decades had seen them lose much to the white man. Traditional lands were taken along with livelihoods, and all too often, dignity. Natives lived on reservations, usually in squalor, with cultural change forced upon them. Because the people were anxious to believe, they readily accepted a vision suggesting that recent defeats and accompanying pain might be forgotten.

The *Messiah Letter*, however, was unusual. More commonly, tribal delegates returned to their people and simply explained the Prophet's teachings to those anxious to listen. It happened this way with the Sioux, who came to hold Wovoka's vision in particularly high regard. Black Elk, the Oglala Sioux dreamer who would place his own mark on the Ghost Dance, remembered what he heard as three band members described their 1889 meeting with Wovoka, whom they called Wanekia.

> *...they saw the Wanekia (One Who Makes Live), who was the son of the Great Spirit, and they talked to him....He told them that there was another world coming, just like a cloud. It would come in a whirlwind out of the west and would crush out everything on this world, which was old and dying. In that other world there was plenty of meat, just like old times; and in that world all the dead Indians were alive and all the bison that had ever been killed were roaming around again.*

This sacred man gave some sacred red paint and two eagle feathers to [the Oglala visitors]. *The people must put this paint on their faces and they must dance a ghost dance that the sacred man taught....If they did this, they could get on this other world when it came and the Wasichus* [white man] *would not be able to get on and so they would disappear.*

The Sioux were intrigued by this vision. They had been among the most feared warriors on the Plains, throughout the 1850s, 60s and 70s providing the United States cavalry with its most determined enemy. By the 1880s, they were on reserves, demoralized, "pitiful and in despair," as Black Elk described it. The notion that the white man would soon be removed kindled the fires that had once burned in their warriors' bellies. Perhaps they might hasten the white man's disappearance? The following year, more Sioux went to see Wovoka. They reaffirmed what had the others had said and they added more, again as remembered by Black Elk.

...people said it was really the son of the Great Spirit who was out there; that when he came to the Wasichus a long time ago, they had killed him; but he was coming to the Indians this time, and there would not be any Wasichus in the new world that would come....This they said would happen after one more winter, when the grasses were appearing.

I heard many wonderful things about the Wanekia, that these men had seen and heard, and they were good men. He could make animals talk, and once while they were with him he made a spirit vision, and they all saw it. They saw a big water, and beyond it was a beautiful green land where all the Indians that had ever lived and the bison and

the other animals were all coming home together....And
once, they said, the Wanekia held out his hat for them to look
into; and when they did this, all but one saw there the whole
world and all that was wonderful. [One of the delegates]
himself told me that, with the power of Wanekia, he had gone
to a bison skin teepee; and there his son, who had been dead
a long time, was living with his wife, and they had a long
talk together.

These messages had a profound impact on the Sioux.
Throughout 1889 and 1890, Ghost Dances were common
on their reservations. Then came the vision of Black Elk.
He had considerable powers of his own, and even before he
was aware of Wovoka's vision, he had seen the rebirth of
the Sioux (or, as he put it, they would be brought "back
into the nation's hoop"). Black Elk was therefore especially
curious about the reports of the Sioux delegates. Eventually
he participated in a Ghost Dance, during which he slipped
into a trance. He had a vision and in it he saw Wovoka's
land of plenty. He also saw two men who "wore holy shirts
made and painted in a certain way." They spoke to him.
"'We will give you something [the holy shirts] that you
shall carry back to your people, and with it they shall come
to see their loved ones.'" After rising from his trance, Black
Elk set about making the ghost shirts.

Black Elk participated in more Ghost Dances and he
continued to have visions that often included the holy shirt.
He made them for other dancers. Those who wore the shirt
believed that it made them bulletproof. Wovoka denied that
he had any such vision. Likely the shirt, which was the most
noted article associated with Ghost Dance, fused understand-
ings of Wovoka's power, Black Elk's vision and the words
and ideas of the returning Sioux delegates. Whatever its ori-
gins, some Sioux came to see the Ghost Shirt as providing

a trail to past glory. Wearing the protective garment, they might return to the warpath to rid the land of the whites, as had been revealed in the vision.

Government officials worried when they heard of the popularity of this new ceremony on the Plains. They didn't put much stock into the vision themselves, but they were concerned that the dance was reinvigorating the Sioux. They were noticeably more restless and increasingly militant, behaviors and attitudes ill suited for the reservation life envisioned by the government. Word of a magical shirt was especially troubling. Officials were hardly concerned about assertions that it could stop bullets. But they were worried that the notions of invulnerability associated with the Ghost Shirt might contribute to increased violence. Officials believed that the Sioux would not hesitate to fight.

Matters came to a head in the late winter 1890, when word came of a proposed large Ghost Dance gathering at the Sioux Pine Ridge Reservation near the southern border of South Dakota. Even more troubling were reports that the great Hunkpapa Sioux chief and warrior, Sitting Bull, would attend. Sitting Bull had participated in Ghost Dances. He had never fallen into a trance, and he doubted the possibility that dead Natives would return to earth. He came to believe, however, that the Ghost Dance could offer his people strength because it united them in a shared vision, with a new hope. The government feared the possibility of Sioux unity, which they saw as a military threat. In their experience, Native dancing was often followed by warfare. They were determined to stamp out any embers before they engulfed the land in flame. Officials especially did not want Sitting Bull to lead the Sioux back onto the warpath. In the fall of 1890, officials ordered Sitting Bull to be arrested, and he was killed in the attempt.

Nevertheless, the Sioux and some neighboring tribes were determined to perform the ceremony. Colonel J.W. Forsyth and the 500 men of the Seventh Cavalry who rode under his command were ordered to stop it. On December 28, the Seventh Cavalry caught up with a band of 350 Miniconjou Sioux (among whom were some vocal proponents of the Ghost Dance). In the band were 230 women and children, and concern for their safety may well have influenced the Sioux decision to surrender. Forsyth marched them back to the Pine Ridge Agency. Along the way they stopped at Wounded Knee Creek to camp. As a precaution, Forsyth ordered the warriors disarmed. Yellow Bird, a medicine man and visitor to Wovoka, began to dance and chant. He urged the warriors to resist, believing that no harm would come to them because they wore their Ghost Dance shirts. A warrior refused to hand over his weapon. A shot was fired. The battle was measured in minutes. The Miniconjou were massacred; 150 died at the scene, and more later from their wounds.

News of the events shocked Wovoka. His message was one of peace. Never had he imagined that it could cause such violence. For a time after Wounded Knee, Wovoka became a recluse. Throughout the rest of his life, he would disappear into the hills surrounding the Mason Valley for months at a time. While he continued to meet with Native delegations and to explain his vision to them, he was not often seen in the company of whites. Perhaps he feared for his own safety. However, he had nothing to fear from the local white community. While some unfounded rumors of Northern Paiute rebelliousness circulated, few in the Mason Valley or surrounding areas saw Wovoka as a threat. They knew him as Jack Wilson, a sometimes ranch hand, and thought that his powers were only deception and trickery. By the mid-1890s his fears subsided, and he resumed a lifestyle similar to that of his pre-visionary days. Similar but

not exact. Nothing was ever quite the same for the Ghost
Dance Prophet.

Although Wovoka had never sought to be a medicine
man, people visited him for his healing powers. Reluctantly
he accepted the responsibility. As with much that Wovoka
did, his healing practices veered from the conventional.
While he shared some of the techniques used commonly
by Northern Paiute medicine men (dancing around the
victim, singing healing songs), he also had his own special
power. Traditionally, Northern Paiute healers sucked poison
or foreign objects from their victims. Wovoka didn't. He
relied on feathers, usually an eagle feather. The feather's
function is illustrated in a story related by an eyewitness to
his healing. The narrator's sister had been shot. She noted
that the local government doctor had failed in his efforts
before the girl was taken to Wovoka.

> *He put the eagle feather near where the wound is, in
> here* [under her arm]. *You know how the feather is. You
> can see the blood was coming through there* [the feather's
> quill]. *That he was getting out his feather in the wound
> and the blood was drawn out. You could see the blood going
> through that feather. Blood went into Jack's mouth and he
> spit it out again. Later, after he had done this a number of
> times, Jack sat down. He said, "She has a chipped bone.
> Piece of bone from her rib." Said he was going to take it
> out. That piece of bone was about as big as a sliver. After
> Jack spit it out, he showed us. Then he put it in the palm of
> his hand and rubbed his hands together. Sang one of his
> medicine songs. When he opened his hands the sliver of
> bone had disappeared. My sister got well and in two weeks
> she was walking again.*

Arapahoe Wyoming
Fremont Co. April 30—11

Dear Father in christ. Jack Wilson,

I today I am thinking of you
and I would like to Write you
afew lines. to you this morning
and to let you know that
I am well with my folks
and also my wife was very
Sickness for along time. But
much. So I wish you Please
tell us if is alright to visit
you. my Brother he is waiting
for his money from Oklahoma
But we would like to hear
from you. before we start
off. to your Place. and I wish
you Please send us little
Painted. if you got to spare
           I am yours truly.
       F. W. Antelope.
    and American Horse,

Excerpts from a letter seeking advice and ochre from the
Ghost Dance Prophet. Wovoka received many such requests.

Wovoka was considered to be a powerful medicine man and he made good money healing. He charged $5 a cure or $10 for a night's work. He never worked past midnight as most medicine men did. Many believed that his ability to heal quickly further demonstrated his powers. Of course, some lived too far away to receive the healing touch of the prophet. Some of those wrote him letters, seeking appropriate remedies for their ailments. Wovoka received so many such requests that he often told his wife to reply that he couldn't help them. Assistance was forthcoming, however, because Tumma prescribed appropriate remedies as Wovoka might, and in dire cases recommending open air and an end to drinking or gambling.

Wovoka also had other sources of income unavailable to the ordinary Toboose tukadu. Reports had it that he charged money for everything from a handshake (people lined up prepared to pay from $.05 to $20 for the privilege), to photographs ($2.50 to $5), feathers (from $2.50 for an eagle feather to $.25 for a magpie or crow feather) and red ochre ($20 per piece). Even his clothing was in demand. Especially popular was his hat, usually a ten-gallon Stetson, for which he expected $20. Often he had to do nothing for money. Natives from across the country sent him cash gifts regularly. Sometimes distant believers were able to give Wovoka gifts in person. While he was not a regular traveler outside the Mason Valley, he did visit other reservations occasionally where a Ghost Dance would inevitably be held in his honor. And, while he received offers to appear at the white man's fairs and exhibitions, Wovoka was not interested. Although he advocated working for the white man, he had little need to do it (and rarely did) after his vision.

Demand for artifacts from Wovoka is explained well enough by his vision of the Ghost Dance and his healing powers, but Wovoka continued to demonstrate his powers for other reasons. One such example was related by a woman whose mother was a contemporary of Wovoka and had seen the described event.

"In five days, Wovoka said a horse will appear on top of a mountain. Sure enough a beautiful white horse appeared on top of the mountain.... Jack, he kept talking to the people same time, motioning the horse to come down. So slowly it came.... It was so beautiful. And when it was coming it looked like its hooves wouldn't even touch the ground.

"My mother thought to herself, *What kind of animal would understand him?*

"'Watch the heavy cloud,' Wovoka then said. And a heavy cloud started to move towards them, coming closer and closer. It came right on top of the horse.

"'This White Horse has pity on you. He wishes you all abundance,' said Wovoka."

When the horse left, rain came. Many stories demonstrating Wovoka's power over the weather were common, and most at the time treated his ability matter of factly. Many amusing stories surround his weather power. On one hot sunny day, Wovoka happened upon a baseball game. The players stopped as they saw him approach.

"Hey, Rain-Maker, let's see if you can make it rain!" they called out teasingly.

Wovoka sang one of his weather songs and clouds formed suddenly in what had been a clear blue sky. The players' tune changed quickly.

"Call off your powers! Don't ruin the baseball game!" they pleaded.

Occasionally anger motivated Wovoka's use of his weather power, as one person remembered: "One time he [Wovoka] want to buy some hay from a man. That man not sell him any. That nite [sic] that man [Wovoka] make that whole stack blow away. All Indian know that."

In the early 1900s, Wovoka took a more active role in Toboose tukadu life. While he supported harmonious living with the white man, he was not a proponent of cultural assimilation and he would not help to bring it about. In 1912, the Walker River reservation superintendent agreed to give Wovoka 20 acres of land if he would work for the government and promote cultural change in the Northern Paiute community. Wovoka longed to own land because it demonstrated wealth by white man's standards. But the price was too great, so he refused. Later he led a delegation of 30 Toboose tukadu to the reservation office requesting communal title to land at the northern end of the valley. The superintendent agreed that there might be some justification for such a transaction, but that the request could not be met because of tangled legal disputes involving traditional Northern Paiute ownership claims.

Wovoka also adopted a firm stand on the matter of drug and alcohol use. He condemned strongly an effort to introduce peyote into the Mason Valley. Users chewed on the peyote button, the above-ground part of the peyote, for its hallucinogenic effects.

"If you keep on using it, you will walk on your hands and feet like a dog. Don't use it," he said. "I don't like that."

Some have suggested that Wovoka's original visions told him that Natives should avoid alcohol. This was apparently not the case, although the mistake is perhaps understandable given his later position on drinking. In 1919 he signed a temperance pledge at a meeting of the Baptist Temperance Society in Mason. The pledge included a promise to assist American officials in arresting whisky sellers. A few years later, alcohol became a problem with the Ute in eastern Nevada. Wovoka sent a telegram to state authorities; if they couldn't solve the problem, he would "with a word." Wovoka's power among his people remained great.

Wovoka, age 56. Wovoka ("Wood Cutter") had long made a living clearing land and cording logs.

Wovoka's positions on these matters suggest that he wanted to shoulder a mantle of leadership. As a prophet and medicine man, pressures were exerted on him to fulfill that duty. Wovoka may have felt added obligation because of the part of his vision that suggested he would be president of the West. He took that matter seriously throughout his life. During World War I, he threatened "to freeze the Atlantic and send all of the Indians over there and equip them with ice," if the Germans won the war. In March 1916, the *Mason Valley News* reported that he hoped to avoid this outcome by visiting President Wilson "to terminate the murderous war in Europe." He never made the trip.

In the late 1920s Wovoka suffered from a series of bronchitis attacks, which had also caused him problems back in the 1890s. Sickness took its toll on the elderly man, and he died of kidney failure on September 29, 1932. He was buried on the Walker River Reservation in the family plot of some friends next to his wife, who had died a month earlier. A Methodist pastor conducted the service.

Wovoka's story does not end there, however. Andy Vidovich, his son-in-law, reported that Wovoka had once said that "when my body is placed in the ground, my body goes back to the earth, where it belongs. And my spirit lives on forever with the Great Messiah." He made it known that the earth would shake if he reached heaven. Three months to the day after his death, the *Mason Valley News* reported that "The most severe earthquakes felt by the majority of Mason valley residents in their lives...shook virtually the entire Western United States and were felt as far north as Canada and as far south as the Mexican border." It was the final prophecy of the Northern Paiute Prophet.

Notes on Sources

AS MUCH AS POSSIBLE, the dialogue in this book is accurate and the accounts described are fictionalized as little as possible.

TECUMSEH

Cwiklik, Robert. *Tecumseh: Shawnee Rebel*. New York: Chelsea House Publishers, 1993.

Sugden, John. *Tecumseh: A Life*. New York: Henry Holt & Company, 1997.

Trowbridge, C.C. *Shawnese Traditions*. Edited by Vernon Kinietz and Erminie Voegelin. Ann Arbor: University of Michigan Press, 1939.

CRAZY HORSE

Ambrose, Stephen. *Crazy Horse and Custer: The Parallel Lives of Two American Warriors*. New York: Doubleday & Company, 1975.

Black Elk. *Black Elk Speaks* (as told through John G. Neihardt by Nicholas Black Elk). 1932. Reprint, Lincoln: University of Nebraska Press, 2000.

Hinman, Eleanor. "Oglala Sources on the Life of Crazy Horse." *Nebraska History*, vol. 57, no. 1, Spring 1976, 1–52.

Sanja, Mike. *Crazy Horse: The Life Behind the Legend*. New York: John Wiley & Sons, 2000.

GERONIMO

Barrett, S.M. (ed). *Geronimo: His Own Story*. 1906. Reprint, New York: E.P. Dutton & Co., 1970.

Debo, Angie. *Geronimo: The Man, His Time, His Place*. Norman: University of Oklahoma Press, 1976.

Opler, Morris E. *An Apache Life-Way*. 1941. Reprint, Lincoln: University of Nebraska Press, 1996.

Schwarz, Melissa. *Geronimo: Apache Warrior*. New York: Chelsea House, 1992.

CROWFOOT

Dempsey, Hugh. *Crowfoot: Chief of the Blackfoot*. 1972. Reprint, Edmonton: Hurtig Publishers, 1976.

Jenish, D'Arcy. *Indian Fall: The Last Great Days of the Plains Cree and the Blackfoot Confederacy*. 1999. Reprint, Toronto: Penguin Books, 2000.

Kidd, Kenneth. *Blackfoot Ethnography* (Archaeological Survey of Alberta, Manuscript Series No. 8). Edmonton: Alberta Culture, Historical Resources Division, 1937.

PLENTY COUPS

Linderman, Frank. *Plenty Coups: Chief of the Crows*. 1930. Reprint, Lincoln: University of Nebraska Press, 1962.

Wagner, Glendolin, & William, Allen. *Blankets and Moccasins: Plenty Coups and His People, the Crows*. Cladwell, Idaho: Caxton Printers, 1936.

Hoxie, Frederick. *Parading Through History: The Making of the Crow Nation in America, 1805–1935*. Cambridge: Cambridge University Press, 1995.

WOVOKA

Bailey, Paul. *Wovoka: The Indian Messiah*. Los Angeles: Westernlore Press, 1957.

Black Elk. *Black Elk Speaks* (as told through John G. Neihardt by Nicholas Black Elk). 1932. Reprint, Lincoln: University of Nebraska Press, 2000.

Hittman, Michael. *Wovoka and the Ghost Dance*. Lincoln: University of Nebraska Press, 1990.

Mooney, James. *The Ghost Dance Religion and the Sioux Outbreak of 1890*. 1896. Reprint, Chicago: University of Chicago Press, 1965.

Whiting, Beatrice. *Paiute Sorcery*. New York: The Viking Fund, 1950.